Student Teaching and Field Experiences Handbook

FIFTH EDITION

Betty D. Roe
Tennessee Technological University

Elinor P. Ross
Tennessee Technological University

Upper Saddle River, New Jersey
Columbus, Ohio

Library of Congress Cataloging-in-Publication Data

Roe, Betty D.

    Student teaching and field experiences handbook/Betty D. Roe, Elinor P. Ross.—5th ed.
      p. cm.
    Includes bibliographical references and index.
    ISBN 0-13-028764-4
    1. Student teaching—Handbooks, manuals, etc.   I. Ross, Elinor P. (Elinor Parry),
  II. Title.
    LB2157.A3R59   2002
    370'.71—dc21   00-06654

Vice President and Publisher: Jeffery W. Johnston
Acquisitions Editor: Debra A. Stollenwerk
Assistant Editor: Daniel J. Parker
Editoral Assistant: Penny S. Burleson
Production Editor: Kimberly J. Lundy
Production Coordination: Carlisle Publishers Services
Design Coordinator: Diane C. Lorenzo
Photo Coordinator: Valerie Schultz
Cover Designer: Linda Fares
Cover Art: Super Stock
Production Manager: Pamela D. Bennett
Director of Marketing: Kevin Flanagan
Marketing Manager: Krista Groshong
Marketing Services Manager: Barbara Koontz

This book was set in New Caledonia and GillSans by Carlisle Communications, Ltd. It was printed and bound by Courier Kendallville, Inc. The cover was printed by Phoenix Color Corp.

Photo credits: Scott Cunningham/Merrill, 5, 81, 99, 124, 133, 147, 197; Laima E. Druskis/PH College, 9; Anthony Magnacca/Merrill, 30,116,173, 224; Tom Watson/Merrill, 48; Mike Peters/ Silver Burdett & Ginn, 52; Barbara Schwartz/Merrill, 1, 56; Anne Vega/Merrill, 72, 149, 188, 216.

Prentice-Hall International (UK) Limited, *London*
Prentice-Hall of Australia Pty. Limited, *Sydney*
Prentice-Hall of Canada Inc., *Toronto*
Prentice-Hall Hispanoamericana, S.A., *Mexico*
Prentice-Hall of India Private Limited, *New Delhi*
Prentice-Hall of Japan, Inc., *Tokyo*
Prentice-Hall Singapore Pte. Ltd.
Editora Prentice-Hall do Brasil, Ltda., *Rio de Janeiro*

10 9 8 7 6 5 4
ISBN 0-13-028764-4

Preface

Student Teaching and Field Experiences Handbook is designed for students who are teaching in schools during their teacher-preparation programs, either in pre-student-teaching practicum courses or as actual student teachers. The text is a practical guide for college or university students who are directly involved with elementary and secondary students. This book offers the theoretical background for particular strategies and provides examples of how these are to be used.

This book is not meant to supply all the information students generally require in their methods courses. Rather, it will remind them of what they already know, fill in some gaps that are often not covered by methods courses, offer practical suggestions, and provide a setting for critical analysis of teaching activities. The orientation is toward practical suggestions needed by busy student teachers. We hope that this handbook will give prospective teachers greater confidence as they prepare for their profession and that it will make the preparation more enjoyable.

TEXT FEATURES

Each chapter opens with an introductory vignette to initiate discussion of the material in the chapter. Questions following each vignette and discussion questions at the end of each chapter encourage reflection about the material in the chapters and about ways to apply the information.

Throughout the text, case studies focus on situations that student teachers may encounter. Analyzing these case studies and considering the other discussion questions in the chapter are good seminar activities for student teachers and practicum students.

Activities related to topics in each chapter enable students to apply information from the text to actual teaching situations. A special listing of these application activities follows the table of contents. Each chapter contains sections entitled "For Your Portfolio," which suggest materials for students to include in their professional portfolios. Selected references guide students to additional reading.

TEXT ORGANIZATION

This text is divided into four major parts. Part I, Preparation for Teaching, consists of three chapters that help the student get ready to teach. Chapter 1 addresses observation of teaching and other school procedures, orientation to the school's facilities and policies, extracurricular activities, self-understanding, and practices related to good teaching—all issues students need to know about as background for engaging in teaching activities. Chapter 2 focuses on the relationships a student teacher or practicum student will have with other people in the school. The diversity of students in today's classrooms receives extensive attention in Chapter 3. Because of inclusion and mainstreaming, all student teachers need information on this topic.

Part II, Organization and Management, consists of two chapters. Chapter 4 provides information on several important aspects of classroom administration: grouping, scheduling, keeping records, supervising students, and the classroom environment. Chapter 5 offers practical suggestions about discipline—the main worry of many student teachers.

Part III, Curriculum, consisting of five chapters, deals with many aspects of curriculum. It opens with Chapter 6, Instructional Planning, which offers practical suggestions about planning for both instruction and evaluation. Chapter 7, Language, Thinking, and Learning across the Curriculum, discusses language skills, higher-order thinking skills, and study skills. Chapter 8, Instructional Resources, emphasizes technology, while also considering various other instructional resources that students should know how to use to enhance their teaching. Part III concludes with a chapter on teaching strategies (Chapter 9), which includes motivation and classroom teaching techniques.

The final chapter—Chapter 10, Moving On—constitutes Part IV, Beyond Student Teaching. It provides information about entering the teaching profession and gives suggestions for locating and applying for positions and information about continuing one's professional growth after obtaining a position. It also provides information about professional ethics and legal issues that are important to all teachers.

Three appendixes offer helpful information: Appendix A, Assessment Instruments; B, Sample Unit and Lesson Plans; and C, Sample Learning Center.

CHANGES IN THE FIFTH EDITION

This fifth edition has been reorganized into four major parts: Preparation for Teaching; Organization and Management; Curriculum; and Beyond Student Teaching. This organization gives the reader a logical framework for locating information. Chapters on classroom administration and discipline have been moved closer to the beginning of the text, since they are of immediate and intense concern to student teachers.

New or expanded sections reflect current topics of interest in education, including new or updated information on cultural diversity, conflict resolution, student self-discipline, communities of learners, computer applications and other uses of technology, and the constructivist approach to learning.

Because many prospective teachers create portfolios to show potential employers, we have added a new feature entitled **For Your Portfolio.** This feature appears at least three times in each chapter, except Chapter 1, where it is introduced, and covers a wide range of topics. It enables students to expand their portfolios continually as they gain new insights into education.

All chapters have been updated and include some new material, and the additions or expansions to some chapters are particularly noteworthy. Chapter 1 introduces teaching portfolios and suggests that students begin to collect items for these portfolios. Chapter 4, on classroom administration, addresses conflict resolution; and Chapter 5 considers ways in which students can be more responsible for their own behavior and become part of a classroom community. Chapter 6 has added material on teaching in accordance with standards. Chapter 8 is extensively updated, with new information on computers and the Internet, as well as other technological applications, such as cable television and calculators. Chapter 9 contains an updated version of Howard Gardner's ideas on multiple intelli-

gences, along with sample lessons; and Chapter 10 lists professional organizations with their addresses so that beginning teachers can remain knowledgeable in their fields.

THEORETICAL AND CONCEPTUAL FRAMEWORK

This text follows a widely accepted research-based framework. Although theory is important, it is of little use unless accompanied by practical applications. This text provides both theory and practice activities to involve prospective teachers in implementing theory.

We believe that students should be at the center of learning. Therefore, attention is given to diversity of origin, learning styles, and motivation, with the ultimate goal that students will become self-disciplined, lifelong learners. Relationships and interactions among personnel at all levels are valued, with an awareness that everyone plays a part in the education of young people. Emphasis is placed on learning through technology, since computers are and will continue to be an essential element of society. Believing that students learn best through an integrated curriculum, we stress connections among the language arts and all subjects across the curriculum. We also feel that a prospective teacher's education should not end at the conclusion of student teaching, so we support the idea of future professional development throughout an educator's career.

ACKNOWLEDGMENTS

We thank Allan F. Cook, University of Illinois at Springfield; Sandra L. DiGiaimo, University of Scranton; Barbara P. Elias, Virginia State University; Jeri-Lynn Gatto, Richard Stockton State College; Sara Delano Moore, University of Kentucky; and Rosemary F. Schiavi, Loras College for their helpful reviews of this manuscript. Their insightful comments were greatly appreciated.

We are also grateful to Alice Pleming and Kathy Dooley for permission to use excerpts from their student teaching journals.

Discover the Companion Website Accompanying This Book

THE PRENTICE HALL COMPANION WEBSITE: A VIRTUAL LEARNING ENVIRONMENT

Technology is a constantly growing and changing aspect of our field that is creating a need for content and resources. To address this emerging need, Prentice Hall has developed an online learning environment for students and professors alike—Companion Websites—to support our textbooks.

In creating a Companion Website, our goal is to build on and enhance what the textbook already offers. For this reason, the content for each user-friendly website is organized by topic and provides the professor and student with a variety of meaningful resources. Common features of a Companion Website include:

FOR THE PROFESSOR—

Every Companion Website integrates **Syllabus Manager™,** an online syllabus creation and management utility.

- **Syllabus Manager™** provides you, the instructor, with an easy, step-by-step process to create and revise syllabi, with direct links into Companion Website and other online content without having to learn HTML.
- Students may log on to your syllabus during any study session. All they need to know is the web address for the Companion Website and the password you've assigned to your syllabus.
- After you have created a syllabus using **Syllabus Manager™,** students may enter the syllabus for their course section from any point in the Companion Website.
- Clicking on a date, the student is shown the list of activities for the assignment. The activities for each assignment are linked directly to actual content, saving time for students.
- Adding assignments consists of clicking on the desired due date, then filling in the details of the assignment—name of the assignment, instructions,

and whether or not it is a one-time or repeating assignment.

- In addition, links to other activities can be created easily. If the activity is online, a URL can be entered in the space provided, and it will be linked automatically in the final syllabus.
- Your completed syllabus is hosted on our servers, allowing convenient updates from any computer on the Internet. Changes you make to your syllabus are immediately available to your students at their next logon.

FOR THE STUDENT—

- **Topic Overviews**—outline key concepts in topic areas
- **Web Links**—a wide range of websites that provide useful and current information related to each topic area
- **Lesson Plans**—links to lesson plans for appropriate topic areas
- **Projects on the Web**—links to projects and activities on the web for appropriate topic areas
- **Education Resources**—links to schools, online journals, government sites, departments of education, professional organizations, regional information, and more
- **Electronic Bluebook**—send homework or essays directly to your instructor's e-mail with this paperless form
- **Message Board**—serves as a virtual bulletin board to post—or respond to—questions or comments to/from a national audience
- **Chat**—real-time chat with anyone who is using the text anywhere in the country—ideal for discussion and study groups, class projects, etc.

To take advantage of these and other resources, please visit the Companion Website for *Student Teaching and Field Experiences, Fifth Edition,* at

www.prenhall.com/roe

Brief Contents

Contents

CHAPTER 9

Teaching Strategies   197

Part IV: Beyond Student Teaching

CHAPTER 10

Moving On   224

APPENDIX A

Assessment Instruments   246

APPENDIX B

Sample Unit and Lesson Plans   253

APPENDIX C

Sample Learning Center: Fabulous Fables   265

SUBJECT INDEX   269

NAME INDEX   275

NOTE: Every effort has been made to provide accurate and current Internet information in this book. However, the Internet and information posted on it are constantly changing, so it is inevitable that some of the Internet addresses listed in this text book will change.

Application Activities

Getting Ready

What Am I Supposed To Be Doing?

Mr. Wiley is the cooperating teacher; Mr. Allen is his student teacher; Mrs. Paris is the principal.

Mrs. Paris: Mr. Allen, I just received a call from Mr. Wiley. He's having car trouble and won't be able to get here on time. I realize you didn't expect to be in charge of the class this morning, but you have been observing for a week. You should be able to take care of the attendance and lunch records with no problem. He said the first two classes will be easy to handle, too. In one, you just have to give the test he left in his file cabinet, already duplicated. He should be here before the students finish the test. Good luck! Call on me if you have any problems.

Mr. Allen: Thank you, Mrs. Paris. I'll do my best. (Mrs. Paris exits. Mr. Allen goes to Mr. Wiley's desk and begins searching for the register. He finds it and looks at it in dismay. He can't remember how to fill it out. He watched Mr. Allen do it before, but he hadn't observed carefully enough. Embarrassed, he goes next door to ask another teacher, rather than sending a child to get the principal. In the meantime, the children, left alone in the classroom, go wild. They run around the room, throw things, and yell. When Mr. Allen returns to the room with information about how to fill out his records, chaos reigns. "How does Mr. Wiley quiet them down?" he thinks in panic. "I have to do something fast.")

Mr. Allen (in a loud voice): Class! Be quiet! Return to your seats! (Mr. Allen's voice is hardly heard above the racket and has little effect. He suddenly remembers what he has seen Mr. Wiley do before, in a less chaotic situation. Mr. Allen quickly walks over and flips the classroom lights off, waits a few seconds, and flips them on again. The noise and movement slowly begin to abate. He flips the switch off and on again, and the room becomes quieter still. Now his voice can be heard.)

Mr. Allen: Go to your seats, and listen for your name as I call the roll. (To his surprise and relief, the students comply. The record keeping proceeds smoothly, and Mr. Allen feels more confident. Then he realizes that he doesn't remember which lesson is first on Thursday mornings, since every day is not the same. Once again embarrassed, he turns to the students.)

Mr. Allen: What do we do first on Thursdays?

Chorus of answers: Spelling! Recess! (Mr. Allen knows recess isn't first, so he looks for the spelling book, wondering what activity to do on Thursday. Then he remembers the lesson planner Mr. Wiley keeps in his desk drawer. He finds the planner and verifies that the spelling lesson comes first. He also discovers that Mr. Wiley has planned a trial test for today. He saw Mr. Wiley give a trial test last week, but he doesn't remember the exact procedure. He leaps into the activity anyway, giving each word and a sentence with it, as he vaguely remembers Mr. Wiley doing.)

Randy: You're supposed to say the word again after you give the sentence. That's the way Mr. Wiley does it.

Mr. Allen (frustrated and upset): Well, I'm doing it today, and I'll do it my way.

Rachel: What was the word again?

Mr. Allen: Clothes.

Randy: Mr. Wiley never repeats a word after we've passed it.

Rachel: Like you close a door?

Mr. Allen: Didn't you listen to my sentence, Rachel? Just do your best. (The test proceeds along these lines until it is finished.)

Mr. Allen: Pass your papers to the front.

Joe: But we grade our own trial tests so we'll learn the words better. (Suddenly remembering that this is so, Mr. Allen decides to do it the way Mr. Wiley would. Half the papers have already been passed to the front.)

Mr. Allen: Okay. I'll let you check your own papers. Pass them back to their owners. (Papers are passed back, amid much murmuring. Mr. Allen has to flip the lights off and on again. While this is happening, Mr. Wiley walks in.)

Mr. Wiley: I'm sorry I'm late. I had car trouble. How did things go?

Mr. Allen: Okay.

Mr. Wiley: If you've finished that English test, that's perfect. We can go right on to math.

Mr. Allen: We didn't get to the English test yet. These are the spelling papers.

Mr. Wiley: You took all this time on spelling? I'm going to have to help you budget your time better.

Mr. Allen (shamefacedly): Yes, sir.

1. What is the difference between just watching and truly observing?
2. Had Mr. Allen been a good observer? Why do you say so?
3. Do you observe procedures carefully enough to be able to perform them alone, if necessary?

THE CHALLENGE OF TEACHING

You are about to enter the teaching profession. Before you become a fully qualified teacher, you will have many experiences working with students under the guidance of a cooperating teacher and a university supervisor. With their suggestions and your knowledge, you will discover many techniques for helping students learn. Your introduction to teaching will be gradual, so you will be prepared to assume additional responsibilities as you encounter them.

When you begin teaching, your point of view will change. As a student, you have worried about paying attention to teachers, spending long hours doing homework, and taking tests. As a teacher, you will have different concerns. How do you prepare informative lessons that will keep each student interested? How do you find the time to plan tomorrow's lessons after teaching all day? How do you make up tests that will truly evaluate what each student has learned?

Teaching is both a wonderful opportunity and a serious responsibility. The countless minute-by-minute decisions that teachers make, along with the kind of support and instruction they provide, can make the difference between students' success and failure. Teachers never really know the extent of their influence. What you teach may affect students in such a way that they will, in turn, influence others. As you teach, be sensitive to the needs and feelings of your students, and let them know that you believe in their ability to succeed.

SOME PRACTICAL MATTERS

Undoubtedly, you will have a lot of questions as you begin student teaching or a practicum in teaching. Try to get a policy handbook, as well as a floor plan of the school, to familiarize yourself with procedures and the layout of the building. Find answers to questions such as these:

Where do I park?

What time should I be here, and when should I leave?

Do I need to sign in at the office when I arrive?

What responsibilities do I have for lunch and bus duty?

What should I do if there is a fire drill?

When and where may I make personal phone calls?

What should I do in case I must be absent because of illness or an emergency?

Is there a dress code for teachers that I must follow?

You may also need to resolve some personal circumstances that might interfere with your effectiveness as a teacher. The following case studies present some potential conflicts to consider, and you are likely to know of others.

To become familiar with student and parent handbooks for schools, visit *http://www.prenhall.com/methods-cluster,* "Topic 10: Policies and Handbooks." Compare one or more of the handbooks linked to this site with the one for the school to which you are assigned.

CASE STUDY 1.1

Job Conflict

Nathan works after school at a child-care center, and he needs the money he earns there for tuition and living expenses. School ends at 3:00 and his job begins at 3:00, so there is no time for after-school activities or planning sessions. What are his options?

CASE STUDY 1.2

Sick Child

Ashley, a single parent, has a six-year-old daughter who has chronic ear infections with high fevers. Ashley has no family nearby and feels that she must stay home when her daughter is ill. What are some other options for Ashley?

CASE STUDY 1.3

Missed Connections

Nicole's husband works the night shift and gets home about 7:00 in the morning, unless he misses the bus. When he is late, Nicole is late to school because she cannot leave their baby alone. What can Nicole do if her husband is late?

CASE STUDY 1.4

Car Pool

Sally, Joe, and Curt ride to school together. Sally and Joe are nearly always on time, but Curt keeps them waiting. Then all three are late for school. What should they do?

CASE STUDY 1.5

Personality Conflict

No matter how hard he tries, Cody cannot seem to please Miss Logan, his cooperating teacher. Cody realizes that they are quite different; she is structured and formal and he is holistic and less formal. He tries to be pleasant, prepared, and conforming, but she always finds fault. What should Cody do?

CASE STUDY 1.6

No Clothes to Wear

Tyler comes from a poor home and has had to work hard to pay school expenses. His wardrobe consists of jeans and T-shirts and not much else. He realizes he needs better clothes but cannot afford them. What choices does he have?

OBSERVING THE CLASSROOM TEACHER

When you begin a practicum or begin student teaching, you will probably spend most of your time observing. It is important to learn as much as you can from this observation time. You may want to begin keeping a journal of your thoughts during observations and continue it as you move into teaching. Recording your reactions, exploring your beliefs, and reflecting on your development as a teacher in your journal can be one of your most valuable activities as a student teacher. Your college supervisor may even require such a journal.

What Is Observation?

To benefit fully from your observation period, you need to realize that "observing" and "looking at" are not the same. Observation involves close attention to detail, analysis and evaluation of what is happening, and assimilation of new ideas into your existing store of information.

In the opening vignette of this chapter, Mr. Allen had spent a week *looking at* what was going on in the classroom, not carefully *observing* it. Therefore, he did not gain the maximum benefit from his observation time. If *you* are to use your observation time to best advantage, you need to know *what* to look for and *how* to look at what you are observing.

When you enter the classroom for your first day of student teaching, your cooperating teacher will probably introduce you to the class and suggest that you spend the next few days observing to get the "feel" of the classroom and learn the general procedures of a typical day. The cooperating teacher may mention that you should become aware of the teaching and disciplinary techniques in use, with a view toward developing your own approach to teaching. Whether or not this is mentioned, you should indeed be alert for these techniques, examining them analytically and critically as you consider them for possible use when *you* are teaching.

It is a good idea to ask your cooperating teacher if there is a seating chart to use as you observe. If such a chart exists, copy it, so that you can take it home and study it at night. If one is not available, construct one, with your teacher's help, before the next observation. Learning the students' names is extremely important for developing rapport with them and maintaining classroom control. At the secondary level, with several different sets of students' names to learn, it is extremely important to apply yourself immediately to the task. Learning names is usually easier at the elementary level, because you generally see fewer students each day, but it is no less important to your success.

At the beginning of the day, your cooperating teacher will probably first check attendance, and, at the elementary level, collect lunch money. Don't just *look at* the process. Observe it. Notice how the teacher marks the register. Make notes, if necessary. If there is roll call, look at each student when his or her name is called. Try to fix the students in mind. Note features that will help you remember the students. You may miss a few students on the first round, but study as many as you can; fill in others later in the day or on subsequent days of observations, adding to your notes each day. Study these notes after school, and try to connect all your students with their names as quickly as possible.

Before actually beginning to teach, take advantage of opportunities to observe your cooperating teacher—observe, don't just look.

Get a daily schedule from the cooperating teacher so that you will be aware of the order of classes, times for breaks and special activities, and beginning and dismissal times. Secondary student teachers may find that each day's schedule is essentially the same with the exception of variations for assembly schedules, test schedules, and other special events, or they may find that block scheduling results in days that look very different. Elementary student teachers often have a different schedule for each day of the week. Whichever is the case for you, familiarize yourself with the schedule as quickly as possible. Don't be left, as Mr. Allen was, wondering what comes next.

Areas of Observation

As your cooperating teacher begins to teach, once again, don't just be a *looker*; be an *observer*. To observe properly, you need to know *what* to look for. Activity 1.1 is a form that contains questions that can help you focus on important aspects of your observations. It covers 11 observation areas. Complete it for one of the observations that you do as your cooperating teacher presents a lesson. You may wish to photocopy the blank form to use with other observations for your own benefit or at the request of your college supervisor.

You can facilitate note-taking when you observe by making a separate page for each of these 11 observation areas. Merely recording carefully the details of the lessons you observe will be beneficial, but it is not enough. At this point, you must analyze what you have seen and evaluate it critically. Below the notes you make on each observation area, write a brief analysis and evaluation (or do this mentally). Once again, some structure may help. Here are some questions you can ask yourself about each of the 11 observation areas.

Area 1.   Did the students seem to grasp how the lesson was tied to previous learning? Did the motivational activities seem to arouse students' interest? Why do you think they did or did not accomplish their goal?

Area 2.   Were the purpose and relevance of the lesson made clear to the students? Why or why not? How might they have been better clarified?

Area 3.   Were the teacher's procedures for presenting the content effective? Might some other procedures have been more effective? Why do you think so?

Area 4. Were the lesson materials appropriate and effective? Would other materials have been more effective? Why do you think so?

Area 5. Was the teaching style effective with this particular group and for this particular lesson? Why do you think so? If the style was ineffective, what might have worked better?

Area 6. Did the teacher seem to have adequate knowledge of the subject matter? Was enough outside knowledge brought into the lesson? If not, what else should have been included? Was content effectively related to the students' lives? If not, how might this aspect of the lesson have been improved?

Area 7. Were adequate provisions made for individual differences? If not, what steps might have been taken to improve the situation?

Area 8. Were disciplinary techniques appropriate and effective? Why do you think so? If they were inappropriate or ineffective, what techniques might have been better?

Area 9. Did the teacher's personal qualities advance the lesson effectively? Why do you think so? Might changes in this area be helpful to future lessons?

Area 10. Was the conclusion of the lesson effective? Why? If not, what might have been done to improve it?

Area 11. Were the teacher's evaluation techniques appropriate and effective? Why do you think so? If not, what techniques might have been better?

Even after this analysis and evaluation, you are not through with your observation. Now you must once again examine each observation area and ask yourself these questions: "How can I incorporate this into my teaching? Will I want to use this technique, or an alternative I think would be better? How does what I have seen fit into what I have learned in my methods courses? Are there areas in which I need clarification?" If you answer "yes" to the last question, you should seek clarification immediately from your cooperating teacher, college supervisor, college textbooks, or a combination of these sources.

Policies and Procedures

You should be observing more than lesson presentations. We have already pointed out the need to observe record-keeping processes, but there are many other areas you need to observe carefully: procedures for carrying out bus, lunchroom, hall, or playground duty, or any of the other duties teachers are frequently called upon to perform. Watch for time factors, control methods, procedures for handling special cases, and so on. Inquire about schoolwide rules, if you have not been supplied with a handbook outlining them. Take notes on what you see and hear so that you can adhere strictly to school policy in the future.

Since teachers are also expected to attend faculty meetings, parent-teacher meetings, in-service sessions, and professional meetings, you would do well to attend these with your cooperating teacher for the purpose of observation. Your cooperating teacher may be asked to chaperone a school dance or take tickets for an extracurricular activity, such as a play, concert, dance, or athletic event. Observing these activities will help you understand better just what working as a teacher entails.

Such small details as the method of dismissal in the afternoon are worthy of note. In many schools, not all students leave the room at the same time. If this is true in your school, make it a point to know who leaves when and why. In many schools, you also need to find out how hall passes are handled. Observe your teacher, and ask questions about general procedures if they do not seem clear.

If you observe carefully, you won't end up like Mr. Allen, and you'll be more ready for teaching when your opportunity comes.

EXTRACURRICULAR ACTIVITIES

In some elementary schools and most secondary schools, students participate voluntarily in a number of school-sponsored activities. School sponsorship makes faculty involvement in these activities important. As a student teacher, you will probably be involved in the extracurricular activities in which your cooperating teacher is involved. You may, however, be asked to help with other extracurricular activities in which you have special interest or expertise. You may be asked to do something as simple as taking tickets or chaperoning a dance or something as difficult as directing a dramatization or coaching defensive ends.

Typical extracurricular activities center around clubs (science, photography, mathematics, computer, drama, foreign language, community action, future teachers, etc.); school publications (magazines, annuals, newspapers); athletic teams (football, basketball, soccer, baseball, track, golf, volleyball, wrestling); musical groups (marching band, jazz band, orchestra, chorus); and scholastic honor societies (Beta Club, Quill and Scroll, National Honor Society). School-sponsored dances, carnivals, and festivals also qualify

ACTIVITY I.I   **Observation Form**

Answer the questions or place a check beside the appropriate responses.

Date: _____   Class observed: _____

Area I   How did the teacher:

   I. Start the lesson? _____

       _____

   2. Tie it to previous learning? _____

       _____

   3. Arouse students' interest? _____

       _____

Area 2   How did the teacher make the purpose and relevance of the lesson apparent?

   I. By making direct statements _____

   2. By eliciting reactions from students _____

   3. Other (Specify.) _____

Area 3   What procedures were incorporated into the body of the lesson?

   I. Lecture _____

   2. Discussion _____

   3. Audiovisual presentation _____

   4. Demonstration _____

   5. Student activities _____

Area 4   What materials were used in the course of the lesson?

   I. Textbooks _____

   2. Supplementary books _____

   3. Films _____

   4. Computers _____

   5. Audiotapes _____

   6. Videotapes _____

   7. Television _____

   8. Concrete objects _____

   9. Transparencies _____

   10. Illustrations _____

   11. Models _____

   12. Videodiscs _____

   13. Other (Specify.) _____

Area 5 What was the teacher's style of teaching?

1. Direct _____

2. Indirect _____

Area 6 Did the teacher show a broad knowledge of the subjects area? _____ Did she or he stick to the textbook or bring in information from other sources as well? _____ Did she or he relate the subject matter to other content the students had studied, to current events, or to students' personal interests? _____ If so, how was this accomplished? _____

_____

_____

Area 7 What provisions were made for individual differences?

1. Small-group work _____

2. Individualized assignments _____

3. Differentiated reading materials _____

4. Other (Specify.) _____

Area 8 What disciplinary techniques did the teacher use?

1. Flipping the light switch _____

2. Penalty points _____

3. Deprivation of privileges _____

4. Reward system _____

5. Time-out _____

6. Other (Specify.) _____

Area 9 How did the teacher's personal qualities help advance the lesson?

1. Dressed appropriately, so that apparel did not distract from subject matter _____

2. Displayed no distracting mannerisms _____

3. Used correct grammar _____

4. Used appropriate voice volume and pitch _____

Area 10 How did the teacher end the lesson?

1. Summarized the day's learning _____

2. Assigned homework _____ If so, specify the kind of assignment. _____

3. Other (Specify.) _____

Area 11 What evaluation techniques did the teacher use in the course of the lesson?

1. Oral questions _____

2. Written questions _____

3. Observation of students' verbal responses _____

4. Observation of students' application skills _____

5. Other (Specify.) _____

Student teachers may be asked to help with extracurricular activities.

as extracurricular activities. This variety gives you a wide range from which to choose if you are asked to participate. The list of possibilities for after-hours involvement seems endless. You may help with science fair projects or work at a book fair; you may judge a storytelling contest or a debate; you may coach intramural sports, accompany students on special trips, mend costumes for a play, paint sets, move band equipment, organize the safety patrol—the list goes on and on. Students involved in extracurricular activities are usually highly motivated and therefore make the sessions enjoyable, so go ahead and give a chosen activity a try.

You may think of extracurricular activities as just another intrusion on your already vanishing free time, or you may remember that extracurricular activities were really important to you when you were the age of your students. Contribute some time and effort to give your students some valuable experiences.

If your school has a handbook, read the section on extracurricular activities. Find out what roles faculty members play and the rules and restrictions for each activity. Then you will be able to choose activities or assist with assigned activities knowledgeably.

You should encourage students to participate in extracurricular activities, because they gain experience that will help them succeed in later life. You might point out that these activities provide opportunities for gaining recognition, engaging in new experiences, developing talents, and extending textbook learning into meaningful experiences. You should also watch to be sure that students don't become too involved, however, and thereby place their academic progress at risk.

When you apply for a job, be sure to mention any extracurricular activities that you supported during student teaching. Direct experience with such activities as editing the school paper, constructing sets for a play, or sponsoring the computer club may make you a more valuable candidate for a teaching position.

SELF-ANALYSIS

As you move through your practicum or student teaching program, you should be constantly evaluating your own progress. Although the supervisory personnel with whom you work are providing feedback on your performance, you may be the best judge of your teaching. You can analyze the effectiveness of your lessons in a variety of ways.

Microteaching, Videotaping, and Audiotaping

You may microteach before or along with practicum experiences or student teaching. The idea of microteaching is to teach a brief lesson (about 5 to 15 minutes in length) to a small group of students. A microteaching lesson concentrates on only one or two specific skills, such as asking higher-order questions or incorporating planned repetition. After the teaching, a supervisor, a teacher, or another student critiques the performance. Some evaluative summary may be provided by the students taught. If the lesson is videotaped, there will be opportunity for pre-lesson and post-lesson comments when it is replanned for teaching to a new group of students. In brief, microteaching follows these steps:

1. The prospective teacher receives exposure to a specific teaching skill.
2. He or she practices the technique in a short lesson with four or five students.
3. The lesson is recorded or videotaped for review by the prospective teacher.
4. A supervisor critiques the lesson.
5. The prospective teacher has an opportunity to replan and reteach the lesson to another small group of students. This session may also be recorded and critiqued.

Instead of having only one person critique the lesson, you may wish to cooperate with other students in critiquing each others' lessons, or you may want to critique your lesson yourself. If videotaping equipment is not available, record your lesson on an audiotape and listen to it later at home. By going over tapes of your lessons, you can become aware of your voice control (audibility, pitch, expression), speech patterns (overuse of certain terms, such as "okay?"), use of praise and positive reinforcement, and clarity of directions. You can determine the kinds of questions you ask and the proportion of "student talk" to "teacher talk" during your lessons. If a videotape is used, you can also become aware of your use of non-verbal communication, such as encouraging nods, nervous gestures, or facial expressions.

Critical Analysis of Lesson Success

You and your cooperating teacher may wish to collaborate on evaluating certain lessons by using a form such as that in Activity 1.2. You should agree on the components that are to be evaluated and then separately rate a lesson or series of lessons. Then you should get together to compare notes and reconcile any differences. Over a period of time, you should try to improve those components that are indicated as needing improvement.

Other components that you may wish to include for certain lessons are giving clear directions, considering individual differences, maintaining discipline, organizing activities well, modeling or demonstrating desired learning, using audiovisual aids and resources appropriately, maintaining a positive classroom climate, asking higher-order questions, promoting positive self-concept in all students, encouraging wide student participation, using different teaching strategies, communicating effectively with students, and showing evidence of preparation.

Student Analysis

Your students observe your teaching on a daily basis, and you may be able to learn a great deal from them about your effectiveness. They may volunteer remarks, such as "Can we do that again?" or "Tell us more about whales," that can guide you in planning subsequent lessons. The students may also give you insights into your effectiveness by answering questions that you ask them, such as "What did you learn today?" and "Did you do better when you worked with a partner?"

To get a more formal type of evaluation from your students, administer a checklist to find out how they perceive you. For younger children, you may use a format similar to that in Figure 1–1. For older students, a format such as that in Figure 1–2 is appropriate.

ACTIVITY 1.2   *Rating Key Aspects of Instruction*

Using the form below, rate yourself for each component of instruction according to the following symbols: plus (+) for *good,* zero (0) for *no evidence,* or minus (−) for *needs improvement.* You may want to make a copy for your cooperating teacher to complete so that you can compare ratings. You may also want to make extra copies so that you can rate yourself periodically as you grow in your ability to teach.

COMPONENT	RATING	COMMENTS
1. Gaining and holding student attention		
2. Telling students what they are expected to learn		
3. Reminding students of related knowledge or skills		
4. Presenting new stimuli for learning		
5. Guiding students' thinking and learning		
6. Providing feedback about correctness		
7. Judging or appraising the performance		
8. Helping to generalize what is learned		
9. Providing practice for retention		
10. Other:		

FIGURE 1–1
Rating Instruction by
Younger Students

A. Marking Responses:

1. My teacher usually looks like this:

2. When I ask the teacher for help, he or she looks like this:

3. After I finish the lesson, I feel like this:

B. Oral Interview:

1. If I were the teacher, I would:

2. When I go to the teacher for help, he or she:

3. I would understand my lessons better if:

CASE STUDY 1.7

A Challenge to a Student Teacher's Evaluation

A student teacher, Ms. Downey, was teaching a chemistry class. She was trying to keep a close record of students' performance in her class. Through observation and analysis of students' responses, she quickly noted that three students appeared to have little interest in the subject. Also, their early work was of rather poor quality. After she checked the results of a couple of tests (each covering two weeks of instruction), it seemed clear that the students had not grasped the content presented during that period of time. Ms. Downey thought student-teacher conferences might be helpful. She brought the evidence of her concern to the conferences. During the three conferences, the students responded with comments such as these:

1. The tests were too hard, so I just guessed.
2. Most of the students missed the same questions I missed.
3. Chemistry is mostly for brainy students.
4. You don't make it clear what I'm supposed to learn.
5. You talk all the time.
6. You don't show much interest in us.

What objective data could Ms. Downey present to respond to each of these comments? What could she learn from these responses?

FIGURE 1–2
Rating Instruction by
Older Students

Student Opinion Questionnaire

A.   Circle the best answer.

   1. Are assignments and explanations clear? Are assignments reasonable?

     Rarely   Sometimes   Usually   Almost Always

   2. Is treatment of all students fair? Are students' ideas treated with respect?

     Rarely   Sometimes   Usually   Almost Always

   3. Do students behave well for the teacher?

     Rarely   Sometimes   Usually   Almost Always

   4. Is the teaching interesting and challenging?

     Rarely   Sometimes   Usually   Almost Always

   5. Do you feel free to raise questions?

     Rarely   Sometimes   Usually   Almost Always

B.   Write a short answer.

   1. Mention one or two things you like about this teacher.

   2. Mention one or two things this teacher might do to help you be a better student.

Reflective Teaching

According to John Dewey, *reflective teaching* is behavior that relates to active and persistent consideration of beliefs or practices in view of supporting evidence and the consequences to which it may lead (Canning, 1991). It is a thoughtful analysis of the teacher's actions, decisions, and results in the classroom. Although it requires time and effort, reflective teaching can give you insights about your effectiveness as a teacher. It can also cause you to question your procedures and consider alternatives, change any nonproductive routines, and try new ideas. Activity 1.3 gives some questions to ask yourself as you reflect on a lesson that you have taught.

Reflection can occur through many types of educational experiences—microteaching with self-analysis, conferences with your cooperating teacher, feedback from students, observations of other teachers in which you compare their strategies with your own, and journal writing. Of these, journal writing may be the most helpful way to reflect on your teaching. When you first begin your journal, you may feel that you are just rambling, putting down random thoughts that occur to you. As you continue writing, however, you may find that you begin to question, explore, and, finally, focus.

To get the most from your journal writing, write about incidents, problems, or issues that truly concern you—not your lesson plan or a list of the day's events. Express your feelings about your frustrations and your triumphs. Think deeply about their causes and consider what you need to do now. Writing can help clarify your thinking and enable you to reach conclusions about your teaching. (See Figure 1–3 for an example of a practicum student's journal entry.)

Perhaps your cooperating teacher or university teacher may assign journal writing. In this case, writing would be not only for your personal benefit but also so that someone with more experience could understand your needs and concerns in order to help you. Similarly, you may want to do journal writing with your students in order to get to know them better. To ensure that they won't simply recall the day's events, you may need to model a sample journal entry

ACTIVITY 1.3   **Questions That Reflective Teachers Ask Themselves**

Date: _____

Lesson: _____

Read and seriously consider the following questions. Choose several that pertain to your lesson and write answers for them.

1. Did the students learn anything? If so, why? If not, why not?

2. Did anything significant occur? If so, what and why?

3. Was the strategy I used the most effective one? What other strategies might have been effective?

4. How well did I relate the lesson to the students' knowledge, experiences, and interests? How might I have done this better?

5. How flexible was I in modifying the lesson according to the students' responses?

6. How well did I manage classroom behavior? What other behavioral techniques could I have used? What technique worked best and what didn't work? Why?

7. What connections were there between teaching strategies and students' learning? What does this tell me about what I need to do in the future?

8. What are some alternatives for conducting today's lesson?

9. How did I motivate the students? What are some other ways I might have motivated them?

10. Did I consider learning theory in preparing and implementing the lesson? If so, what theories worked? If not, what theories should I have considered?

11. Did I give students opportunities to direct their own learning? If so, how? If not, how could I have done this?

12. As a result of this lesson, what have I learned about teaching? How might I change to become a better teacher?

Teacher's signature _____

FIGURE 1–3
Excerpts from a Reading Practicum
Student's Journal

Oct. 19
I had to reteach what I taught yesterday. I really had to discipline a lot too. I feel that they understood the content of what we were doing better after we went over it again. We went over question by question to ensure that everyone was listening—learning? I really want to establish myself before I get off the strict basal lesson. When they deserve to do something fun, we will. I'm enjoying this. This is a real-life classroom. I am learning so much!

Oct. 20
They were so "bad" today, or was it me? It seemed those same three boys always cause so much trouble. I gave them something that really challenged them—it was obvious that they are not often challenged. They acted so completely confused. I took it up and they were doing, mostly, okay on it. The ones with the lower grades were obviously intentionally not trying. I will go over it tomorrow.

Nov. 4
I have to constantly tell them to be quiet!! Why won't they learn—they are going to get into trouble when they're loud. I gave them a skills test—they did great! No one has to retake it!! I felt so proud of my teaching!

Nov. 13
I almost lost it today. I had assigned them homework. Five of them had it and even remembered it. They never stopped talking! I didn't know what to do. It is so discouraging. Forget all the good stuff I've learned and heard to say and do. It makes me feel so bad.

Nov. 14
We started back on basal. Boy, did they hate it. This class is definitely "dynamic" and likes something besides plain old reading class. This will challenge me to add more creativity to these lessons.

Nov. 19
We had an interesting class today. First, Tommy was sent to alternative school ... today. The teacher was out of the class at a meeting because of that. Another lady sat in while she was gone. Two girls from my class observed me. I got evaluated. The principal came in and out about Tommy. That makes five extra people in the classroom besides myself and the students. They managed to stay tuned in fairly well. And I think I had them challenged with interesting issues about the story.

based on your own reflections about the lesson. You may do this on the chalkboard, a chart tablet, or a transparency, and then discuss what you wrote and why. A practical procedure is to provide time for students to write in their journals each day and for you to write a response to them about once a week. Here are some guiding questions to help your students write in their journals:

1. What did I learn?
2. What do I want to know more about?
3. What don't I understand very well?

PORTFOLIO DEVELOPMENT

When you apply for a job in the teaching profession, you are likely to be asked to provide a portfolio that reflects the work you have done in the field. Those who are seeking teaching jobs for the first time will need to have a portfolio of material that they have compiled from their practicum and student teaching experiences. Development of a portfolio is discussed thoroughly in Chapter 10. As you move through teaching and other educational activities in the schools, you should be collecting your best center, lesson, and unit plans; examples of your involvement with extracurricular and professional development activities; examples of your evaluations from supervisors and students; and your personal reflections on your experiences. Don't forget to save artifacts, such as audiotapes, videotapes, disk copies of websites you have developed or helped develop, and sample work from your students. At the end of your student teaching experience, you should have abundant evidence that you can perform the jobs for which you apply.

To start your portfolio, choose one or more of the following items:

1. an artifact from an extracurricular activity with which you are working—a program from a play you directed, a diagram from a marching band show you helped develop or field, a copy of a school publication for which you were an adviser, or something similar.
2. a videotape of a microteaching lesson.
3. the results of an evaluation by your students, your cooperating teacher, or your university supervisor.
4. a self-reflection about your teaching, similar to Activity 1.3.

STRESS

As a practicum student or student teacher, you face many pressures: teaching lessons for the first time, preparing to enter the job market, and handling social, family, and monetary demands. These pressures can cause stress, and stress can affect your teaching. It can also affect your physical and emotional well-being. How you deal with stress will determine to a great extent how successful you will be in teaching.

Understanding Stress

Stress results from anxiety. It occurs when people have trouble coping with the demands of a situation. The most stressful situations are those that people are least able to control.

An increase in stress and subsequent "burnout" has become a major concern in the teaching profession. This high rate of stress is caused by many factors, including lack of respect from students, potential violence among students, run-down school buildings, and unreasonable expectations from the public. Teachers often even have to be monitors of the clothing that students wear, as dress codes in schools become more prevalent and/or more restrictive. Teachers are held accountable for helping students attain certain levels of achievement; additionally, they find they must also act as counselors and stand-in parents. They are pressured to individualize, evaluate, motivate, and maintain discipline. Good teachers must combine all their knowledge, skill, and training in their daily encounters with students.

Although too much stress can cause physical and emotional problems, a certain amount of stress is desirable. Stress can give you a burst of energy and get your adrenaline flowing. In the right amount, stress will enable you to "rise to the occasion" and put forth the extra energy to get the job done.

Sources of Stress

Any situation involving worry or tension may cause stress. You may encounter some of these sources of stress:

1. *Too much work for the time available*—You find you are staying up late at night and working on weekends to get everything done. You have practically no free time and not enough social life. The day moves too quickly, and extra responsibilities—working on the school newspaper, bus duty, playground supervision—further intrude on your time.
2. *Unpleasant working environment*—Not everyone faces this problem, but those who do face it are disturbed by overcrowded classrooms; poorly maintained buildings; or old, drab schools with poor lighting in potentially dangerous inner-city neighborhoods.
3. *Lack of resources*—Some schools have old audiovisual equipment in need of repair. Books and materials you would like to use with your unit may be unavailable or outdated. Videotapes or films may need to be ordered so far in advance that they cannot reach you in time to be used.
4. *Poor relationships with coworkers*—You may not get along with your cooperating teacher or other personnel. You may feel they are not interested in helping you, expect too much from you, do not give you enough freedom, or are too critical.
5. *Evaluation by supervisors*—Being evaluated is probably stressful for you. You worry about how your supervisors regard your efforts, especially if they observe one of your less successful lessons.
6. *Job market*—The job market may be tight when you graduate and seek employment. You may worry about how you will support yourself if you can't get a teaching job.

If you allow stress to affect you negatively, you may develop physical and emotional reactions. Some of these are probably already familiar to you—sweaty palms, rapid breathing and heartbeat, tense muscles, and queasy stomach. This kind of stress is normal and temporary, but continued stress cannot only affect you physically and emotionally but also have a detrimental effect on your teaching. You will tend to be grouchy, impatient, and short-tempered with your students. In order to prevent this, consider the positive responses to stress in the next section.

Positive Responses to Stress

There is no doubt that teachers encounter stressful situations in their profession. What makes the difference between job satisfaction and burnout is the way teachers cope with these situations.

Figure 1–4 describes several stressful situations, reactions to them, stress ratings, and strategies for avoidance and management. The ratings rank from 1 (lowest stress) to 10 (highest stress). Make a similar chart for one day of your student teaching, including your own ideas for avoidance and management strategies (see Activity 1.4). If four or more stressful situations are rated 8 or above, you will need to give serious attention to reducing the stress in your life.

Attitudes

Your attitude toward yourself is important in how you handle stress. Recognize and accept your strengths and weaknesses. For instance, instead of envying another practicum student's or student teacher's artistic talent, make the most of your own special skills. If you can play a guitar, find a way to include a guitar selection in your lesson. If you can do some magic tricks, use magic to get the students' attention when you introduce a lesson. Know your limitations as well, and don't try to do something that probably won't succeed.

Be well prepared for each lesson. Thorough knowledge of content and methods will help you feel confident as you teach. Then, even if things don't go exactly as you expect, you can complete the lesson so that the students get the message.

Think positively! Don't say to yourself, "I'll never get all this work finished" or "These students are impossible." Instead, tell yourself, "I really got that point across" or "I think I'm finally making some headway."

Avoid worrying. Many things you worry about never happen. Other things work themselves out without the serious consequences you feared. Worrying doesn't solve problems; it only makes you less effective as a teacher. Don't worry about things you can't change; do something about things you *can* change.

Relationships

Find time to be with friends during student teaching. Unlike practicum experiences, student teaching is very intensive in its focus. You don't move from one set of circumstances to another throughout the day as you did in your earlier preparation program. You are concentrated on your responsibilities to the school and students to which you have been assigned.

Therefore, you need some change of pace in your life. Some friends should be outside the field of education so that you can get your mind off school. You need to forget your students and teaching obligations for a while and laugh and talk about other things. You will also want some friends in whom you can confide about problems with your student teaching. By sharing your difficulties with each other, you may see things from a different point of view and be willing to try a new approach.

Your working relationships with supervisory personnel and other student teachers also are important. If you have a conflict with someone, it is usually best to discuss the problem with that person instead of worrying about it. Perhaps it is based on a misunderstanding and can be readily resolved. If there is simply a personality conflict or a basic difference in point of view, accept the situation, and get along the best you can. The relationship is only temporary.

Don't forget that your students may also be under stress. They don't know exactly what to expect from you. Let them know what your standards of behavior are and what will happen if they violate them. Give warnings only when you are prepared to act on them. Give assignments clearly so students will know what to do. Show them that you care and are willing to help. Be fair and consistent. If you can relieve your students' stress, they will perform better for you.

Dealing with Stress

One of the first steps in dealing with a problem that produces stress is to decide if the problem is really *yours*. If it isn't, turn it over to the person responsible for it. If it is your problem, brainstorm ways to solve it. If you don't know how to solve it, get help. Then proceed to solve the problem the best way you can.

When you feel stress because you have so many things to do, make a list of all the tasks that must be done, in order of their importance. Consider what must be done right away so that it will be completed when it is needed, such as starting a science experiment that takes two weeks to reach fruition. Set deadlines for getting these things done, and stick to your schedule. As you finish each task, check it off. This way you are aware of your accomplishments and aren't as likely to fall behind.

Don't worry about assignments that seem too big. Break them into manageable chunks, and work on them one piece at a time. Do the hardest parts first, and save the most interesting tasks until the end. Each time you successfully complete one portion of the assignment, you will be motivated to try another until you are finished.

Time	Stressful Situation	Reactions	Rating	Avoidance/Management Strategies
6:30 a.m.	Can't decide what to wear. Out of cereal for breakfast. Can't find car keys.	Felt rushed, tense, annoyed at self, hungry.	4	Decide what to wear the night before; check food supplies and keep adequate stock; always put car keys in same place. Set alarm clock 15 minutes earlier to allow for unexpected problems.
7:20 a.m.	Have to wait 10 minutes for car pool passenger.	Hated to waste time, especially after rushing around to get ready.	5	Use waiting time productively. Check over lesson plans; think about what to do about the problems Marty is having.
9:15 a.m.	Fire drill while introducing lesson. Students are excited and won't settle down again.	Felt angry with school for ruining my lesson. Why can't they have fire drills when nothing is going on?	8	Can't avoid fire drills. Need to stay more relaxed, give students more time to get back to the lesson. Don't push them—or myself—so much.
11:30 a.m.	Jack pulled a knife on Eddie. Kids gathered around. Looked as though a mean fight was coming.	Panic! Didn't know how to handle this one. Stood there like an idiot. Principal stopped it.	8	Must check with teacher about what to do. Need to be prepared to deal with such situations.
1:45 p.m.	Spied the university supervisor out of the corner of my eye as he entered to observe my lesson.	Couldn't remember what I was supposed to say next. Worried about the students' restlessness.	9	Be well prepared and know exactly what to do. Don't let the students get out of control. Do the best job I can and forget about Mr. Henry's being there.
3:00 p.m.	Cliff's mother accused me of being unfair to him. She claimed Cliff says I am "picking on him."	Felt unjustly accused, completely bewildered by her unfair statement. Wanted to shout, "It's not true!"	9	There has been a misunderstanding. Discuss the matter calmly. Find out why Cliff feels this way. Possibly include him in our conversation. Don't get angry!
7:30 p.m.	Left my teacher's manual at school. Will have to wait until morning to plan my lessons. Probably won't do well.	Felt disgusted with myself for forgetting it, worried about not being prepared for tomorrow's lesson.	5	Can I find an extra copy of the manual in the storeroom to keep at home? Need to put everything to take home in a special place so I won't forget. Get some any-occasion ideas to fill in.
10:00 p.m.	Just realized I have to put up a bulletin board tomorrow! I'll have to make it tonight.	Felt overwhelmed with so much to do and not enough time, angry at cooperating teacher for making so many assignments.	8	Keep a calendar of due dates. Try to keep ahead on assignments. Must get my sleep or I'll be a nervous wreck the next day.

FIGURE 1–4
A Day of Student Teaching

ACTIVITY 1.4   **One Day of Student Teaching**

TIME	STRESSFUL SITUATION	REACTIONS	RATING	AVOIDANCE/ MANAGEMENT STRATEGIES

Keep your sense of humor. Be able to laugh with the children at your own mistakes. It is better to laugh with them when something goes wrong than to get angry. Even though it may not seem funny when it happens, you may see the humor later. Besides, laughter reduces stress, while anger increases it.

Feel free to say "no" to people when you feel you can't handle another responsibility. Do what is required of you and a little more, but don't accept unreasonable demands on your time. Someone may be taking advantage of your good nature. If you take on more responsibilities than you can manage, you will not do well in anything.

Taking Action

Some activities will keep stress from getting the better of you. Exercise—jogging, walking briskly, playing tennis or racquetball, working out in the gym—is good for you as a change of pace. Even though these forms of exercise can be physically tiring, they leave you with a pleasant, relaxed tiredness, rather than the tense exhaustion you may feel at the end of a school day. Be careful to avoid highly competitive games, though, or you may defeat your purpose of reducing stress.

Getting enough sleep is important in staying fit for the classroom and avoiding nervous tension. For some people, a nap after school relieves that drained feeling. When you go to bed, try not to go over what happened in school or what you plan to do tomorrow. You need to relax before you can sleep, so try reading a magazine or watching an entertaining television show.

You can't do schoolwork all the time, so turn to hobbies or relaxing mental activities for those free times when you are alone. Read a novel, or solve a crossword puzzle. Do something easy that involves a different sort of mental activity. You can't worry about school when you are thinking about something else.

You may want to fill out the questionnaire in Activity 1.5 to analyze how you manage stress. Most reactions to stress fall into one of four categories: freeze, flee, fight, or compromise. Learn your most effective ways of dealing with stress, and use these techniques to relieve future stressful situations.

FOR YOUR PORTFOLIO

Consider putting Activity 1.4 or 1.5 in your portfolio, if either one shows qualities that you want potential employers to know about.

PRACTICES RELATED TO GOOD TEACHING

One way to be successful in your student teaching is to know and apply teaching practices that are supported by research, such as the following (Goodlad, 1994):

Using positive reinforcement and providing feedback

Assigning learning tasks at appropriate levels

Redirecting activities that are not going well

Varying the length of learning experiences

Making sure students understand the learning tasks

Keeping students actively involved

Varying instructional techniques

Some guidelines for good teaching are listed below, and Activity 1.6 gives you an opportunity to assess your proficiency in using each practice.

1. Organize the material you teach around a limited number of significant concepts or a central theme.
2. Support and respond to students' learning instead of just presenting information.
3. Encourage students to *make sense* of what they read and learn.
4. Give assignments that are authentic tasks dealing with real-life situations.
5. Integrate higher-order thinking skills and opportunities for problem solving into your lessons.
6. Create a social environment that resembles a learning community so that students can learn from and with each other.
7. Emphasize conceptual understanding instead of skill mastery.
8. Take advantage of "teachable moments" to develop ideas.
9. Relate new information to students' prior knowledge.
10. Actively engage all students in learning activities.

Using the chart in Activity 1.6, rate yourself on your use of good teaching practices.

SUGGESTIONS TO HELP YOU BE SUCCESSFUL AS A STUDENT TEACHER

During your first days in the classroom, you may feel somewhat unsure of how to act or dress. Following these general tips will help alleviate some of your anxiety. Some have been mentioned earlier but bear repeating here because of their importance to your success.

- Be pleasant and polite to everyone with whom you come into contact—students, parents, your cooperating teacher, other teachers, administrators, and support personnel. In your anxiety about the new situation, don't forget how to *smile*.
- Be enthusiastic about the prospect of teaching. Show your cooperating teacher that you are energetic and willing, rather than lethargic and reluctant. Volunteer to help with tasks such as grading papers, giving individual assistance, and making instructional aids, as the opportunity arises. The greater and earlier your involvement, the more comfortable you will be when you begin teaching.
- Be punctual. Punctuality reflects a professional attitude.
- Dress like a teacher. Don't wear faded jeans and sweatshirts. If you don't look like a teacher, the students won't treat you like one. This aspect becomes more and more important as the grade level increases. It is easy for a secondary student teacher to look like "just one of the gang," but classroom management suffers when this happens. In most cases, you can take your cue from your cooperating teacher or other teachers in the school. Remember, however, that they are probably older than you and have already established their authority, whereas you are in the process of trying to establish yours.
- Check with your cooperating teacher about school policies *before* a crisis occurs in which you need to know those policies.
- Learn the students' names quickly. This helps you both to build rapport and to maintain class control.
- Always use good grammar. You are supposed to be a model for the students, so you must take care to meet this responsibility in speaking and writing.
- Write legibly. You may be asked to construct worksheets or study guides for the students or write assignments on the chalkboard. Use the form of writing appropriate for your students (manuscript or cursive), and make sure that you form the letters properly, that spacing and size of letters are appropriate, and that the overall product is legible. Once again, you are a model for the students.
- Keep calm. Do not allow yourself angry outbursts in school, even if things are not going well.
- Observe all school policies related to teachers, including those about tobacco use (which is a trouble area for some student teachers).

- Never criticize your cooperating teacher to another teacher or criticize other teachers in the school to each other. This is unprofessional behavior.
- Become familiar with the school's resources well before you are expected to take charge, so that you will be able to locate the things you need when you need them.
- Learn the daily routine thoroughly, so that you can manage it smoothly when you take over responsibility.
- Speak with pride about becoming a teacher. In these days of criticism of education, you should stand up for your chosen profession.

Later, when you begin teaching, you will need to remember the preceding tips, which apply to all your field experiences, including student teaching, plus the following additional tips, which apply to your direct teaching activities. Learn them so that you can perform acceptably.

- Be aware of the students' comfort. Adjust the temperature if the room is too hot or too cold, or have the appropriate person do so. Adjust the blinds if there is a glare from sunlight. See that there is adequate ventilation. Before, your cooperating teacher saw to these details; now, they are your responsibility.
- Don't lecture about something you have written or drawn on the board while standing in such a way that you block the students' view of the material.
- Use your voice well when teaching. A droning monotone bores students. An overly loud voice may intimidate some students, especially younger ones. A too-quiet voice may not carry well enough to reach students at the back of the room.
- Use only disciplinary methods sanctioned by your cooperating teacher. Avoid inappropriate practices such as punishing everyone for the misbehavior of a few and making unrealistic threats.
- Don't call on the same students all the time. Distribute classroom participation as evenly as possible.
- Vary activities to keep students' interest. Avoid relying exclusively upon one teaching approach, such as the lecture method.
- Plan each lesson thoroughly, no matter how well you think you know the material. Consider the level of the students, and adjust your explanations and procedures accordingly. For example, a one-hour lecture is completely inappropriate for a second-grade class.

ACTIVITY 1.5   ***Analyzing Stress***

1. Identify a recent stressful situation._____
   _____
   _____
   _____

2. Why did this particular situation cause you to feel stress?_____
   _____
   _____
   _____

3. How did you react? _____
   _____
   _____
   _____

4. Could the situation have been avoided? If so, how? What else could you have done? _____
   _____
   _____
   _____

5. Should you have reacted differently? What else could you have done? _____
   _____
   _____
   _____

6. What was most effective in helping you overcome your feelings of stress? _____
   _____
   _____
   _____

7. Could you have used this situation in a positive way? How?_____
   _____
   _____
   _____

8. How could you have reduced the intensity of the stress?_____
   _____
   _____

9. If the same thing happens again, how can you manage the stress better? _____

_____

_____

_____

ACTIVITY 1.6   **Practices for Good Teaching**

Read the list of guidelines related to good teaching practices near the end of the chapter. Periodically, consider your quality of performance in each of these areas and rate yourself on a scale of 1 (lowest) to 5 (highest) for each guideline.

	RATING PERIODS			
GUIDELINES	1	2	3	4
1. Organize content around concepts.				
2. Support and respond to students.				
3. Encourage meaning making.				
4. Make authentic assignments.				
5. Integrate thinking skills.				
6. Create a learning community.				
7. Stress conceptual understanding.				
8. Use teachable moments.				
9. Relate material to prior knowledge.				
10. Actively engage students.				

For each rating period, identify your strengths and weaknesses according to the guidelines. Consider how you might develop your strengths and reduce your weaknesses.

First period:

Strengths:

Weaknesses:

Second period:
Strengths:

Weaknesses:

Third period:
Strengths:

Weaknesses:

Fourth period:
Strengths:

Weaknesses:

Reflect on your overall teaching style and identify those guidelines that you follow most closely.

- Make clear and unambiguous assignments, and give students an opportunity to ask for clarification if they need it.
- Grade and return all assignments promptly. Students will learn more from assignments with immediate feedback.
- Don't assign busywork. Make sure that all assignments contribute appropriately to instructional goals.

If you take these suggestions seriously, you will greatly enhance your chances of success in student teaching.

DISCUSSION QUESTIONS

These discussion questions and those near the end of the other chapters may be handled in different ways. Questions may be discussed by the entire class, shared with partners, considered in small groups, or adapted for role playing.

1. What are some things that cause stress? What are some ways you can reduce the effects of these stressors? Can you think of a time when you handled a stressful situation especially well?
2. What are some common areas of stress that you can share with other practicum students or student teachers? Can any changes be made in policies or assignments to reduce the stress?
3. Consider the guidelines for good teaching (Activity 1.6, and the fuller list in text). What are your reactions to them? Which ones are in accord with your personal philosophy of teaching? Which ones might cause you difficulty?
4. Think of the teachers you have had. Which characteristics of good teaching did they possess? Which characteristics were often lacking? Do you think you would have learned more if your teachers had implemented the guidelines in this chapter?
5. What can you do to help with extracurricular activities? What have you done so far? Can you think of a way to help that no one else is doing? What is it?

6. What special talents or interests do you have that could help you become involved with extracurricular activities?
7. How can you make your observations of your cooperating teacher or other teachers most useful to you? Would it help to keep a log of ideas for future use?
8. Do all the teachers you have observed use the same teaching and disciplinary techniques? Why do you believe this might be so?
9. What are the most effective ways for practicum students and student teachers to evaluate their own teaching?
10. How valid are students' evaluations of teachers' performance?
11. How important is it for you to start developing a portfolio now? Why?

SELECTED REFERENCES

Bennett, W. J. (1986). *What works: Research about teaching and learning.* Washington, D.C.: United States Department of Education.

Beyond 'effective teaching.' (1992, April). *Educational Leadership, 49.* (Series of articles.)

Brophy, J. (1992, April). Probing the subtleties of subject-matter teaching. *Educational Leadership, 49,* 4–8.

Canning, C. (1991, March). What teachers say about reflection. *Educational Leadership, 48,* 18–21.

Cunningham, P., & Allington, R. (1994). *Classrooms that work.* New York: HarperCollins.

Goodlad, J. (1994). *What schools are for* (2nd ed.). Bloomington, Ind.: Phi Delta Kappa.

Knowles, J. G., & Cole, A., with Presswood, C. (1994). *Through preservice teachers' eyes.* New York: Merrill/Prentice Hall.

Miller, W. C. (1979). *Dealing with stress: A challenge for educators.* Bloomington, Ind.: Phi Delta Kappa Educational Foundation.

Sturtevant, E., & Linek, W. (Eds.). (1994). *Pathways for literacy:* Sixteenth Yearbook of The College Reading Association.

Selye, H. *Stress without distress.* (1974). Philadelphia: Lippincott.

Wentz, P., & Yarling, J. (1994). *Student teaching casebook for supervising teachers and teaching interns.* New York: Merrill/Prentice Hall.

Human Relations

Self-Improvement Activities

Mrs. Sanchez is a cooperating teacher. Miss Mosley is her student teacher.

Mrs. Sanchez: Miss Mosley, there is going to be a special in-service education program at the teacher center Thursday evening at 8:00. Would you like to attend the session with me?

Miss Mosley: What's the topic?

Mrs. Sanchez: Our reading program. I know you aren't required to attend, but this is an excellent opportunity for you to learn about the materials you'll be using for the remainder of the semester. I thought you'd want to take advantage of it. I'll be glad to drive you over there, if you need transportation.

Miss Mosley: Yes, I'd like to go. Thank you for inviting me.

At the end of the semester, Miss Mosley is pleased to see that Mrs. Sanchez has made the comment: "Interested in self-improvement of teaching skills."

1. Did Mrs. Sanchez have a good basis for her evaluative comment? Why or why not?
2. Do you show interest in self-improvement of teaching skills when opportunities are presented?

FOCUS ON SPECIFIC RELATIONSHIPS

An important part of student teaching and other field experiences is developing appropriate relationships with a variety of people—students, college supervisors, cooperating teachers, other school personnel, other student teachers, and parents. Your interaction with these people can be a major factor in your overall success as a student teacher or practicum student. Let us first look at each of these relationships separately.

STUDENTS

The most important and most demanding relationships you must handle as a student teacher or practicum student are those with your students. The students are the ones whose learning you hope to facilitate. It is important to develop a positive and cooperative relationship with each student in the class. Some student teachers and practicum students misunderstand the nature of this relationship. They want to be "buddies" with the students because this seems the best way to be liked. Unfortunately, being liked is not sufficient for this relationship; respect is also important, as is recognition of the student teacher as an authority figure. The students' respect must be earned, and earning it takes time. It is not automatically accorded. Development of a "buddy" relationship can undermine the students' respect for you as an authority figure, and thus adversely affect classroom control.

What, then, should your relationship with your students be? An appropriate relationship will require a great deal of perceptiveness and understanding on your part.

General Guidelines

First, you must treat each student as a worthwhile individual. You must react positively to all students and show them you care about their progress and well-being. Something as simple as learning the students' names quickly can have a positive effect on your relationships with them. Noticing that a student was absent the day before and inquiring about his or her health or indicating that he or she was missed shows the student that you care. When students perform well, your approving comments help establish a positive relationship.

It is important to let the students know you respect them as individuals. You can do this by listening to their opinions and expressions of feelings and responding to them in a way that shows you have given careful thought to their ideas. Dismissing students' ideas as trivial or worthless will indicate that you feel they are unable to contribute effectively to the class. Such actions can cause students to withdraw from the learning environment, rather than participate in classroom activities.

Nonverbal behavior can also promote good relationships with students. *Smile* at them often. Show them that you enjoy them. Let all the students know you are there to help them. *Listen* to them when they voice problems, and try to help each one. Let them know that you are on their side.

One important aspect of respecting students' individuality is to avoid labeling them according to racial, ethnic, socioeconomic, or sex stereotypes. Expectations should not be the same for all Asian-Americans, all African-Americans, all whites, all Hispanics, all people whose ancestors were of any particular nationality, all poor people, all rich people, all boys, or all girls. Each of these groups has industrious individuals and others who are lazy; bright individuals and others who are dull; honest individuals and others who are dishonest; clean individuals and others who are not; athletic individuals and some who are not; and so on. Each member of a group should be looked upon as an individual with a variety of traits acquired through interaction with the environment. As a student teacher, you are an important part of that environment, and, therefore, you help to shape some of the traits your students develop. Don't be so narrow-minded as to expect all members of a group to be alike.

Avoiding Sexism.   The following case study shows a situation involving sex stereotypes.

CASE STUDY 2.1

Sex Stereotypes

Miss Chambers was a student teacher in a fifth-grade class that was studying Mexico. She thought that staging a fiesta, which would give the children an opportunity to sample many Mexican foods, would be a good teaching device.

She told the boys to plan and construct a set to look like a festive Mexican home, while the girls located and prepared the foods to be tried. Darren, who liked to cook at home, wanted to prepare the tamales. Miss Chambers responded, "Surely you don't want to cook with the girls. You need to help the boys with the construction."

1. What is your analysis of Miss Chambers's reply to Darren?
2. What would you have said?

3. Do you suppose some of the girls might have enjoyed the construction project better than the cooking?
4. How would you have handled the entire project?

Sex stereotypes, such as the one Miss Chambers demonstrated, are unfortunately not uncommon. Certain activities, toys, and manners of speaking are arbitrarily attributed to boys and others to girls. A boy or girl who fails to fit the stereotype may be treated as abnormal, instead of as an individual with a right to behave in a way that does not fit the stereotype. Teachers often discourage boys from cooking or sewing, indicating that these are not appropriate activities for boys, just as other activities are considered inappropriate for girls.

Sexism is an issue you should be aware of when you choose materials and work with male and female students. Sexist practices can restrict what a person becomes by limiting choices of behavior and careers. Title IX of the Education Amendments Act of 1972 was enacted by Congress to prohibit discrimination against males or females in federally assisted education programs. Even though it is no longer legal to discriminate, many people continue to do so through their attitudes toward sex roles.

Consider your own feelings by answering the following questions: Should the wife or husband be the primary provider for a family? Are girls or boys likely to be better at each of the following: reading, math, science, cooking, industrial arts, or sewing? Who will cause more discipline problems—boys or girls? If you have a definite choice of one sex in each of your answers, you are probably reflecting the sex-role stereotypes in our society.

According to research, there are very few innate differences between the sexes. Although biological factors are significant in shaping some masculine behavior, cultural factors can override biological impulses (Thompson, 1986). Some of the differences that appear to exist may be the result of different expectations for boys and girls as they grow up. You may be helping to cause the differences. Instead, you should be helping both boys and girls to recognize the breadth of their behavioral and career choices. Boys should be permitted to try cooking and sewing as well as carpentry, and they should be allowed to show emotions, ask for help, and be gentle and cooperative, without having their masculinity questioned. Girls should not just be allowed but should be encouraged to engage in athletic activities or use computers. They should also be encouraged in their study of math and science, for this is one way of acknowledging that girls may wish to enter technical fields that require knowledge of these subjects.

It may be desirable for you to talk about how both men and women are found in careers, such as nursing and construction work, that were once considered the domain of a particular sex. A girl who says she wants to be an airplane pilot should be given as much reinforcement as a boy who says the same thing.

In addition, you should try to give your attention to girls and boys equally. All students need to be given chances to respond and receive feedback from the teacher.

Your language may unintentionally support sexist stereotypes. When you speak of the builders of our nation as *forefathers,* for example, it may seem to young children that women had no part. Use of the generic *he* may also cause young, and even adolescent, students to assume that only males are the topic of conversation. Use of terms such as *mailman* and *policeman* to refer to letter carriers and police officers seems to close these careers to females. You should attempt to eliminate such usages from your speech patterns.

Dealing with Cultural Diversity.   Some people have grown up hearing derogatory language referring to certain racial, ethnic, or socioeconomic groups. This language must be eliminated from your vocabulary, or you can damage the self-concepts of some of your students.

The classes you are asked to teach may be culturally diverse. It is part of your responsibility to help each student develop a positive cultural identity and accept classmates with other cultural backgrounds. The students need opportunities to read material by and about people from their own cultural backgrounds and from a variety of other backgrounds. They also need to be led to see that there are many ways that people from other cultures are like them: they often share similar dreams, emotions, and experiences. Students also need to be helped to understand why some differences exist and to learn to value those differences for the variety and interest that culturally diverse people add to our nation and the world.

Classrooms that have culturally diverse populations should direct attention to the contributions and values of all cultures represented, as well as some that are not, in order to allow the students involved to feel a part of the educational experience and to experience an increased sense of self-worth. In social studies classes, for example, inclusion of such material should be a natural occurrence. Contributions to our society, other societies, and the world at large made by people from different cultures, as well as difficulties faced by these people, can be emphasized as you teach history, geography, political science, and current events. In science, scientific contributions of people from varying cultures should be emphasized. You may need to point out the cultural background of the scientist in question, or else the students may simply assume that the person was from their own culture or the culture that they expect to produce scientists. In literature, selections by and about people from different cultures should be included. You may also want to locate books in the primary languages of your ESL students. You may use the Internet to help you locate appropriate books. For example, the Center for the Study of Books in Spanish for Children and Adolescents' website, *http://www.csusm.edu/campus_centers/csb/*, can help you locate books in Spanish. Use a search engine to find sites for books about different cultures, by authors and illustrators from different cultures, or written in different languages. (Complete Activity 2.1 to see how your classroom rates in this area.)

FOR YOUR PORTFOLIO

Include a copy of Activity 2.1 in your portfolio, along with evidence of adjustments in materials that you made, if any were needed, to help combat any cultural bias that you detected.

On special occasions in school, students from different cultural backgrounds should be allowed to explain, if they wish, how celebrations of those occasions differ for them or how they celebrate similar things at different times of the year. Special attention to the effects that the landing of Columbus in the New World had on the Native American inhabitants, for example, or consideration of the points of view that groups such as the Tories, Native Americans, British, and French had toward the American Revolution may be appropriate in expanding multicultural awareness and understanding.

Instructional materials in the classroom should be free of cultural bias. Even math activities may show cultural bias by the situations described in statement problems. Teachers must be vigilant and de-emphasize material that could cause some children to feel that they do not "fit in" with the class.

Cooperative learning groups (described in detail in Chapter 4) should be formed in a way that results in multicultural groupings. In such situations, the students will learn from each other and come to respect the contributions made by the other group members.

In classrooms where there is little or no cultural diversity, an even more urgent need exists to make students aware of the ways in which people may be different from them, while sharing some characteristics with them. They need to realize that not all contributions to society have come from their own restricted group, but that all kinds of people have influenced their world. Not only printed materials, but also audiovisual resources, should be brought to class to help make the discussions of other cultures as vivid and complete as possible.

Understanding of the culture or cultures represented in your classroom is very important for you as a student teacher. For example, a child from one culture may look down and fail to meet your eyes as a sign of respect, but you may use your cultural background to give this action a negative interpretation. One beginning teacher gave a test to a group of Navaho children and was upset when she saw them helping each other. She interpreted their actions as cheating, but in their culture cooperation and helping others are considered desirable. On the other hand, there is much diversity within cultural groups, and you should avoid having the expectation that all students from a particular group will respond to the same situation in a similar manner. (Complete the Class Culture Survey in Activity 2.2 to help you plan ways to adjust for multicultural class membership.)

Some of your students may speak little or no English, while you may not speak their language. How can you relate positively to such students? It takes persistence and effort, but you can have a positive impact. From the first moment they enter the classroom, include these students in classroom activities that require little language. At the elementary level, these activities may include playing active games at recess, drawing and painting, and viewing displays and demonstrations. At the secondary level, the activities may include almost all aspects of a physical education class or some vocational classes and viewing displays and demonstrations in other areas. You should attempt to communicate with each student through gestures, pictures, and any words you know from her or his language. Whatever you do, even though attempting to communicate with these students may be frustrating, always be positive. Encourage other students to include a new student in their activities, explaining that they are already at home in this school and can make the new student comfortable by helping him or her learn the standard procedures and popular activities. Students often take behavioral cues from their teachers.

Some of the students in your class are likely to speak nonstandard dialects of English. Part of your

ACTIVITY 2.1   *Checking for Cultural Bias and Stereotypes in Reading Materials*

1. Are a variety of cultures represented in the illustrations in the materials? _____

2. Are a variety of cultures represented in the written texts of the materials? _____

3. In the illustrations, are the people from any particular cultures shown in stereotyped occupations or activities? _____ If so, which ones? _____

   _____

   _____

   _____

4. In the written texts, are the people from any particular cultures described or represented in stereotyped occupations or activities? _____ If so, which ones?_____

   _____

   _____

   _____

5. From what cultures do the main characters in stories or featured characters in expository text come? _____

   _____

   _____

   _____

6. Are any of the materials written by people from other cultures? _____ If so, which ones?_____

   _____

   _____

7. Are any of the materials illustrated by people from other cultures? _____ If so, which ones? _____

   _____

   _____

8. What do the results of your analysis of the reading materials in your classroom indicate that you need to do in order to provide your students with positive multicultural reading experiences? ____

   _____

   _____

   _____

ACTIVITY 2.2   **Class Culture Survey**

1. What different cultural backgrounds are represented by the students in your classroom?

CULTURES   NUMBER OF STUDENTS

a.

b.

c.

d.

e.

f.

2. What are some important holidays or events for the various cultural groups in your class?

a.

b.

c.

d.

e.

f.

3. List any students in your class who speak a language other than English as their primary language. Make a checkmark by the language if you can speak it.

STUDENT'S NAME   OTHER LANGUAGE   CAN YOU SPEAK IT?

a.

b.

c.

d.

e.

f.

job as a teacher is to expose them to standard English so that they can become upwardly mobile in society. On the other hand, you must model standard English and reinforce its use in school settings without discrediting their home language. Home language should be treated as one communication system and standard English ("school language") as an alternative system that can be useful for them to know. Students should not be reprimanded for using their home language for communication with other students in informal settings, but they should practice standard English in formal situations, such as giving oral reports and producing written reports. Elementary classroom teachers and secondary English teachers especially must approach this task with understanding and sensitivity.

It is the purpose of multicultural education to promote understanding among the varied people in our country. Teachers have to find ways to accomplish this in their own classrooms.

Showing Respect for and Fairness to All Students.

You can show respect for your students by allowing them to take on responsibilities. Giving students tasks for which they are responsible, no matter how small the tasks may be, shows that you trust them to fulfill the duties and recognize their ability to do so. This attitude can have an enormous effect upon the way a student responds to you. Let us look at the case of Randy as an example.

CASE STUDY 2.2

Showing Respect for Students

Randy was a sixth-grade student who had failed two previous grades. As a consequence, he was a 14-year-old in a classroom with many 11- and 12-year-olds. He was larger than any of the other students and had different interests. To make matters worse, he was poor, and most of his clothing was worn and faded. The heels of his boots were worn out, and his sleeves were a little too short for his arms.

Randy was generally quiet and obedient in class, but rarely made any attempt to do his assignments. He displayed an extremely negative self-concept, informing the student teacher, Miss Davis, "I'm too dumb to do that," when she encouraged him to try some of the work.

Miss Davis tried very hard to treat Randy the same way she treated the other students. She called on him to respond in class and listened respectfully to his replies. She greeted him when he entered the class-

room in the morning. She smiled and spoke when she passed him in the hall. She gave him much encouragement and assistance during directed study periods. Still, she felt she was making little headway. To be sure, he talked a *little* more in class than he had previously, and turned in a few more assignments, but Miss Davis still did not feel she had reached Randy.

One day, as Randy was leaving the classroom to go home for lunch, Miss Davis realized she had a letter that needed to be mailed and remembered that Randy passed by a mailbox on his way home. She called to him and asked him if he would do her a favor and mail the letter. Randy looked at her in disbelief. *Nobody* at school had ever trusted him to take responsibility for *anything.* He hesitated and said, "You want *me* to mail it?"

Miss Davis replied, "I'd appreciate your doing it, if you don't mind."

Randy walked over and picked up the letter, glancing around to see if others had heard this exchange. "I'll be sure it gets mailed," he told Miss Davis rather loudly, and walked out of the room proudly holding the letter.

Upon returning to the room after lunch, the first thing he told Miss Davis was, "I mailed your letter." He said it with a smile of satisfaction.

Thereafter, Randy began to respond more and more to Miss Davis's encouragement to do assignments. He seemed to try much harder to do what she thought he could do. He did not become a scholar overnight, but he improved in all his work and once even earned a 100 in mathematics. And he continued to carry Miss Davis's letters with pride.

1. What is your analysis of the way Miss Davis handled Randy?
2. Would you have treated the situation differently in any way?
3. Would it have been wise for Miss Davis to give a crucial piece of mail, such as a bill payment, to Randy before she was sure that he was trustworthy?

It is important to give attention to all students. Do not favor a few with your attention and ignore or avoid others. This may be difficult, for some students are not as appealing as others. Some dress carelessly or shabbily, fail to wash, or have belligerent attitudes. It is your challenge to be as accepting of and positive about the appropriate behaviors these students exhibit as you are of the actions of the neat, clean, cooperative students. This does not mean you should accept behavior that deviates from school rules, but it does mean you should show acceptance of the individual, even when you show disapproval of her or his behavior. It also means you should find traits in each person to which you can react positively. Try to develop a sense of community in your classroom—a feeling of togetherness in which all students can feel they are valued members of the class. Now complete Activity 2.3 to help you focus on this behavior.

After you have completed Activity 2.3, attempt to use as many of the comments from the activity as you can. Then do Activity 2.4 as a follow-up procedure to help you analyze your results.

To have a good relationship with your students, absolute fairness is important. If you have a rule, enforce it equally for all students. Any hint that you have "teacher's pets" will cause poor relationships between you and the majority of the class.

Honesty is also important in your relationship with your students. Students quickly recognize insincerity and resent it.

Therefore, to establish good relationships with students, you should do the following:

1. Treat each student as a worthwhile individual, worthy of respect.
2. Use appropriate nonverbal behavior in your interactions with students.
3. Avoid labels and stereotypes when working with students.
4. Offer students chances to take on responsibilities.
5. Give attention to all students.
6. Be positive toward all students.
7. Be fair to all students.
8. Be honest with all students.

COLLEGE SUPERVISORS

Your relationship with your college supervisor is also important. He or she has the responsibility for overseeing and critiquing your work in the classroom. The college supervisor is there to help you throughout the student teaching experience, as well as to determine your grade at the end. Therefore, the college supervisor will be offering, either orally or in writing, suggestions for improving your teaching. These suggestions are intended to help you analyze what you are doing and make the most of your field experience. They are not meant as personal attacks upon your competence. Try to consider the suggestions objectively and ask questions about points that may be unclear, rather than react defensively and produce excuses for mistakes you may have made. If you show your college supervisor that you are open to suggestions and will make an effort to benefit from constructive criticism, your relationship is likely to be a good one.

A way to show that you are eager to improve and that you welcome your college supervisor's help is to try to put his or her suggestions into practice as soon as possible. When your supervisor makes a suggestion and subsequently sees no attempt on your part to change, he or she is likely to view your behavior negatively. On the other hand, if your supervisor sees you working to incorporate the suggestion into your teaching, he or she is likely to perceive you as a serious student with a desire to become a good teacher.

FOR YOUR PORTFOLIO

Put one of the written evaluations from your college supervisor in your portfolio, along with a written explanation of how you changed your teaching practices as a result of this evaluation.

Asking pertinent questions of your college supervisor shows a desire to improve and an interest in seeking new knowledge—desirable attributes that are likely to be appreciated. After observing your teaching, your college supervisor will probably hold a conference with you or with both you and your cooperating teacher. It is a good idea to take the written comments your college supervisor has made about your performance to these scheduled conferences. If conferences are not automatic, don't hesitate to request them if you feel the need for more feedback.

ACTIVITY 2.3   **Attending to Students***

List the students in your class (if you have a self-contained classroom) or one of your classes (if your students change classes throughout the day). After each student's name, note something that you could say to this student to make him or her feel accepted and appreciated. Consider positive comments about schoolwork, athletic exploits, personal appearance, behavior, or family.

STUDENT'S NAME   COMMENTS

1. _____   _____

2. _____   _____

3. _____   _____

4. _____   _____

5. _____   _____

6. _____   _____

7. _____   _____

8. _____   _____

9. _____   _____

10. _____   _____

11. _____   _____

12. _____   _____

13. _____   _____

14. _____   _____

15. _____   _____

16. _____   _____

17. _____   _____

18. _____   _____

19. _____   _____

20. _____   _____

21. _____   _____

22. _____   _____

* If you have several classes with different students, you may want to duplicate these pages and carry out this activity for each class.

STUDENT'S NAME   COMMENTS

23. _____   _____

24. _____   _____

25. _____   _____

26. _____   _____

27. _____   _____

28. _____   _____

29. _____   _____

30. _____   _____

31. _____   _____

32. _____   _____

33. _____   _____

34. _____   _____

35. _____   _____

36. _____   _____

ACTIVITY 2.4   ***Analyzing Student Interactions****

Examine the list of students and possible comments that you made for Activity 2.3. Below, write down the name of each student for whom you tried the comments. After the student's name, indicate her or his reaction to the comment. Did she or he smile, frown, make a positive comment in response, make a negative comment in response, make a gesture of acceptance, or ignore the comment? Consider what the student's response indicates to you about future interactions with her or him. Did you strike a responsive chord, or do you need to think of another approach? Why did your comment elicit the reaction that it did?

STUDENT'S NAME	COMMENTS
1.	
2.	
3.	
4.	
5.	
6.	
7.	
8.	
9.	
10.	
11.	
12.	
13.	
14.	
15.	
16.	
17.	
18.	
19.	
20.	
21.	

* If you have several classes with different students, you may want to duplicate these pages and carry out this activity for each class.

STUDENT'S NAME COMMENTS

22. _____   _____

23. _____   _____

24. _____   _____

25. _____   _____

26. _____   _____

27. _____   _____

28. _____   _____

29. _____   _____

30. _____   _____

31. _____   _____

32. _____   _____

33. _____   _____

34. _____   _____

35. _____   _____

36. _____   _____

Notes for the future based on my results:

Fear of Exposure

Dale Martin was a secondary school student teacher, assigned to two classes of algebra, a class of plane geometry, and a class of trigonometry. His college supervisor had visited him several times, but all visits had been during one of his algebra classes. Dale felt very confident and comfortable teaching the algebra classes, and the comments from his college supervisor had all been positive. He was really struggling with the trigonometry class, however, and could sense that his cooperating teacher was displeased with his efforts. Dale confessed his concern to Alvin James, a student teacher in physical education.

Alvin suggested that Dale ask Mr. Walsky, their college supervisor, to make a point of sitting in on the trigonometry class on his next visit to the school, so that he could give Dale some feedback. Dale told Alvin that he thought he had better leave well enough alone—Mr. Walsky had seen him only in successful experiences. Perhaps if he saw the trigonometry class, Mr. Walsky's overall evaluation at the end of the quarter would be lower. Acting on this reasoning, Dale said nothing to Mr. Walsky.

1. How do you feel about Dale's situation?
2. What is your opinion of Alvin's advice?
3. What would you have done?
4. What is likely to be the result of Dale's decision?

When you are speaking with your college supervisor, it is important to be straightforward about your problems. He or she is the person best equipped to act as liaison between you and your cooperating teacher or other school personnel, if the need arises. Your honesty will make the supervisor's job easier and will probably ultimately improve your situation. Your openness about problems will also improve the rapport between you and the college supervisor.

The college supervisor is there to help you. Your openness, honesty, and willingness to accept suggestions will create a good relationship that makes it easier for the supervisor to help.

COOPERATING TEACHERS

A good relationship with your cooperating teacher is vital for achieving maximum benefit from the student teaching experience. Whereas your college supervisor may be in contact with you once or twice a week for a period or two, your cooperating teacher is with you every day. You and your cooperating teacher will be working together for the best interest of the students.

It is important to remember that the cooperating teacher has ultimate responsibility for the classroom to which you are assigned. She or he is legally responsible, and because of the responsibility, some cooperating teachers are more hesitant than others to relinquish control. The way you conduct yourself initially will have a strong influence upon how the cooperating teacher feels about leaving you in control. Taking an interest in everything that is going on in the classroom, asking questions about appropriate procedures and classroom rules, and making notes on information the cooperating teacher offers may be helpful. Being responsive to requests for assistance (putting up bulletin boards, grading test papers, etc.) will show the cooperating teacher that you are a willing worker.

Your appearance and manner are also important. Your cooperating teacher will feel more comfortable entrusting you with her or his charges if you dress appropriately (look more like a teacher than a student), speak correctly (use standard English), and exhibit self-confidence.

Appropriate Dress

Susan Granger was in a secondary English practicum class. Her cooperating teacher was Mrs. Barfield, a 50-year-old English teacher.

On the first day of her practicum, Susan reported to her assignment wearing a pair of jeans, a T-shirt, and a pair of tennis shoes. Before Susan had a chance to introduce herself, Mrs. Barfield made the mistake of asking her if she was a new student in the class. When Mrs. Barfield learned who Susan was, she said, "Ms. Granger, I believe you need to dress more appropriately for teaching in the future."

Susan, who noticed that Mrs. Barfield was clad in casual slacks and shirt, was furious. Later that day she said to her roommate, "Who does she think she is, telling me what to wear? She had on pants herself."

1. What do you think about Mrs. Barfield's comment to Susan?
2. Was it justified?
3. Was there a difference in Mrs. Barfield's dressing as she did and Susan being dressed as she was? If so, what was the difference?
4. Might Susan's attire affect her relationship with Mrs. Barfield? Might it affect her relationship with her secondary students?

Currently, many schools have dress codes for both teachers and students. You must conform to the dress code for teachers, if one is in place. Your college supervisor may provide you with information about the dress code for the school to which you are assigned, or you may be expected to discover it by reading the school's handbook for teachers. Do not assume that there is no dress code. Check to be sure before you cause yourself avoidable difficulties.

When you are given an actual teaching assignment, careful planning is likely to evoke a positive response from your cooperating teacher. Showing responsibility in small ways will encourage the cooperating teacher to give you larger responsibilities. (Chapter 6 has tips for good planning.)

Although you may be very eager to begin teaching, do not demand that your teacher let you start. Demonstrate your readiness; then suggest that you are ready. If this fails, you may wish to consult your college supervisor, who can act as a liaison.

Your teacher may want to team-teach with you before letting you strike out on your own. Teaming with another teacher is a valuable experience, and it will prepare you for an organizational plan that you may encounter in the future. Team teaching allows teachers to take advantage of the special skills of team members. For example, if you have musical knowledge and skill, you may help drama students add a dimension to their production that the classroom teacher could not have supported as well. On the other hand, the classroom teacher may be able to help much more with blocking of scenes than your skills would have allowed you to do. Each of you may work with the students on the production, utilizing your unique talents. A member of a team with particular expertise may plan the lessons in that area and do the primary teaching in it, while the other team member provides support and follows the plan provided for specific activities.

You may find that your cooperating teacher does some things differently from the way you would do them or the way you have been taught. Do not criticize her or his methods; ask why she or he does things that way. Weigh the pros and cons of the teacher's method. If you feel it is not the best way, simply ask if you can try another way in which you have some background. Most cooperating teachers expect some experimentation and will allow this without your resorting to an attack on an existing procedure. This approach can certainly help your relationship with the teacher, and, upon examination, you may find things of value in the teacher's approach that you will wish to use also. Just because you have not been exposed to an idea or approach before does not mean it is not a good one.

Most programs have specified minimum requirements that student teachers are expected to meet. If you are willing to do only the minimum expected of you, your relationship with the cooperating teacher may be less than perfect. Dedicated educators do not settle for doing the least they can get by with doing.

Your cooperating teacher, like your college supervisor, will be giving you oral or written suggestions (or both) and constructive criticism. Accepting these comments as avenues to improvement will enhance the rapport between you and your cooperating teacher. If the teacher sees that you are attempting to put the suggestions to work, she or he will be more likely to have positive feelings toward you as a prospective member of the profession. Ignoring suggestions or indicating that you cannot or will not change will not promote a good relationship.

CASE STUDY 2.5

No Desire to Change

In his first conference with his cooperating teacher, Leon Garritt was told, "Mr. Garritt, you must watch your English when you are speaking to the class. I noticed you saying 'he don't' and 'I seen' several times during this single lesson."

Leon responded, "That's the way everybody talks back home. I've talked that way all my life. It's too late to change now. Besides, I'm going back home to teach. I want to sound like everyone else."

1. How do you think Leon's teacher responded to Leon's explanation?
2. Do you think Leon's reaction affected his relationship with the teacher? In what way?
3. How would you have responded if you had been in Leon's position?
4. How would you have responded if you had been Leon's teacher?
5. Does where Leon plans to teach have any relevance to the issue at hand?

FOR YOUR PORTFOLIO

Put a copy of a written evaluation of your teaching by your cooperating teacher in your portfolio along with an explanation of the adjustments to your teaching that were made in response to this evaluation.

Taking the initiative and offering assistance before it is requested shows the teacher that you are ready to be a part of classroom activities. Waiting to be told every move to make is a sign of immaturity and lack of confidence.

Showing the cooperating teacher your preparedness, willingness, and ability to perform in the classroom can do much to enhance your relationship. Appropriate reactions to suggestions and criticism and willingness to work cooperatively are also important.

OTHER SCHOOL PERSONNEL

In addition to building a good relationship with your cooperating teacher, you need to develop positive relationships with other school personnel, including other teachers, administrators, counselors, supervisors, secretaries, the custodial staff, and cafeteria workers. From time to time you will have occasion to interact with all these people.

On your first day in the school, introduce yourself to the school personnel with whom you come in contact. Tell them that you are pleased to meet them. Explain that you are a student teacher or practicum student and may need their assistance in the future. They will appreciate your acknowledgment that you may need their help, and they may seek opportunities to help you. Even if you do not need their aid, just knowing them and realizing that they know who you are will make life in the school more comfortable.

CASE STUDY 2.6

Pleasantness Pays Off

Miss Garcia, a student teacher in first grade, had gone out of her way to meet and be pleasant to the school custodian, Mr. Nabors, who some of the teachers thought was an uncooperative person. She had cause to be glad she had done so on the first day her cooperating teacher left her in charge of the class.

The children were moving down the hall toward their classroom following a milk break, when Mario started throwing up. The children squealed and scattered as Mario's snack gushed onto the floor. Mario burst into tears.

Mr. Nabors, hearing the commotion, hurried over to help Miss Garcia. He made certain that the remainder of the class lined up again and became quiet, while Miss Garcia calmed Mario. Then he assured Miss Garcia that he would take care of cleaning the hall immediately, while she continued with her normal procedures.

1. Do you think Miss Garcia's friendly approach to the custodian worked in her favor?
2. In your opinion, is it possible that the custodian's reputation is unjust?
3. How might the other teachers elicit more cooperation from him?

Other teachers may offer valuable suggestions about teaching or disciplinary actions and may provide you with support and counsel in the absence of your cooperating teacher. Administrators can help you become acclimated to the school and school policies and may also offer useful information about your responsibilities as a member of the profession. Supervisors may offer critiques of your teaching procedures, or they may provide materials that will be helpful to you in your lessons. Custodians may help with incidents such as the one cited in the previous case study, as well as with major and minor spills of food, paints, or other materials in the classroom. Cafeteria workers may alert you to problems developing in the cafeteria before they are beyond control.

In brief, you should be pleasant to all school personnel and cooperate with them as necessary. Your friendliness and cooperation will be returned in kind.

OTHER STUDENT TEACHERS AND PRACTICUM STUDENTS

There are probably other student teachers or practicum students assigned to your school; if not, you have probably been assigned to a seminar with student teachers or practicum students from other schools. These peers are facing the same challenges that you are, even though the different situations make each assignment unique. If you are willing to share your experiences openly with these peers, you may find that they can help you analyze and solve the problems you face. At the same time, solutions you have discovered yourself may benefit others in the group. Openness and willingness to cooperate can make your relationships with the other student teachers or practicum students very rewarding.

Just because another student teacher or practicum student is teaching in an elementary school and you are teaching in a secondary school, or another teacher is a physical education teacher and you are a chemistry teacher, do not assume that you cannot learn from each other. Regardless of level or subject area, many of the problems student teachers and practicum students encounter, especially in human relations, are similar.

Sharing experiences with other student teachers can help you analyze and solve problems.

CASE STUDY 2.7

Learning from Others

Troy was assigned to a secondary geography class for his student teaching experience. He had planned for and taught several lessons but had trouble estimating the amount of time his plans were going to take. As a result, he had twice run out of instructional material before the period ended. He hadn't known what to do, so he had just let the students have a study period each time. He mentioned his problem in his student teaching seminar.

Carol was teaching in a sixth-grade self-contained classroom but was expected to conduct certain classes during specified periods of the day. She had run into the same problem that Troy had. Her cooperating teacher had suggested planning several extra filler, or sponge, activities for each subject area in case her lessons did not take as much time as she expected. The practice had worked well for her. She mentioned several filler activities she had used for social studies, including blank outline maps to be filled in with data pertinent to the current topic, vocabulary card games, and construction of time lines. Troy adapted several of her ideas to meet the needs of his particular class and found that they worked well for him too. (See Chapter 4 for suggestions for filler activities.)

1. Do elementary and secondary student teachers and practicum students have many common concerns such as the one Troy and Carol shared?
2. What are some of the common concerns?

Treat your fellow student teachers and practicum students with the same respect you show the other teachers with whom you have contact. Listen to what they have to say in your seminars, and share your knowledge with them. The relationships can be mutually beneficial.

PARENTS

As a practicum student you probably will not have much contact with parents. As a student teacher, you may or may not have much contact. If such contact occurs, however, it is vitally important that you develop good relationships with parents.

One factor in effective interaction with parents is knowing about the community in which you are teaching. Awareness of the types of businesses, industries, and recreational facilities in the community will give you some insight into the background from which the parents come. Awareness of the general socioeconomic, racial, and ethnic balance of the community also will be helpful. Knowing that the people in the town generally are avid football fans and enthusiastically support the local high school team or realizing that many work in the coal mines and may have associated health problems can give you a basis for interacting with community members with greater understanding and empathy. For this reason, it is a good idea to spend some time familiarizing yourself with the community and its people. Walk around the downtown area and observe the businesses and the people. Attend recreational activities, such as ball games, concerts, dances, and festivals, and note community interests. Drive around the residential section, and observe the types of homes in which your students live. These experiences will help prepare you for encounters with parents.

Many parents are uncomfortable in the school environment, so when parents come to the school to discuss their child's progress, the teacher (or possibly you as the student teacher) must make an effort to put them at ease. Open the conversation with a nonthreatening comment, perhaps about the weather or some recent local event. Then express your appreciation to the parent for taking the time to come to the school. It is difficult for many parents to schedule such visits, and your acknowledgment of this fact may put the parent more at ease. It is also best to begin the discussion about the student on a positive note. Almost all students have attributes that can be praised—a pleasant manner, creativity, talent in art or music, athletic ability, cooperativeness, or excellence in a particular academic area. Be honest with parents about problems, but do not be abrupt or unkind in your comments. Have documentation to illustrate the existence of the problems that you are describing, for example, portfolios that contain samples of the student's work, test papers, records of homework, or records of disciplinary conferences with the student. Explain the procedures you plan to implement to correct the problems, and express anticipation of improvement. Try to end the interview with another positive note. Always stress your desire to help the child in any way you can, and urge the parents to consult you if they have any concerns. Throughout the conference, remain pleasant, calm, and objective.

If you can think of ways that the parents can help with educational activities, ask your cooperating teacher if it is acceptable to invite them to do so. Some may be able to serve as resource persons and provide information to the students during a special unit; for example, a parent who is a doctor might come to school to talk about a particular disease, the importance of sanitary practices to healthy living, or the importance of immunizations. A police officer, firefighter, or public official may be able to share information in a social studies class. Some parents may be able to share cultural information from their heritages when other countries are being studied. Some may be able to share knowledge of foreign languages, music, dances, and art forms that they know. Others may be able to perform needed tasks, such as building a piece of scenery or making costumes for a play, chaperoning a field trip, listening to students read orally for practice, reading to students, and teaching team sports to students. If you make parents welcome to participate in your classroom in various ways and show your appreciation for their knowledge and helpfulness, they will tend to look favorably upon you as their child's teacher.

It is important that the parents perceive you as a competent professional who is truly concerned about their children. If you put your best foot forward in any encounter with parents, they are more likely to be supportive of what you attempt to do with the students.

Listen to what parents have to tell you about their children. They can often give you information that will help you understand the students' strengths and weaknesses and thus help you plan instruction that will be most beneficial to the students. Parents will also be favorably impressed with your willingness to listen to what they have to say.

If you meet parents outside the school setting, smile and speak to them. Do not bring up problems at chance meetings. These should be covered in carefully planned conferences.

CASE STUDY 2.8

Careless Comments Cause Problems

Mr. Meadows, a student teacher in a junior high school, saw the father of Joe Mills, one of his general science students, in the supermarket. Mr. Meadows walked over to Mr. Mills and said, "If Joe doesn't start coming to class more regularly, I will have to give him a failing grade. I think he cuts class to sneak off and smoke."

Mr. Mills was visibly upset. "Why haven't I been notified of this?" he demanded. "Why don't you keep parents adequately informed?" Then he turned and stalked away.

The next day, Mr. Meadows' cooperating teacher, Mrs. Daily, told him that Mr. Mills had called the principal and spoken angrily to him about the way the general science class was being handled. The principal demanded an explanation from Mrs. Daily. Now Mrs. Daily demanded an explanation from Mr. Meadows.

1. What mistakes did Mr. Meadows make in his contact with Mr. Mills?
2. What should he have done instead?
3. What would you have done?

Parents are potential allies. If you make an effort to communicate with them appropriately, they can help you better understand your students. Parents have their children's best interests at heart and will respond favorably to you if they believe you do too.

For websites that focus on parent involvement in the schools, visit *http://www.prenhall.com/methodscluster,* "Topic 9: Parents and the Community." Read about the ways parents may be involved in schools and the benefits of such involvement.

DISCUSSION QUESTIONS

1. What conditions could cause you to have problems in developing good relationships with your students? How might you work to overcome these difficulties?
2. Are there any special problems in developing good relationships with students of racial or ethnic groups different from yours? What are they? How can they be overcome?
3. How may the fact that the college supervisor is giving you a grade affect your relationship with him or her? Should this happen? Why or why not?
4. Why should you avoid criticism of your cooperating teacher's methods?
5. Why is it a good policy to develop positive relationships with many school personnel?
6. How can your relationships with other student teachers benefit your student teaching?
7. How could your poor relationships with parents inhibit a student's progress?
8. What will you do if:

   a. You are a student teacher in second grade, and an apparently bright and curious Vietnamese boy, who speaks no English, is in your class. Your cooperating teacher has ignored him, letting him entertain himself during lessons. The boy's father is an engineering student at a university who speaks broken English. The boy's mother is free during the day, but she speaks only a few words of English. No one in your school speaks any Vietnamese.

   b. You are student teaching in sixth grade, and a girl in your class comes from an impoverished home with no running water. The child's clothes are filthy. Her face and hands are encrusted with grime, and she smells bad. The other children make fun of her and refuse to sit next to her.

9. A student teacher in a secondary school located in an area with little racial diversity wrote the following entry in the journal she kept of her reactions to daily events at school: "Students from other counties were visiting the school for some FFA event. One of my students walked out in the hallway (before class) and spoke to a visiting student, using a racial slur. I'm so tired of all these racial problems. They seem to get worse every year." How should she have handled this situation?
10. The student teacher in Question 9 was told by her supervisor, "You could approach a situation like this by asking the student to put himself in the other person's place and think how the remarks would make him feel."

   a. Do you think this advice would work? Why or why not?
   b. What other advice could have helped her to deal with such a situation?

SELECTED REFERENCES

Arthur, B. M. (1991, May). Working with new ESL students in a junior high school reading class. *Journal of Reading, 34,* 628–631.

Au, K. Heu-Pei, & Kawakami, A. J. (1990, October). Reviews and reflections: Understanding and celebrating diversity in the classroom. *Language Arts, 67,* 607–610.

Commeyras, M. (1999, February). How interested are literacy educators in gender issues? Survey results from the United States. *Journal of Adolescent & Adult Literacy, 42,* 352–362.

Cox, C., & Batstone, P. (1997). *Crossroads: Literature and language in culturally diverse classrooms.* Upper Saddle River, NJ: Prentice Hall.

Diller, D. (1999, May). Opening the dialogue: Using culture as a tool in teaching young African American children. *The Reading Teacher, 52,* 820–828.

Dudley-Marling, C. (1997, Spring). "I'm not from Pakistan": Multicultural literature and the problem of representation. *The New Advocate, 10,* 123–134.

Early, M. (1990, October). Enabling first and second language learners in the classroom. *Language Arts, 67,* 567–575.

Fredericksen, E. (2000, March). Muted colors: Gender and classroom silence. *Language Arts, 77,* 301–308.

Garcia, E. (1994). *Understanding and meeting the challenge of student cultural diversity.* Boston: Houghton Mifflin.

Goldenberg, C. (1990, October). Research directions: Beginning literacy instruction for Spanish-speaking children. *Language Arts, 67,* 590–598.

Greever, E. A. (2000, March). William's doll revisited. *Language Arts, 77,* 324–330.

Heathington, B. S. (Ed.). (1981). *Breaking barriers: Overcoming career stereotyping in early childhood.* College Park: University of Maryland Press.

Hadaway, N. L., & Mundy, J. (1999, March). Children's informational picture books visit a secondary ESL classroom. *Journal of Adolescent & Adult Literacy, 42,* 464–475.

Jackson, J. F. (1999, December). What are the real risk factors for African American children? *Phi Delta Kappan, 81,* 308–312.

Koskinen, P. S., Blum, I. H., Bisson, S. A., Phillips, S. M., Creamer, T. S., & Kelley, T. B. (1999, February). Shared reading, books, and audiotapes: Supporting diverse students in school and at home. *The Reading Teacher, 52,* 430–444.

Krupp, J. A. (1991, October). No, you can't build someone else's self-esteem. *Teaching K-8, 21,* 67–68.

Lee, L. C. (1991, Winter). The opening of the American mind: Educating leaders for a multicultural society. *Human Ecology Forum,* 2–5.

Martinez-Roldan, C. M., & Lopez-Robertson, J. M. (1999, December/2000, January). Initiating literature circles in a first-grade bilingual classroom. *The Reading Teacher, 53,* 270–281.

Miller, H. (1998, April). Teaching and learning about cultural diversity: Victims, heroes, and just plain folks. *The Reading Teacher, 51,* 602–604.

Moore, S. A., & Moore, D. W. (1991, December). Linguistic diversity and reading. *The Reading Teacher, 45,* 326–327.

Newkirk, T. (2000, March). Misreading masculinity: Speculations on the great gender gap in writing. *Language Arts, 77,* 294–300.

Norton, D. E. (1990, September). Teaching multicultural literature in the reading curriculum. *The Reading Teacher, 44,* 28–40.

Pine, G. J., & Hilliard, A. G. (1990, April). Rx for racism: Imperatives for America's schools. *Phi Delta Kappan, 71,* 593–600.

Pritchard, R. (1990, Fall). The effects of cultural schemata on reading processing strategies. *Reading Research Quarterly, 25,* 273–293.

Pugh, S. L., & Garcia, J. (1990, September). Portraits in black: Establishing African American identity through nonfiction books. *Journal of Reading, 34,* 20–25.

Ramsey, P. G. (1987). *Teaching and learning in a diverse world: Multicultural education for young children.* New York: Teachers College Press.

Rasinski, T. V., & Padak, N. D. (1990, October). Multicultural learning through children's literature. *Language Arts, 67,* 576–580.

Reimer, K. M. (1992, January). Multiethnic literature: Hold fast to dreams. *Language Arts, 69,* 14–21.

Reyes, M., & Molner, L. A. (1991, October). Instructional strategies for second-language learners in the content areas. *Journal of Reading, 35,* 96–103.

Rigg, P., & Allen, V. G. (1989). *When they don't all speak English: Integrating the ESL student into the regular classroom.* Urbana, Ill.: National Council of Teachers of English.

Schon, I. (1999, October). Enticing Spanish-speaking adolescents: Recent books in Spanish for every taste. *Journal of Adolescent & Adult Literacy, 43,* 126–132.

Singham, M. (1998, September). The canary in the mine: The achievement gap between black and white students. *Phi Delta Kappan, 80,* 9–15.

Tarvin, W. L., & Al-Arishi, A. Y. (1990, September). Literature in EFL: Communicative alternatives to audiolingual assumptions. *Journal of Reading, 34,* 30–36.

Thompson, D. C. (1985, December/1986, January). A new view of masculinity. *Educational Leadership, 43,* 53–56.

Trachtenberg, S. J. (1990, April). Multiculturalism can be taught only by multicultural people. *Phi Delta Kappan, 71,* 610–611.

Villegas, A. M. (1991). *Culturally responsive pedagogy for the 1990s and beyond.* Princeton, NJ: Educational Testing Service.

Teaching to Diversity

Making a Breakthrough

In January, Carlos, a 9-year-old boy from Puerto Rico, enters a mostly white, middle-class school in a suburb of a northern U. S. city. Carlos is a shy child who knows only a little English. Mrs. Hearn, the cooperating teacher, and Carol Vaughn, the student teacher, encourage the class to accept Carlos and try to make him feel part of the class. Sam Ray is a student teacher in a fourth-grade class.

Mrs. Hearn: Boys and girls, I'd like you to meet Carlos. He has just moved here from Puerto Rico, and I want you to make him feel welcome. Carlos, we're glad to have you. Here is your seat, right between Leslie and John.

John (at recess): Come on, Carlos. We're going to play kickball. You can be on my team.

Carlos: No. I no play ball.

Terry: We'll show you how. It's easy.

Carlos: No. (He moves away from the boys and stands off by himself.)

John: Suit yourself. Let's get started.

Hank (at lunch): Did you bring your lunch, Carlos?

Carlos: Sí.

Hank: Here, you can eat at our table.

Carlos: No. I eat over here. Myself.

Hank: Okay. Whatever you say.

Miss Vaughn (one week later): Mrs. Hearn, I'm worried about Carlos. I think the class tried to make him feel welcome at first, but now the children ignore him. He just stays by himself and looks so sad and lonely. We should be able to do something.

Mrs. Hearn: I'm concerned about him too, but I don't know what to do. I've talked to some of the children about him, and they say he never wants to do anything with them, so they don't ask him anymore.

Miss Vaughn: What's even worse is that some of them are beginning to laugh at him and make fun of him because he brings unusual food to lunch and acts strangely sometimes. I'll try talking to him about it and see how he feels.

Miss Vaughn: Carlos, how are you getting along?

Carlos: Not so good. Boys and girls, they no like me.

Miss Vaughn: Sure, they like you. They want you to be their friend.

Carlos: No. I no like them.

Miss Vaughn (to herself): I didn't get anyplace with him. I've just got to think of something.

Miss Vaughn (a few days later): Sam, aren't you teaching a unit on Mexico?

Mr. Ray: I'm right in the middle of it.

Miss Vaughn: How would you like your children to learn some Spanish words?

Mr. Ray: That'd be great. What do you have in mind?

Miss Vaughn: I've got this little guy from Puerto Rico who is having a really hard time in our class. I thought maybe you could ask him to help you with some Spanish words.

Mr. Ray: Sure. Could he come to our class tomorrow about 10:30?

Miss Vaughn: That'll be fine.

Miss Vaughn (back in her own class): Carlos, the class down the hall is learning about Mexico. The teacher can't speak Spanish. Could you go there and tell them some Spanish words tomorrow?

Carlos: I don't know. They no like me either.

Miss Vaughn: They'll like you. Don't worry about that. Anyway, you know Spanish words, and they don't know any.

Carlos: Well, maybe.

Mr. Ray (next day at 10:30): Class, this is Carlos from Mrs. Hearn's room. He knows how to speak Spanish and is going to tell us some words we need to know.

Jean: Terrific! I'm working on a scrapbook. I can put in some Spanish words. Carlos, how do you say *family* in Spanish? How about *dinner*? And *school*?

Barry: Can you teach us how to count in Spanish?

Elaine: Say something to us in Spanish.

Mr. Ray: Whoa. Wait a minute. Give Carlos a chance to answer. Carlos, can you tell Jean the words she wants to know first?

Carlos (beginning very cautiously): Sí. Word for *family* is *familia*. What else you want to know? (Carlos answers more questions, gradually builds confidence, then seems eager to answer questions about Spanish.)

Mr. Ray: That's great, Carlos. You've helped us a lot. Maybe you can come back again.

Carlos (with a big grin): Sí. I come back.

Mr. Ray (that afternoon): Thanks, Carol. Having Carlos come was really good for my class.

Miss Vaughn: It seemed to help Carlos, too.

John (three days later): Hey, Carlos. I hear you've been teaching the kids down the hall to speak Spanish. How about teaching us?

Carlos: Sí. I teach you. What you want to know?

Terry: I know. You teach us some Spanish, and we'll teach you how to play kickball. Is it a deal?

Carlos: Okay. Now we go play ball. You show me. Okay? Then I teach you Spanish.

1. Why do you think Carlos had trouble getting along with the boys and girls?
2. What are some indications that he is beginning to feel more comfortable in his new school?
3. Why did Miss Vaughn's idea about having Carlos teach Spanish to a group of children seem to help him when other attempts to help had failed?
4. Can you think of other plans that might have helped Carlos adjust to his new class?

RECOGNIZING THE EXCEPTIONAL STUDENT

It probably comes as no surprise that you will find all types of students when you enter the classroom. Students will probably be culturally diverse and range in ability from academically gifted to slow learning. Some may be learning disabled and some may be physically challenged. Today's policy of inclusion means that nearly all students are placed in regular classrooms, regardless of physical, intellectual, or emotional disabilities. In addition, you are likely to find a rich diversity of cultural backgrounds, including students whose first language is not English. You must give your best efforts to challenge, help, provide for, and understand these students.

Instead of focusing on differences, however, recognize the many ways in which these students are alike. They have many of the same needs in terms of acceptance, achievement, and interactions, and their interests are also likely to be similar, centering around friends, ball games, popular television shows or films, and the like. You should help each student reach his or her potential and find a niche in the classroom.

Challenging the Gifted Student

Gifted students often make much faster academic progress in a year than do average students. Usually, they have some of these characteristics:

1. Interest in books and reading
2. Large vocabularies and the ability to express themselves verbally in a mature manner
3. Curiosity and long attention spans
4. High levels of abstract thinking
5. Wide ranges of interests

Whereas gifted students are able to direct many of their own activities, some direction from the teacher is needed. Marty Williams describes her experiences in teaching some gifted students in Figure 3–1.

Within the school program, look for opportunities to challenge gifted students. Here are some ideas.

1. Make available a wide selection of resource materials.
2. Develop theme studies that provide opportunities for in-depth and long-term learning experiences.
3. Create a kit of challenging problems, puzzles, riddles, and the like.
4. Support students in creating and directing their own projects.
5. Encourage students to prepare oral and written reports on current theme studies.

6. Place gifted students in cooperative learning groups where they can work with less able students.

As a student teacher, you should begin collecting a file of creative and unusual ideas for use with gifted students. Figure 3–2 shows one card with which you can start your file.

Educational opportunities beyond regular classroom instruction may be available for gifted students in the school in which you are a student teacher. These options may include special programs outside the classroom, use of resource teachers, minicourses, summer programs, independent study, advanced placement, community programs, curriculum compacting, and study groups. In addition, your school system may have a special teacher for the gifted and talented, who can give you a great deal of help with materials and program planning.

As the student teacher, you can enjoy learning from gifted students as you become involved in their projects and support their efforts. Respect their ideas and encourage a wide range of activities. As you work with these students, you will certainly need a sense of humor. How helpful it is to be able to admit mistakes and laugh at yourself!

CASE STUDY 3.1

Options for Gifted Students

Ms. Tompkins was a busy teacher, and she was pleased to have an intern, Samantha Briggs, coming to help her. As Miss Briggs began observing, she was struck by the range of levels in this sixth-grade class. Some children were struggling to keep up, and others finished their work quickly and easily.

Miss Briggs watched Gwynne in particular, who always finished quickly and looked around for something to do. One day Miss Briggs heard Gwynne ask Ms. Tompkins if she could check a book out from the adult section of the town library instead of choosing one from the recommended reading list. Ms. Tompkins agreed, so Gwynne began reading a full-length novel during free reading time.

As Miss Briggs continued to work with Gwynne, she noticed that sometimes when Gwynne finished her work early, Mrs. Tompkins asked her to clean out the storage closet. Gwynne seemed pleased to be asked, and she happily sorted and organized the materials. Miss Briggs wondered, however, if this was the best use of time for an obviously gifted student.

1. What, if anything, should Miss Briggs do about this situation?
2. Could she suggest alternatives for Gwynne? If so, what might she suggest?
3. Was Gwynne being challenged in this class? Why or why not?

Helping the Student Who Is Academically Challenged

The main characteristic of students with low-normal ability is that they do not learn as quickly as do others of the same age. You will have to make some adjustments for instructing these students, such as:

1. Carefully developing readiness for each learning task
2. Moving through instructional material slowly and gradually
3. Developing ideas with concrete, manipulative, and visually oriented materials
4. Using simplified materials
5. Varying activities to accommodate short attention spans
6. Relating learnings to familiar experiences (such as school, lunchroom, gymnasium, current events, community projects, and holiday celebrations)
7. Providing for large amounts of practice to master new learnings
8. Reviewing with closely spaced, cumulative exercises to encourage retention

If a student of low-normal ability is having difficulty with a particular concept or idea, you may need to use corrective exercises and materials, such as the one shown in Figure 3–3.

Many such students, accustomed to years of placement in low groups, have negative self-concepts. It is important for them to experience success in some way—perhaps through athletics, art, or some other

FIGURE 3–1
Math Wizard: A Course in Informal Geometry

During the summer, I taught a mini-course in informal geometry geared to gifted children in grades 4–6, as part of the Summer Enrichment Program. Since geometry is an indispensable tool of mankind, used constantly in many professions—by the builder, the engineer, the navigator, the astronomer, the artist, the musician, the inventor—gifted children should learn this material to have a solid foundation on which to build more complex geometric skills as their education progresses.

Some of the concepts taught and investigated in this mini-course were the three basic shapes; the ideas of proximity, separation, order, and enclosure; the relationship of sides and angles; the ideas of congruent, similar, and different; the Platonic Solids and Euler's Formula; and the visualization and creation of two- and three-dimensional objects.

Gifted children need to begin by working with concrete objects, even though these students are quick to perceive the abstract. From concrete objects they can move to semiconcrete or pictorial representations and then to abstract thinking.

Integration of mind and body is also essential for the gifted student, and with this in mind, I made it a point to involve the students physically with the concepts we studied. For example, they used their and/or other students' bodies to demonstrate the ideas of proximity, separation, order, and enclosure, and we had a relay race as a follow-up to the section on visualization and creation of two- and three-dimensional objects.

Every few days we had a "Tricky Puzzle"—a mathematical brain-teaser—to serve as a follow-up of the lesson. These puzzles also served as a lesson carry-over to get things rolling the next day by having the students present their solutions of the previous day's puzzle. "Tricky Puzzle" time was definitely the highlight of the day!

As the culminating experience for this mini-course, the students created box sculptures from "trash" they had been collecting since the first day of class. The only criteria were that (1) the students have a "guiding idea" for their construction, and that (2) they be able to name the geometric shapes involved in their sculptures. This exercise served as a good way to wrap up the course and ended things on a pleasant note.

FIGURE 3–2
Sample Activity Card for
Gifted Students

BOX O' BALLADS

Have a copy available of Carl Sandburg's book *The American Songbag*. Provide time
and materials for students to do one of the following related projects after discussing and enjoying some of the ballads:

1. Draw a panorama representing one of the cowboy ballads.
2. Write some imaginative ballads of your own about the pioneers or the
   railroad workers.
3. Create a shoe-box diorama representing one of the lumberjack ballads.
4. Plan and present a short creative drama representing the ballad of your choice.
5. Read in several sources about the historical period represented and prepare
   a report.

talent or skill. Consider those students in your class
who have less academic ability than others, and then
do Activity 3.1.

To develop and maintain positive attitudes toward
school subjects, provide students who are academically challenged with situations that relate to their
experiences and to the real world in which they live.
Identify basic life skills, and relate them to subject
content. For example, in math, teach skills related to
such everyday tasks as reading price tags, calendars,
road maps, recipes, coupons, timetables, thermometers, clocks, and sales slips; understanding money
values and measurement units; and making change.
Similarly, you can present subject matter concepts
through such readily available materials as newspapers and magazines, "how to" books, telephone
directories, mail-order catalogues, television guides,
scouting manuals, menus, greeting cards, hobby
materials, food and medicine containers, road signs,
and nature guides.

Some secondary school programs focus instruction
for the student who is academically challenged on
practical applications, such as planning a budget; filling out job applications; learning social skills needed
in family and job situations; and using independent
living skills, such as food preparation, home management, attention to personal hygiene practices, and
safety practices. Other functional curriculum programs incorporate career education, specific vocational skills, or on-the-job training in certain areas.

Even gifted children need to begin
by working with concrete objects.

FIGURE 3–3
Sample Corrective Exercise for Slow Learners

If you're still having trouble with these words . . .

"That's my son."

"The sun is high in the sky."

sun
A

son
B

1. Do <u>sun</u> and <u>son</u> sound alike?
2. What is different in the spelling of the words?
3. Draw a picture to fit these sentences.
   a. The <u>sun</u> is shining.
   b. Mother is with her <u>son</u>.
4. Write a sentence using the word <u>sun.</u> Then write a sentence using the word <u>son.</u>
5. Circle the picture word that fits these sentences.
   a. The _____ was behind the clouds.
                     (sun, son)
   b. Bill is Mr. Brown's _____.
                             (sun, son)

Providing for Students with Learning Disabilities

Students with learning disabilities usually demonstrate a significant discrepancy between intellectual potential and actual level of performance. They have some sort of difficulty learning in one or more subjects, but they are usually not below average in intelligence, visually or hearing impaired, or educationally deprived.

The following guidelines may help you understand how to work with students who have learning disabilities.

1. Increase attention span by removing distractions, including any materials other than those necessary for the assigned task.
2. Teach the student how to organize his or her desk, belongings, and materials.
3. Try to improve one behavior at a time, rewarding appropriate behavior and involving the student in recording progress.
4. Carefully structure the learning environment and tasks with specific standards, limits, and rules, and be consistent in your expectations. Make consequences for violations clear.
5. Assign one task at a time, at first using a step-by-step procedure. Use short, sequential assignments, with breaks between tasks.
6. Find a variety of media to present content (such as videos, audiotapes, and transparencies), and use active methods (such as simulation games, experiments, and role playing) as instructional strategies.

Practices frequently used with secondary students who have learning disabilities include teaching generalized learning strategies (such as note-taking, test-taking, outlining, and study skills), putting greater emphasis on multimedia presentations of material than on lectures or textbooks, and making provisions for alternatives (such as oral instead of written tests).

Students with Attention Deficit Disorder (ADD).
You may have heard teachers discussing students with attention deficit disorder (ADD), a form of learning disability. Although ADD can occur without hyperactivity, these teachers are probably referring to hyperactive students who are difficult to manage in the classroom. ADD is most common among elementary school children and tends to slow down by adolescence. The child with ADD is likely to:

1. Be inattentive and unable to remain "on task"
2. Become impatient while waiting for his or her turn during games
3. Blurt out answers to questions
4. Fidget with his or her hands or feet
5. Be easily distracted
6. Turn in careless or incomplete work
7. Talk excessively and interrupt others
8. Lose things necessary for school tasks (e.g., pencils, books, assignments)
9. Engage in potentially dangerous acts without considering the consequences (e.g., darting into the street without looking)
10. Shift from one activity to another without completing anything

Since this disorder occurs in about 3% of children, you are likely to have an ADD child in your class—one who constantly disrupts the class and has several of the characteristics listed above. A guidance counselor or your cooperating teacher may have some suggestions for dealing with such a student, and the following ideas can also be helpful:

1. Reward the child for remaining on task and completing work.
2. Set up study carrels or private areas where the child can work without distraction.
3. Keep lessons short.
4. Use progress charts and contracts.
5. Ignore inappropriate behavior whenever possible.
6. Stick to schedules and routines.

Helping At-Risk Students

Educators often use the term *at risk* when referring to certain students. What does *at risk* mean, and what can you do to help these students?

At-risk students are those who lack the skills necessary for succeeding in school and later life. They are likely to become dropouts, runaways, suicide risks, delinquents, or teenage parents. Family or societal conditions are generally the reasons why students are at risk. Some of these conditions are the following:

Homelessness

Abuse

Poverty

Unstable family situations

Immigration, involving students who have trouble adapting to the language and behaviors of typical classrooms in the United States

Persistent health problems and malnourishment

High rate of absenteeism

These students will need a great deal of support and understanding. As a student teacher, you may not be able to become directly involved in such issues, but here are some ways you may be able to help.

Be a good listener.

Intervene when you sense a problem developing.

Offer encouragement for efforts.

Give positive reinforcement to build self-esteem.

React sensitively to situations.

Visit homes or meet with caregivers to understand family situations, if possible.

Assign a buddy or a tutor to a student who needs help.

Develop a sense of community within the classroom so that all children feel welcome and respected.

Provide opportunities for achieving success.

FOR YOUR PORTFOLIO

Write a case study of a specific student who may be at risk. Describe ways you tried to encourage and support the student.

MAINSTREAMING AND INCLUSION

Because students who in the past would have been enrolled in special education classes are now being integrated into regular classes, you will probably be responsible for a number of exceptional students. The practice of including exceptional students in the regular classroom is referred to as *mainstreaming* or *inclusion*.

ACTIVITY 3.1   ***Building the Self-Esteem of Less Able Students***

Some students in a class may be less able than others. List ways that you can help the less able students build their self-esteem and succeed, and try these techniques in the next two weeks.

Two weeks later: Identify the techniques that were most effective by putting an asterisk (*) in front of them. Put an X in front of the least effective techniques. Can you think of other strategies to use?

Mainstreaming means integrating students with disabilities into regular classrooms for part of the day and allowing them to meet elsewhere with special teachers at other times. Inclusion, on the other hand, means that students with mild to severe disabilities remain in the regular classroom for the entire day, and special teachers come into the classroom to provide support services.

You should be familiar with Public Law 101-476, the Individuals with Disabilities Education Act (IDEA), which is the reauthorization of Public Law 94-142, the Education for All Handicapped Children Act. These laws affect services provided to individuals with disabilities in public schools and provide for including students with disabilities in regular classrooms.

On the basis of test materials and appropriate records, an evaluation is made by a multidisciplinary team, or M-team. The team is composed of the student's teacher, one or both of the parents, and a representative of the local education agency (other than the teacher). It may include the student and additional professional personnel, and you may also be invited to participate.

The M-team writes an Individualized Education Program (IEP), which provides assessment information, as well as classroom modifications and instructional plans that you should know about when you work with these students. The format will probably include items such as these:

1. Student's present levels of educational performance
2. Student's learning style
3. Annual goals
4. Short-term instructional objectives
5. Specific educational services needed
6. Date when those services will begin and length of time the services will be given
7. Evaluation of student's ability to meet goals and objectives

FOR YOUR PORTFOLIO

If you have the opportunity, be a member of an M-team. Include a copy of the IEP, with the student's name deleted, that you helped to create.

The following ideas may be useful in teaching included or mainstreamed students:

1. Build rapport with the students. Let the students know that you are genuinely interested in seeing that they overcome difficulties. A comfortable, relaxed atmosphere also enhances rapport.
2. Make a plan for alleviating their difficulties as much as possible. Tailor instruction to meet the needs of each individual student, and relate instruction to the student's learning characteristics and potential. Different approaches may succeed with different students, so you must be familiar with many different approaches and flexible in your use of them.
3. Adjust the length of the instructional sessions to fit the students' attention spans. In fairly long sessions, you will need frequent changes of activities.
4. Learn the students' interests and use them as the focus of your instruction. A student will tend to put forth much effort to master a particular concept or skill that relates to a special interest. Give authentic, meaningful assignments and emphasize the values and usefulness of completing tasks.

Special education teachers and other personnel can offer you help when you work with exceptional students (see Activity 3.2). A paraprofessional may be available, and peers, either students from the same classroom or students from higher grades, may act as tutors.

CASE STUDY 3.2

Planning for Differences

Mr. Hernandez, a student teacher, is planning a study of the Civil War for his American history class. He is aware of the need to adjust instruction for varying achievement levels and personal needs. He plans to encourage several advanced students to read widely and present information to the class in the form of reports, panel discussions, and dramatizations.

Some students will read chapters from the textbook and search for answers to a list of questions. Mr. Hernandez will prepare study guides to help these students focus on particular information.

Several slower-learning students will use some easy-to-read books and other supplementary materials to prepare for a group discussion about the Civil War. They will also view a video as part of their study. Mr. Hernandez will assign a student tutor to help when difficulties arise.

During this theme study, Mr. Hernandez plans to place students in cooperative learning groups with each group consisting of an advanced student, a slow learner, and two or three average students. Working as a team, these students will investigate different aspects of the Civil War and share their findings with the rest of the class.

Other students will read about Harriet Tubman and role play her efforts in freeing the slaves. One student with ADD will work on short, sequential assignments, with a specific "date due" schedule. Mr. Hernandez will help Felipe, a visually impaired student, by providing audiotapes and by asking a good reader to read key information aloud to Felipe. In these and other ways, Mr. Hernandez hopes he has made appropriate adjustments for the needs of the students in the classroom.

1. What is your opinion of the way Mr. Hernandez adjusted assignments to meet differing needs?
2. What additional ideas can you suggest for meeting individual differences?

UNDERSTANDING THE NEEDS OF CULTURALLY AND LINGUISTICALLY DIVERSE STUDENTS

Students differ in cultural background because of their ancestry, language, religion, physical characteristics, or customs. Some are not native to the United States, or come from the inner city or from rural areas, such as parts of Southern Appalachia. Various groups exist within a larger, dominant society, but they exhibit different language patterns, attitudes, or behaviors from those in the mainstream population. Teachers should be aware of concerns related to culturally diverse students.

Ethnic groups include Caucasians, Hispanics, African Americans, Asian Americans, and Native Americans. In dealing with students from diverse groups, your knowledge of their language and culture can be valuable. Research reveals typical learning patterns within ethnic groups. For example, many Mexican Americans seek close personal relationships with their teachers and prefer learning general concepts to learning specific facts; African Americans tend to like discussion, collaborative work, and active projects; and many Native-American students value quiet times for thinking and the use of visual stimuli for creating images. Remember, however, that the variations among students within any cultural group are as great as their similarities, so avoid the temptation to stereotype by ethnic group (Guild, 1994).

Because Latino cultures value interactions among family members, children are taught to work together and be helpful to others. Therefore, instead of expecting all independent work, try letting students work in pairs, do choral reading, and discuss answers to homework questions before writing them on their own.

Each school setting will have a different cultural mix. Try to familiarize yourself with the cultural backgrounds of the specific students you are assigned to teach.

Multicultural Education

Multicultural or multiethnic education is a way of affirming the value of various cultural groups within the schools. Supporters of multicultural education believe that material related to ethnic groups should be an integral part of the curriculum, beginning in kindergarten and continuing throughout the grades. In social studies, you may want to have students study world events from different perspectives. Instead of having the students consider only prevalent views in the United States, you can lead them to consider how people from other countries view international events. In literature, you can have them read stories with varied ethnic and racial content. You can also incorporate multiethnic themes into art, music, science, mathematics, and physical education.

A much less effective approach to multiethnic education that some teachers take is the "heroes and holidays" observance. Two or three times during the year, certain periods are set aside to celebrate a particular event related to an ethnic group. For example, at Thanksgiving children may dress as Native Americans and construct tepees, or in observance of Martin Luther King's death, students might prepare a "soul food" meal. Such observances do little to promote understanding of racial and ethnic groups, but rather reinforce misconceptions and stereotypes. As a student teacher, you should consider taking a more meaningful approach to multiethnic education.

Multiethnic content in the curriculum can offer relevant reading material for students of particular ethnic groups. Many African-American students will be more interested in reading stories about Harriet Tubman's heroic efforts to free slaves or George Washington Carver's ingenuity in finding ways to use peanuts than about many situations involving no African-American characters. When students have greater interest, they will be more enthusiastic about learning.

In recognition of the learning preferences of non-mainstream ethnic groups, Coelho (1994) recommends that you consider two major educational strands when planning instruction:

- Cooperative learning for developing both social and academic skills
- Exploratory talk to connect language and learning

ACTIVITY 3.2   **Support Personnel for Students with Special Needs**

Identify a student with special needs in your class, and identify several people who might help you work with this student, such as your cooperating teacher, a resource teacher, or a guidance counselor. Interview them, and then write an informal plan for helping the student.

Comments from support personnel:

Informal plan:

Reflection: How effective is my plan? Who else might be able to help? What else could I try?

Many studies indicate that cooperative learning is particularly beneficial for minority students, for promoting race relations, and for enhancing self-esteem.

Here are some specific strategies you can use with students of varying ethnic backgrounds (Garcia, 1994).

1. Hold high achievement expectations for all students.
2. Focus on teaching reading, writing, and math.
3. Maintain an orderly, safe environment.
4. Provide continual feedback on academic progress.
5. Give recognition for academic success.

Be conscious of ways to use multicultural content in your lessons. Keep in mind that multicultural education is not simply a matter of adding a bit of information about a minority group to your lessons now and then. It is a commitment to presenting material from a global perspective that values the contributions and cultures of each ethnic group.

You might want to subscribe to *Teaching Tolerance,* a free semiannual journal designed to combat racist attitudes (Education Department, Southern Poverty Law Center, P.O. Box 548, Montgomery, AL 36101-0548). Used in about 55,000 schools, it includes practical materials, resources, and strategies for elementary and secondary classroom teachers. A book entitled *Responding to Hate at School* and video-and-text teaching kits are also available free if you write for them.

Attitudes toward Diversity

You need to be sensitive to the special needs of the culturally diverse students in your classroom. Respect their ethnic and racial backgrounds. While some students have no problems with their ethnicity, others feel insecure and ill at ease in a different culture. You should respond in helpful and constructive ways to students with ethnic adjustment problems.

Several strategies can be used to encourage students to accept their peers who come from different racial or ethnic origins. Role playing can help students understand how it feels to be a member of a different ethnic group. Assigning children of different ethnic heritages to work together on a committee helps them realize that each member of the group can make an important contribution. You can create other situations in which problems can be solved only through the cooperation of each member of an ethnically mixed group.

Culturally different students need to acquire the values and behaviors essential for success in the dominant society while retaining important aspects of their own subcultures. (See Activity 3.3, on valuing diversity.) Whereas you cannot do a great deal to further this ideal in a short period of time, your awareness of cultural differences, your attitudes toward your students, and the focus of your lessons can make a difference (see Activity 3.4).

FOR YOUR PORTFOLIO

Using your lesson plan from Activity **3.4** as a basis, show how you could adapt it to meet the needs of diverse learners.

Language-Minority Students

Every year, many people who do not speak English enter the United States from a variety of nations. Students who speak only a language other than English need your help in learning English as quickly as possible in order to benefit from the educational experiences offered in an English-speaking school. Don't be too concerned about having these students acquire mastery of English grammar and rules. Coelho (1994) points out that students learn English more easily by using it purposefully in real situations than by learning information about the language. Others (Willis, 1994) agree, saying that a different language is best learned when students use it with literature and content rather than through a grammar-based approach.

You should purchase a foreign-language dictionary to refer to when trying to communicate with students who are trying to learn English. If a student reads her or his own language fluently, you should provide a dictionary with English equivalents of familiar words for that student.

In the lower grades, you can construct a picture dictionary of English words for such a student. You may make use of pictures and concrete objects to supply needed vocabulary words. For example, you may show the student a picture of a dog or an actual dog and point to the picture or the animal while saying the word *dog.* Coloring books and picture books were successfully used with one 8-year-old child from Thailand, whose vocabulary grew rapidly, due to her desire to communicate. Classmates spent countless free hours identifying objects in these books for her, listening to her repeat their names, and helping her correct her pronunciation. In return, she taught the names for the items in her own language to her highly receptive classmates. The result was mutual respect and enjoyment.

It is often helpful to assign buddies to students who speak little or no English. Students who speak the new students' languages would be good choices for buddies. Including new students in cooperative learning groups and classroom activities in which they can listen to the language being used can also be helpful. As the students learn English, they can help familiarize other students with a second language, as Carlos did in his school and as the Thai girl did in her class.

CASE STUDY 3.3

Learning English through Collaboration

Lori, Mr. Chowdhuri's student teacher, observed that there were several Korean students in her second-grade class. They were eager to learn English and were making good progress, but Lori wanted to find a way to help them feel more comfortable with their new language.

Aware of the benefits of cooperative learning for language-minority students, Lori decided to form groups, each of which would include a Korean child, so far as possible. Lori knew the children loved the big books that Mr. Chowdhuri shared with them during reading lessons, so she decided to ask each group to make an original big book to share with the rest of the class. Since the children were enthusiastic about the project, Lori got the supplies they needed and let them get to work.

As she listened in on the groups, she heard the children eagerly suggesting ideas. The Korean children listened carefully, joined in, and gladly accepted the corrections in language usage that their native-English speaking peers offered. Whewon was especially full of ideas, and Lori noticed that he wanted to dictate the text. As he spoke the lines, group members approved his ideas, but sometimes changed verb endings and word order to correspond with English usage.

As a result of this collaboration, the Korean children learned many of the fine points of English—without a grammar book and in a mutually satisfying endeavor. Lori felt that she had taken a big step toward realizing her goal.

1. What are some other ways to help language-minority children learn English in a constructive, purposeful way?
2. Compare the advantages of teaching English to non-English speakers with purposeful conversation instead of with grammar rules.

DISCUSSION QUESTIONS

1. How could you identify the following types of students: (a) gifted; (b) learning disabled; (c) culturally diverse?
2. Consider one content or subject area. How would you challenge the gifted student?
3. How could you make a "heroes and holidays" observance more meaningful?
4. How would you help a student with a learning disability? Relate your answer to a specific content area.
5. How can you consider the needs of culturally diverse students in the instructional program?
6. What are your responsibilities toward the mainstreamed or included student?
7. How can you and special resource personnel cooperate to ensure the best program for the exceptional student?
8. In the ninth-grade history class where you are a student teacher, there is a student named Pedro who speaks fluent Spanish but refuses to try to learn more than the small amount of English he already knows. Many of the other students are Mexican Americans like Pedro, but unlike him, they are learning English rapidly. When it is time to give a test over the unit you have been studying, Pedro is the only one who has difficulty reading the questions. What would you do? Would you translate into Spanish for him (assuming you can), read the questions to him in English, or let him do the best he can with the test on his own? Explain your answer.

SELECTED REFERENCES

Allain, V., & Pettus, A. (1998). *Teaching diverse students: Preparing with cases.* Bloomington, IN: Phi Delta Kappa.

Au, K. (1993). *Literacy instruction in multicultural settings.* Fort Worth, TX: Holt, Rinehart and Winston.

Bertrand, J., & Stice, C. (Eds.). (1995). *Empowering children at risk of school failure: A better way.* Norwood, MA: Christopher-Gordon.

Choate, J., & Rakes, T. (1998). *Inclusive instruction for struggling readers.* Bloomington, IN: Phi Delta Kappa.

Coelho, E. (1994). *Learning together in the multicultural classroom.* Markham, Ontario: Pippin.

Educating for diversity. (1994, May). Themed issue. *Educational Leadership, 51.*

Faltis, C. (1993). *Joinfostering: Adapting teaching strategies for the multilingual classroom.* New York: Macmillan.

First, P., & Curcio, C. (1993). *Implementing the disabilities acts: Implications for educators.* Bloomington, IN: Phi Delta Kappa.

Fouse, B., & Brians, S. (1993). *A primer on attention deficit disorder.* Bloomington, IN: Phi Delta Kappa.

ACTIVITY 3.3   *Valuing Students' Diversity*

Refer to the Class Culture Survey that you did in Activity 2.2 to focus on students who represent various ethnic backgrounds. For additional information about teaching in a diverse society, check the website *http://www.prenhall.com/methods-cluster*. Go to "Topic 5: Diversity in the Classroom," where you will find information on cultural, racial, linguistic, and gender diversity. Plan some experiences for valuing the diversity of students in your class. Briefly describe them here.

Experiences:

Reflection: How effective were the experiences? What else could you try?

ACTIVITY 3.4   *Adapting Lessons to Students with Special Needs*

Briefly outline a lesson plan for a subject you are teaching.

How would you adjust this plan for the following students? (You may consider other types of diversity, particularly those of students you are teaching.)

Hearing Impaired Students:

Visually Impaired Students:

Students with Limited Use of English:

Academically Challenged Learners:

Gifted Students:

French, M. & Andretti, A. (1995). *Attention deficit and reading instruction.* Bloomington, IN: Phi Delta Kappa.

Garcia, E. (1994). *Understanding and meeting the challenge of student cultural diversity.* Boston, MA: Houghton Mifflin.

Guild, P. (1994, May). The culture/learning style connection. *Educational Leadership, 51,* 16–21.

Inclusion. (1995, December). Themed issue. *Phi Delta Kappan, 77.* The inclusive school. (1994, December/1995, January). Themed issue. *Educational Leadership, 52.*

Kranz, B. (1994). *Identifying talents among multicultural children.* Bloomington, IN: Phi Delta Kappa.

Lombardi, T. (1994). *Responsible inclusion of students with disabilities.* Bloomington, IN: Phi Delta Kappa.

Menkart, D. (1999, April). Deepening the meaning of heritage months. *Educational Leadership, 56,* 19–21.

Parks, S. (1999, April). Reducing the effects of racism in schools. *Educational Leadership, 56,* 14–18.

Pawlas, G. E. (1994, May). Homeless students at the school door. *Educational Leadership, 51,* 79–82.

Responding to hate at school. (1999, Fall). *Teaching Tolerance, 16,* 54–56.

Rothstein-Fisch, C., Greenfield, P., and Trumbull, E. (1999, April). Bridging cultures with classroom strategies. *Educational Leadership, 56,* 64–67.

Spangenberg-Urbschat, K., & Pritchard, R. (Eds.) (1994). *Kids come in all languages: Reading instruction for ESL students.* Newark, DE: International Reading Association.

Wang, M., Haertel, G., & Walberg, H. (1998). *Building educational resilience.* Bloomington, IN: Phi Delta Kappa.

Willis, S. (1994, October). Making schools more inclusive. *ASCD Curriculum Update, 36,* 1–8.

Willis, S. (1994, June). Teaching language-minority students. *ASCD Update, 36,* 1, 4–5.

Classroom Administration

Chaos in the Classroom

Miss Collins, a student teacher, has been successfully using the Newspaper in Education program with her ninth-grade students. As a culminating activity for the unit, she expects the students to publish a newspaper of their own. She has divided them into groups for writing their paper.

Li-Jan: Miss Collins, what am I supposed to do?

Miss Collins: What is your job?

Li-Jan: I'm supposed to be the sports editor.

Tony: Miss Collins, where are we supposed to work?

Miss Collins: What is your group, Tony?

Tony: Feature stories.

Miss Collins: Well, try to find a place over by the bulletin board.

David: That's where you said we could work, Miss Collins.

Miss Collins: Well, find another place then, Tony. What is your group, David?

Li-Jan: Miss Collins—

Miss Collins: Just a minute, Li-Jan. What did you say, David?

David: We're writing the ads.

Miss Collins: Oh, that's right. Now, Li-Jan, what did you want?

Li-Jan: What is the sports editor supposed to do?

Miss Collins: Look at the sports section of the paper, and see if you can figure out what's supposed to be in there.

Li-Jan: Who's supposed to be in my group? I can't find anyone to work with me.

Miss Collins: Let's see. I know I have that list here somewhere. It must be under these papers.

Linda: Miss Collins, Joe says he's in charge of the news stories, but yesterday you said I could do that.

Miss Collins (to the whole class in a raised, agitated voice): Boys and girls. You must get quiet! We can't work in here with all that noise. Get busy now.

Li-Jan: Is it okay if I just write something about what our softball team did over the weekend?

Miss Collins: Yes, that'll be fine, Li-Jan. Just do that. I can't seem to find who the other members of your group are.

Phil and Steve: Miss Collins, you said we needed to go interview some other teachers. Is it okay if we do that now?

Miss Collins: I'm not sure.

Joe (approaching Miss Collins angrily): How come Linda says she's supposed to do news stories? I thought you told me to do that.

Linda (addressing Joe): She told me to do them!

Miss Collins: Why don't you two work together on them?

Joe (shuffling off and muttering under his breath): I can't stand that girl. She's a creep. She can do it by herself for all I care.

Phil and Steve: What about it? Can we go?

Miss Collins: Go where? Oh, yes, I remember. Did you make appointments with anyone?

Phil and Steve: No, were we supposed to?

Miss Collins: Well, you really should.

Diane: It's almost time for my bus. Shall I get ready?

Miss Collins: I had no idea it was that late already. Yes, go get ready.

Miss Collins (addressing the class): Class! (No one hears.) Class! (Still no one hears amidst the laughter, talking, and running around the room.) Boys and girls! (now shouting to be heard) Clean up your work, and get in your seats. The buses are coming.

The students finally hear her and begin to gather their things together. The buses arrive before they finish, and Miss Collins must straighten up the rest of the room herself. At this point, her cooperating teacher walks in and asks, "Well, how did everything go?"

Miss Collins (with a heavy sigh): I'll never try that again. These kids don't know how to work in groups.

1. Was Miss Collins's idea for a culminating activity a good one? How might it have been handled more successfully?

2. What mistakes did Miss Collins make in assigning group activities? How could she have prevented some of the problems?

3. Why do you think Miss Collins ran out of time? What factors should be considered in scheduling activities such as this one to be sure there is enough time?

4. What could Miss Collins have done to get the children's attention instead of shouting at them? How could she have reduced the noise level while the boys and girls were working?

5. Do you agree with Miss Collins that these children can't work in groups? Do you think she was right to say she'll never try group work again?

SUPPORT SYSTEM FOR TEACHING

Knowing your subject and how to teach it is important, but students won't learn if your plans go awry because of poor classroom management. What can you do about providing a classroom environment conducive to learning, scheduling activities within limited time frames, grouping students for different purposes, and keeping records for future reference? Unfortunately, there are no easy answers to these questions. Each situation is unique. You *can*, however, observe your cooperating teacher and read this chapter for some useful ideas on classroom management. You may find a tutorial on classroom management to be helpful. You can access on the Internet at *http://www.prenhall.com/methods-cluster*, "Topic 3: Discipline/Classroom Management."

CLASSROOM MANAGEMENT

Traditional and Learner-Centered Classrooms

Schools and individual teachers within the same school observe different degrees of formality in their approaches to learning. Classrooms range along a continuum from being highly structured to extremely flexible. One teacher may assign seats arranged in perfect rows, whereas another may have a room filled with clusters of chairs for small-group work and areas designated for learning centers. Regardless of the amount of structure or flexibility in your classroom, you must do a great deal of planning and classroom management. In traditional, structured classrooms, the rules are already pretty clearly established, and you simply need to enforce them. Prepare lesson plans carefully and keep the students on the subject during discussions. Try to meet each objective and cover the material adequately.

In learner-centered classrooms you will find exploration, discovery, and spontaneity—a community of learners. Students may negotiate learning experiences with their teachers, make choices about how and what they study, and take an active part in classroom decision making. If students express interest in a particular aspect of a lesson, the teacher may allow them to pursue that special interest, rather than conforming rigidly to the lesson plan.

In this type of classroom you should set up situations and make resources available to stimulate the desire to learn. Your class may actually resemble a museum—a place for students to investigate and learn (Fogarty, 1998). Be sufficiently knowledgeable in your subject to expand on your lesson in response to the interest your students show. You may permit, and even encourage, differences of opinion in your classroom, but know how to help students resolve disagreements and conflicts.

Conflict Resolution

Conflict resolution skills are useful for helping students work out their own differences peacefully. These skills include understanding different points of view, recognizing personal feelings and the feelings of others, avoiding put-downs, controlling anger, listening attentively, and finding win-win solutions (Carlsson-Paige & Levin, 1998). The three problem-solving strategies of conflict resolution are *negotiation*, with only the two parties involved meeting face to face to resolve the dispute; *mediation*, in which a mediator assists the two parties in arriving at a solution; and *consensus decision making*, which is a group problem-solving process for creating a plan of action supported by all parties (Bodine & Crawford, 1998). Constructive conflict resolution advances the students' sense of community and promotes such values as concern for others, self-respect, devotion to the common good, and respect for diversity. Read the following case study to see an example of how Highlands Elementary School employs conflict resolution (Johnson, Johnson, Stevahn, & Hodne, 1997).

CASE STUDY 4.1

Loose Ball

During a soccer game, a ball rolls out of bounds. One student from a group of students passing by kicks the ball away just as one of the players is trying to get it. When an argument begins, a pair of peer mediators ask the two disputants if they'd like some help resolving their conflict. Mediation continues until the disputants reach a solution that satisfies them both. They shake hands and separate as friends, then return to their activities. The peer mediators record the event and the resolution.

At a time when school violence appears to be escalating, conflict resolution offers one possible solution (Bodine & Crawford, 1998). Conflict resolution education programs offer students "the understandings, skills, and strategies needed to choose alternatives to self-destructive and violent behaviors when confronting intrapersonal, interpersonal, or intergroup conflicts" (p. 11).

You may want to learn more about conflict resolution because you can apply strategies to situations both within and beyond school. Training is available and necessary for fully understanding how to implement the procedures, but understanding the basic skills, strategies, and values provides a starting point for enabling students to resolve disputes peacefully.

ORGANIZATIONAL PLANS

Individualization

Each student is unique in terms of personality, experience, language facility, academic potential, attitude, cultural influences, and home environment. Ideally, teachers would work with each student as an individual, but such an idea is impractical, of course. Nevertheless, teachers should provide opportunities for students to work individually on some occasions in order to pursue special interests and proceed at their own paces. Some ideas for independent activities follow.

1. *Sustained silent reading (SSR)*—In this program, students, teachers, and perhaps the entire school staff read materials of their choice during an agreed-upon period each school day (generally between 15 and 30 minutes long).
2. *Journal writing*—Each student writes a daily entry in a notebook. Entries may consist of reactions to lessons, communications with the teacher, or special concerns. Teachers may read the journal entries and respond to them.
3. *Computer-assisted instruction*—Students work on computer programs to practice skills, play games, write compositions, or solve puzzles. Chapter 8 provides information on using computers.
4. *Learning centers*—Students work independently on special projects at learning centers. They are useful for giving students choices of activities that extend classroom learning.
5. *Research reports*—Students choose topics to investigate. They find reference materials in the library, organize the content, and prepare oral or written reports.

Grouping

Grouping is a compromise between totally individualized and whole-class instruction. Individual differences can be reduced to some extent by achievement grouping, but many differences remain.

By this time, you are probably well acquainted with the school at which you are a student teacher or are getting your field experience. You may already know whether students are grouped homogeneously (according to ability) or heterogeneously (without regard to ability) schoolwide. Secondary schools may offer a multiple-track curriculum that groups students into a college preparatory, business, or general curriculum. There may also be special programs for groups of students with different needs. For instance, your school may group students who are learning English as a second language, who have been identified as potential dropouts, or who are recognized as gifted. Grouping patterns that cut across classrooms and grade levels are known as *interclass* groupings.

You will be concerned primarily with *intraclass* groupings (grouping within the classroom). Your cooperating teacher may already use small groups. As you teach, you may want to try grouping as a way to meet your objectives.

You can set up groups for different purposes. During some reading instruction, children with similar achievement levels meet together in groups, and math groups may be formed for students having difficulty with a particular skill. In social studies, students may work together in research groups, and groups in science classes may perform experiments that illustrate certain concepts. Physical education classes may be divided into homogeneous groups according to skill level, or into heterogeneous groups so that less able students can benefit from interaction with more proficient students. Groups may be short-term or long-term, depending on the length of time required to meet objectives.

Friendship groups allow friends to work together. Students in these groups are often highly motivated because they enjoy being with each other. Be careful of two things when forming friendship groups, however. First, students may enjoy one another's company so much that they won't get any work done, so you will have to warn them that they can work with their friends only as long as they produce results. When they cease to work, the groups will be disbanded and other activities substituted. Second, there will probably be some students who do not seem to have any friends. You might tactfully approach one or two popular students about including these isolates in their groups.

Interest grouping is another kind of classroom organization you may wish to try. Ask students to list topics of interest; then identify the most popular topics and ask students to sign up for their first, second, and third choices. Form groups based on your findings.

Achievement groups can reduce the range of individual differences that the teacher must meet in a specific lesson and help the teacher focus on each group's strengths and needs. However, when groups are set up on the basis of achievement levels, low-achieving students often develop poor self-concepts. They think of themselves and others in their group as "dummies." By forming project and interest groups, you encourage students of differing achievement levels to work together, and students contribute according to their particular knowledge, skills, or talents.

The types of groups you form and the way you conduct them can make a big difference in the way students respond. Read the following case studies and notice the way each teacher uses groups.

CASE STUDY 4.2

Let's Find Out about Dinosaurs!

After surveying his students' interests, Mr. Barnes placed the children in groups according to their preferences. The group that chose dinosaurs consists of three children from the low-achievement group, two from the middle group, and three from the high group. Their assignment is to create a room display and give a presentation at the end of two weeks.

Before they realize what's happening, the students are excitedly delving into books, working on drawings, sharing models from home, and planning their presentation. Jessica suggests they contact the librarian, who may have some videos, and Seth wants to share a kit he got for Christmas for the display. Amy offers to draw a backdrop for the display, and Andy says he'll find some leaves and moss that will make the display look more natural. Robert is studying the habitats of dinosaurs so that the display will be as authentic as possible, and Ruth is outlining topics for a report she plans to write. At least during this period, achievement levels are forgotten.

CASE STUDY 4.3

Which Invention Will It Be?

Ms. Ting wants to get all her students involved in a unit on inventions, so she decides to form groups. She includes in each group one or two leaders and three or four students who have not been participating actively in class. The assignment for each group is to decide which invention has had the greatest impact on the progress of the human race.

Working secretly in their groups, the students investigate inventions, select the one they feel is most

influential, and build a case to support their choice. They know they'll have to support their selections with facts, so they seek evidence from many sources in the library, as well as from teachers and others whom they consider to be authorities. Instead of only a small number of students participating, everyone is working creatively to prove to the rest of the class that his or her group's invention is most significant.

1. How did Mr. Barnes and Ms. Ting use grouping? How successful were they? What benefits resulted from such groupings?
2. What are some ways you have observed groups working well? How could you organize your class into groups that would actively involve all students?

The preceding case studies demonstrate the importance of getting all students involved as active and productive participants in the learning process through effective grouping. Here are some guidelines to help you form and manage groups. (Miss Collins in the opening vignette should have observed some of these pointers!)

1. Don't begin impulsively. Think your plan through carefully before you start.
2. Try to make your groups a workable size, small enough that everyone must participate but large enough to develop a worthy project. Generally, four to six students will work well.
3. Avoid putting in the same groups students who cause trouble when they are together.
4. Be sure that resource materials—references and supplies—are available and that students know how to use them.
5. Set up guidelines so that students know their privileges and limitations. Make sure before starting that all the students understand exactly what they are to do. Allow them freedom to talk quietly and move around the room. If possible, let them go to the library for additional information.
6. Suggest that each group appoint a leader who will be responsible for the group's activities.
7. Experiment with the length of time for maintaining groups; allow enough time to get something accomplished but not so much that students lose interest and stray off task.
8. Give each group space to carry out its activity without interfering with the other students.
9. Be available to offer ideas.

Complete Activity 4.1 on grouping patterns to help you analyze the uses of grouping in your classroom situation.

ACTIVITY 4.1   ***Grouping Patterns***

Place a checkmark (✓) beside each type of grouping that is currently being used in your class-room. Place a plus sign (+) beside any type of grouping not currently being used that you intend to try. Note your reasons at the bottom of the page.

_____   Achievement or ability grouping to put students of similar achievement or ability together

_____   Needs, or skills, grouping to correct problems

_____   Research grouping to investigate topics or themes

_____   Project grouping to perform experiments or carry out construction activities

_____   Friendship grouping to increase motivation

_____   Interest grouping to allow students to pursue special interests

Cooperative Learning

Cooperative learning is a form of classroom organization in which students work in groups or as teams to help each other acquire academic information. Sometimes students discuss material or practice skills that the teacher has presented; at other times they use cooperative methods to discover information on their own. Two key elements are individual accountability and positive interdependence (Slavin, 1990, 1991).

Cooperative learning has been used successfully at all grade levels and in every subject area. Its benefits include increased self-esteem, better intergroup relations, more positive attitudes toward school, higher academic achievement, and acceptance of academically mainstreamed students. Cooperative learning is especially effective with students from diverse cultural backgrounds, including English as a Second Language (ESL) students, who acquire social behaviors, learn content, and practice English during group interactions. Also, for students from many cultures cooperative arrangements seem to be more natural than competitive situations.

Because cooperative learning has possible academic and social benefits, you may want to try it with your classes. Workshops and courses can provide training, but some self-study and guidance from other teachers may be enough to help you get started. You need to become familiar with some of the most widely used models of cooperative learning so that you can choose one that is appropriate. Figure 4–1 shows five methods of Student Team Learning (STL), a type of cooperative learning.

Here are some features of effective cooperative learning.

1. A teacher who facilitates by circulating, first by checking to see that everyone understands, then by asking individuals questions about content.
2. A problem, goal, or task that requires higher-order thinking skills and is viewed as important by the students.
3. Active participation by each group member, often by assignment of specific roles or responsibilities.
4. Individual accountability by having each member take a test, make a presentation, write a paper, or provide a product.
5. Positive interdependence by making group members dependent on each other for meeting goals.
6. Group size appropriate for the task (usually four to six students), with more complex tasks requiring more members.
7. Heterogeneous group composition, with members from high-, low-, and average-achievement levels.
8. Acceptable social behaviors and interactions.

FIGURE 4–1
Methods of Student Team Learning (STL)

Student Teams-Achievement Divisions (STAD)—After the teacher has presented the lesson, four-member student teams of mixed ability help each other learn the material. Each member takes an individual test, and scores are computed to arrive at team scores. Teams that meet certain criteria earn rewards, which are usually certificates.

Teams-Games-Tournament (TGT)—This procedure begins like STAD, but weekly tournaments replace quizzes. Groups of students of similar achievement levels, representing their home team, compete at tournament tables. Points earned in the tournment are taken back to home teams. Points of team members are averaged.

Team Assisted Individualization (TAI)—Combining cooperative learning with individualized instruction, TAI is used to teach math to students in grades three through six. Team members usually work on different units but help each other with problems and check answers. Groups earn points as members complete units and do extra work.

Cooperative Integrated Reading and Composition (CIRC)—Teachers use CIRC to teach reading and writing from literature-based readers to students in grades 3 through 5. Students work in pairs as they read to each other, make predictions, write responses to stories, and so on. They take quizzes and may also "publish" team books.

Jigsaw—The teacher divides information to be studied into categories and puts students in home groups, with each student responsible for learning a different category. Expert groups, consisting of all students who have studied the same category, meet to review content and prepare to teach it. Experts return to their home groups and take turns teaching the material.

9. Reasonable time period set for reaching goals.
10. Thoughtful group discussions in which members provide reasons for their responses.
11. Appropriate room arrangement to facilitate group work.
12. Understanding of goals, procedures, tasks, and methods of evaluation by each group member.

CASE STUDY 4.4

Cooperative Learning— What Went Wrong?

After a lesson on the signing of the Declaration of Independence, Ms. Grady decided to form groups to reinforce the lesson. She placed students in groups of five and asked them to look through the textbook to find answers to factual questions on a worksheet. One student in each group would be responsible for finding the answer, and another would be the recorder.

As the students began working, Ms. Grady checked to see if they were finding the answers. The first group was on task, but the second group was having some problems. Ms. Grady sat with this group for the remainder of the class period, helping them locate answers in the text. Whenever the class got too noisy, she reminded the students to work quietly.

At the end of the period, each group turned in a worksheet. Ms. Grady marked their papers and gave each group member the grade that the group made. Some students complained that the grading wasn't fair because they didn't have a chance to participate, but Ms. Grady said that's the way cooperative learning works.

1. Was this task appropriate for cooperative learning? Did it cause students to think, or was it simply a literal question-answer exercise? How could Ms. Grady create a stimulating task from this topic for cooperative learning?
2. How did Ms. Grady perform as a facilitator? What could she have done differently to be more effective?
3. Was each student actively involved? Why did some students resent the grading procedure? How could each student have been an active participant?
4. Was there evidence of both individual accountability and positive interdependence? Why or why not?
5. Considering your answers to the previous questions, did Ms. Grady understand how cooperative learning works?

CASE STUDY 4.5

Cooperative Learning— A Challenge for All

Wanting to get her students actively involved in studying the possible effects of global warming, Ms. Greer decided to introduce them to the topic by presenting background information and asking them to brainstorm questions. The class came up with the following list of questions:

- How might global warming affect coastlines?
- If glaciers start to melt, what might happen?
- How might global warming affect our health?
- How might global warming affect trees and crops?
- What effects might global warming have on weather systems?
- What can we do to prevent global warming?

Ms. Greer asked students to sign up to work on the topic that interested them most, and she divided them into groups of four or five according to their choices. In each group she asked students to perform the roles of resource manager, researchers, recorder, and checker. She asked the groups to share their findings at the end of the week.

Eagerly, the students began investigating their topics. Finding accurate, current resource materials was a challenge, and deciding what information to include and how to organize it involved all group members. They questioned one another and found that they had to substantiate their reasons for believing as they did. As students worked, Ms. Greer checked with each group, questioning individual members about what they were learning, and intervening if problems developed. By Friday each group was ready to report.

1. Did Ms. Greer's idea cause students to get involved in higher-level thinking? How? Was problem solving part of the task?
2. How did Ms. Greer make sure each student was an active participant?
3. Was there evidence of individual accountability and positive interdependence? Why or why not?

Whole-Class Instruction

On many occasions whole-class instruction is most effective. Good activities for the entire class include listening to a resource visitor, contributing ideas for a theme study, seeing a video, participating in a discussion, watching a demonstration, listening to an ongoing story, and creating a semantic map. Whole-class activities have the advantage of building esprit de corps, so that all students are likely to feel a sense of belonging and share the concerns of their classmates.

Integrated Curriculum

Believing that students learn best when concepts are interrelated and reinforced, many teachers are implementing theme studies that span the curriculum. Instead of teaching fragmented, isolated subjects throughout the day, these teachers are identifying worthy themes that enable students to see real-world connections. Students use reading and writing all day in authentic situations as they investigate topics related to themes.

If you want to teach through themes, you will need to consult your cooperating teacher and the curriculum guide in selecting a significant topic. Be sure that your theme merits the time that you will need to give it! Then you will need to plan extensively, thinking of ways to apply the theme to different areas of the curriculum. You need to involve your students in the planning, so they will become actively involved in gathering resources, researching topics, learning concepts, designing projects, developing a culminating activity, and evaluating their progress. Ideally, teachers carry out theme studies throughout the entire day, but you may feel more comfortable if you begin in a limited way, perhaps by integrating language arts and social studies and teaching other subjects separately.

Theme studies are easier to develop in self-contained classrooms where the teacher can focus on the theme throughout the day. Although they are more difficult to manage in departmentalized situations, they are possible if teachers agree to focus on certain topics and coordinate their planning. For example, teachers of American history and American literature may work together to coordinate integrated study of these subjects.

FOR YOUR PORTFOLIO

Outline a unit in which you integrated learning across much of the curriculum. If you teach a single subject, you may still have been able to integrate other subjects, particularly language skills.

CASE STUDY 4.6

To Integrate or Not To Integrate

As Kathy Jenkins sat in a seminar listening to a discussion of integrated curriculum, she reflected on her two experiences as a student teacher. Her first assignment had been in the second grade at Spring Street School. She recalled planning lessons for handwriting,

Listening to a visiting storyteller is a large-group activity, sometimes involving whole classes.

spelling, grammar, and reading. Each subject was taught from a different book, and no lesson related in any way to another. She remembered doing a unit on animals of the forests, but it didn't tie in with what the students were doing in any other subject. Her lesson plan book had been filled with small blocks of time, each centered on a different subject or skill.

She was in a fifth grade class at Northside School now, and her teacher was centering instruction around the theme of *survival*. Kathy was amazed at the way Mr. Sundaram was able to relate this theme to nearly every subject, although he did teach math lessons from the math book. "Perhaps what impresses me most," thought Kathy, "is the way the children are planning so many of the activities themselves. They are discovering material on adventurers, on national heroes, and on people who showed courage in various ways. They're creating projects on endangered plants and animals in the rain forests, and they're writing books on survival skills in the wilderness. They've found dozens of books—fiction, nonfiction, and biography—to use as resources. They've invited a forest ranger to speak on survival in the woods and a nurse to speak on health hazards. They've learned new words related to the theme—and how to spell them. I never imagined there were so many ways to tie survival skills into the curriculum."

Comparing the two experiences, Kathy remembered the way the second-graders sat quietly in orderly rows with the teacher doing the talking, but those fifth-graders were a different story! They were constantly moving about and talking with each other. It was hard to tell exactly what they *were* doing sometimes. "Even though I find theme studies exciting," Kathy thought, "I'm not sure I could manage them successfully."

1. Compare the advantages for the students of a segmented and an integrated curriculum. In which of Kathy's classrooms do you believe the students were learning more? Why do you think so?
2. What are some problems created by integrating the curriculum? How can you be sure you are covering everything if you don't follow a textbook in each subject?
3. What are some ways to involve students in planning and implementing theme studies? How can you use their ideas?

SCHEDULING

Time enters into nearly every phase of your teaching. It has a lot to do with how much you accomplish, how well you hold the interest of your students, and how you feel as you proceed through the day. Good time management will make teaching a lot easier, as well as more effective, than rushing helter-skelter through the day.

Flexibility within a Routine

Routine and flexibility seem to be contradictory ideas, but you need some of each to build a balanced program. A well-planned routine helps you cover everything you are supposed to accomplish, fosters good classroom control because students feel secure when they know what to expect next, and is comfortable because you don't have to wonder all day long what to do next.

You will probably begin teaching by following the schedule already set by your cooperating teacher. Don't be a slave to your schedule, however. The schedule is for your convenience; don't let it become an obstruction to learning. Sometimes, to develop a concept fully, you will need more time than what is scheduled. You may want to use audiovisual media, invite a resource person, or take a short field trip. You may get into an activity and realize that some really creative experiences are taking place. Whenever possible, allow these learning experiences to continue, even if it means extending them beyond the scheduled time limit.

One way to have flexible scheduling within a fixed schedule in a self-contained classroom is to plan on a weekly instead of a daily basis. Perhaps you will spend 20 minutes extra on math today because you are working with manipulative materials and cut 20 minutes out of language arts. You can pay back this time later in the week.

Some schools provide for flexibility through modular, or block, scheduling. Modules are blocks of time arranged to meet instructional needs. For instance, a field trip would require several connected modules, whereas reviewing a test might require only one module. Check with your cooperating teacher to see if your school uses this plan or a similar one.

Some students report to supportive classes. A handful may go to remedial reading from 10:10 to 10:40 three times a week; another group may go to a class for gifted students from 1:15 to 2:15 every Friday. Don't plan an activity for the whole class when some students will be elsewhere.

Using Time Effectively

Your time, both in and out of the classroom, is precious. Many of the procedures that have become habitual for experienced teachers will require detailed planning for you. In order to have time for yourself, make use of planning periods during school.

Don't depend on this time, however, as unexpected interruptions occur frequently during any school day.

Evenings and weekends are not entirely your own during student teaching. You may be working with your cooperating teacher on the yearbook, sharing late afternoon bus duty, or coaching the football team well into the evening. Sometimes you will have a parent-teacher conference after school or a meeting in the evening. Record keeping also takes a great deal of time. For these and other reasons, many universities do not permit student teachers to take additional courses. If you have held a part-time job during your college years, you may have to quit or reduce your hours. Avoid committing too much time to extracurricular or social activities. Full-time student teaching is generally much more demanding of your time than 15 or 18 hours of coursework.

Plan well ahead. Order or reserve materials in advance. If you will need to make several games or posters, buy all the materials at once. A single trip to the library can serve many purposes if you get resource material you will need over a period of time. Instead of spending hours searching through curriculum guides for ideas, sit down and think hard for a few minutes. Your own ideas are often as good as or better than those you find in other sources. Combine social activities with school functions—take your date, a friend, or your family with you on a Sunday afternoon hike while you collect specimens for a terrarium.

The following tips will help you keep things moving in the classroom:

1. Have learning centers ready for action, fully equipped and neatly arranged.
2. Put markers in your books so that you can turn quickly to the right pages.
3. Be sure all the resource materials you will need for the day are readily available, including supplies you will ask students to distribute.
4. Make sure students can move from one activity to the next with little disruption or confusion.
5. Have everything ready for the next day's lessons before you go home in the afternoon. If you are an early riser, however, you may prefer to come early and get things ready in the morning.

Here are some questions and suggested answers for using time effectively.

Do the students take five minutes to change from one lesson to another as they yawn, stretch, sharpen pencils, drop books, and talk to each other, or do they quietly put away one book and get out another?

If it takes too long for students to change from one book to another, practice doing this one day. Have a race against time to see if they can make the change in 45 seconds, 30 seconds, or less. They won't always work this quickly, but knowing what they *can* do should speed things up.

Do you have to repeat instructions three or four times before everyone knows what to do, or do the students listen the first time?

It's important to train students to listen well the first time you say something. Not only is repeating yourself a time waster, but it also teaches students that they don't really have to listen the first or second time; they know you'll keep repeating what you want them to hear. You can break this habit by warning them that from now on you will say something only once. Get their attention, speak clearly, and don't repeat yourself. Some students may do the wrong assignments or miss out altogether on an activity, but if you really mean it, most of them will eventually learn to listen the first time.

When you ask them to line up or get into groups, do they make a mad dash, sit and stare in confusion, or do what you expect of them?

If the students don't know what to do when you tell them to line up or get into groups, the fault is probably yours. This was undoubtedly the case with Miss Collins. Have you told the students what you expect? Are your directions clear? You may have to practice these activities one day so you won't waste time on other occasions.

When it's time for class to start, are students still roaming around the room, or do they get into their seats?

Students must realize that, as soon as they come to class or at a certain signal, they are expected to get into their seats and be ready to begin.

Do you spend a lot of time organizing materials and straightening the room?

Instead of assuming these responsibilities yourself, let students volunteer to carry out various tasks. They may even think of them as privileges!

Are students constantly interrupting you by asking to use the bathroom or sharpen pencils?

Minimize interruptions by letting students know in advance what you expect. For example, students won't need to raise their hands and interrupt the lesson if they already know what they can do. With young children, establish regular times for using the rest rooms. After that, if a child really has to leave, allow her or him to go alone without asking permission. Encourage students to sharpen pencils before school starts, but if a point breaks, allow a student to sharpen the pencil without first asking you.

Do students interrupt with irrelevant stories that they relate in great detail?

If a student interrupts discussion with an irrelevant story, ask him or her to tell you later. Responding this way allows you to continue the lesson and satisfies the student by letting him or her know you will listen later.

Do you find yourself spending a disproportionate amount of time with one or two students?

While it's true that some students need more individual attention than others, you must be careful to attend to all students' needs. Avoid spending so much time with an individual student that you neglect the rest of your class. Perhaps you can help a particularly needy student by arranging peer tutoring, working with the student before or after school, or conferring with a parent to get assistance at home.

No class must always operate on schedule. Sometimes something funny happens, and everyone needs to take time for a good laugh. You may lose some time from a scheduled activity by taking advantage of a "teachable moment," but this time is well spent. For instance, when the first snow falls, let the students go to the window and watch. Then share a poem or a song about snow, or talk about how snowflakes form, and note their delicate beauty. After a particularly tense test-taking session, students may need time to relax. Remember—schedules do keep things moving along, but they are not cast in concrete.

Filler, or Sponge, Activities

Even the most experienced teacher cannot predict exactly how long a lesson will take. As a relatively inexperienced teacher, you will often find yourself running out of time—or having time left over. When you realize that your lesson will end five or ten minutes before the class is over, you should have some ideas in the back of your mind. The best filler (or sponge) activities are those that directly relate to your lesson or unit. For instance, if you are teaching a unit on energy, the students could brainstorm several ways to conserve or produce energy. Try to plan one or more filler activities for each lesson in case you have time left over. Here are some filler activities that could be adapted to specific subject matter areas or used for other occasions:

1. Read or tell a story—good at any age level.
2. Play "20 Questions." Students try to guess what you're thinking by asking questions to be answered only by *yes* or *no*.
3. Get a paperback book of brainteasers, riddles, and puzzles, and ask the class for answers.
4. Ask students to do mental arithmetic.
5. Let students play storybook charades by acting out favorite stories or portraying famous characters.
6. Introduce a new vocabulary word that has an interesting meaning or origin. This can be a "Word of the Week" activity.
7. Sing a folk song or round with the class.

8. Let students dictate headlines about current news stories for you to write on the board.
9. Name a topic, and see how many facts the students can tell you about it.
10. Let students pantomime their favorite sports or hobbies, and have the class guess what they are doing.
11. Start a story with a one-line introduction, and have each student add a line to the story. (A possible starter: "It was a cold, dark, dreary night. I was alone in the house. Suddenly I heard a noise.")
12. Have a question box, and let a student pick a question. It could be serious (What can we do for senior citizens to improve their lives?) or silly (Why would a grasshopper make a good pet?). Students answer the question.
13. Role-play a recent classroom conflict.
14. Play "Gossip." Whisper a sentence to one student, who whispers it to the next, and so on. Compare the original sentence with the final result.
15. Give students, one at a time, a series of directions to follow, and see if they can remember to do everything in the correct sequence.
16. Write the months of the year on the board. Poll the class to find out how many students' birthdays fall in each month.
17. Divide the class in half to create two teams. Name a country, and let a student from each team try to locate it on a world map or globe within 10 seconds.
18. Brainstorm solutions to a problem. (See Chapter 7 for suggested topics.)
19. Review assignments.
20. Discuss plans for an upcoming event.
21. Let students have free reading time, finish their class work, do their homework, or clean out their desks.

RECORD KEEPING

Every teacher has the responsibility of keeping records. The amount and type of record keeping varies from one school system to another, and your cooperating teacher will show you what records your school requires. Many schools are currently using portfolio assessment (see Chapter 6 for more on portfolios). When you are responsible for keeping records, record the information promptly so that you don't forget to do it later. Keeping accurate records is an important aspect of professionalism.

Personal Record Keeping

As part of your student teaching or practicum assignment, you may keep a journal to record the lessons you teach, your feelings about teaching, or both. You may write some of the funny things the students say or insights about teaching you don't want to forget. Later, looking back, you will probably notice how your attitudes changed and your confidence grew as the weeks passed.

School Records

The attendance register is one of the most important school records. Class roll must be taken daily or every period of the day, and all absences and cases of tardiness recorded. These records are used for various purposes, including computing average daily attendance for state funding. The state allocates a certain amount of money for each child counted in the average daily attendance record. Records are sometimes used in court cases to verify a student's presence in school on a particular day. This information is summarized at the end of every month. Even though these records may be handled by a computer or by office personnel, you should learn how to do them yourself, especially since you may need access to them when help may not be available. You need to know when students have been absent and may have missed an important lesson so that you can help them catch up.

You will have to keep other records when you are teaching. Many schools require each teacher to turn in a milk-money or lunch-money report every morning. Some schools have fund-raising activities that require a great deal of bookkeeping; if you are involved in these efforts, you will have to keep an accurate account of the money collected and each student's sales record. If you (through your cooperating teacher) sponsor an extracurricular activity, you may be responsible for keeping membership and financial records. You also need to keep records of students with special programs or problems, such as those who are excused from physical education or who go to special classes at specific times during the day. Additional records are required for students in federally funded programs.

As a student teacher, you will probably have very little responsibility for ordering books and supplies or keeping inventory. It would be a good idea to learn these procedures anyway, so that you will know what to do when you are in your own classroom. Become familiar with school supply catalogs so that you know what materials are available, what they cost, and how to order them.

You will also have to keep records related to your teaching. Record in a daily lesson plan book brief outlines of your lessons and page numbers of material you expect to cover in each class. You can never be sure exactly how far you will get in your lesson, so you will probably have to modify these plans slightly from day to day. If you schedule a field trip in connection with a lesson, you will be responsible for keeping records of parents' permission notes and any money you collect. If you use audiovisual media, you may need to fill out request forms. You may want to give the school media specialist a list of topics you will be covering and request help in locating appropriate books and materials.

FOR YOUR PORTFOLIO

Photocopy a page or pages from your daily lesson plan book when you were teaching full-time.

Reporting Students' Progress

Keeping track of students' progress is one of the most important forms of record keeping. You should keep records of daily quizzes and completed daily assignments, as well as scores of major tests. Your cooperating teacher probably has a grade book with the scores of each student before you arrived. You may be expected to record your grades in this book, or you may have your own grade book.

Some teachers keep tests in folders or portfolios at school in order to have a record of each student's progress throughout the year. Teachers who feel that parents should be kept aware of their child's performance may send tests home. If you decide to send papers home but are not sure all the students are showing the papers to their parents, ask the students to have a parent sign each test paper and then return it to you.

Some computer-managed instructional systems in areas such as reading and mathematics generate reports on students' progress. These reports may indicate what skills each student needs, what skills have been mastered, and sometimes what assignments have been given. Some reports are for your use as a teacher, whereas other reports are for parents.

Reporting to parents is usually done through report cards, although it is sometimes done with descriptive letters or orally at parent-teacher conferences. Your cooperating teacher may ask you to assist in assigning grades on report cards or to assume the full responsibility for grades during the period you do most of the teaching. In either case, be sure you thoroughly understand the school's grading system. Most schools give grades according to achievement, but some give marks for attitude and effort, and some grade on the basis of students' ability. Most report cards have a place for comments, which you may or may not wish to use. Putting grades on report cards requires some hard decisions. If the responsibility is yours, be sure to have good records of students' work on which to base your decisions.

You may want to send notes to parents of students who have behaved or achieved unusually well. Notes of this type are always welcome and help build positive relationships among the student, parents, school, and you. These notes will be especially appreciated by students who rarely receive praise and are often in trouble. If you make a practice of sending favorable comments home, the students are likely to do better work for you.

CASE STUDY 4.7

No Records for Support

Miss Patel is a student teacher. Recently, she has been concerned about Vinetta's behavior. Vinetta doesn't do her homework and doesn't seem to be doing good work in class. Miss Patel decides to ask Vinetta's mother, Mrs. Kolsky, to come for a conference. Mr. Kent is the cooperating teacher.

Miss Patel: Good afternoon, Mrs. Kolsky. I'm Miss Patel, Vinetta's student teacher. I'm glad you were able to come to talk with me about Vinetta.

Mrs. Kolsky: Yes. I hope Vinetta is getting along all right.

Miss Patel: That's just it, Mrs. Kolsky. Vinetta doesn't seem to be doing as well as she could be.

Mrs. Kolsky: Why not? What's wrong? Is there a problem?

Miss Patel: She isn't doing her homework, and she isn't doing very well in her classwork, either.

Mrs. Kolsky: Well, this is the first I've known anything about homework. And what do you mean she isn't doing well in her classwork?

Miss Patel: I've been assigning homework for each night, but Vinetta never has hers done. As far as classwork is concerned, she just doesn't seem to be doing her best work any more.

Mrs. Kolsky: May I see her grades on her classwork and her test grades?

Miss Patel: I'm afraid I don't have any records of her classwork. I've given some quizzes, but I've let the students take them home. I have the scores but not the papers. I can remember, though, that she didn't do very well on any of her classwork. And the test scores are low. Didn't she bring her tests home?

Mrs. Kolsky: No, she hasn't brought any of them home. It seems to me you don't really know what you're talking about. You say she isn't doing well, but you can't show me any papers. When I ask you what she isn't doing well in, you don't seem to have any definite answers. These test grades are just numbers. *What is she having trouble with?* I don't think there's anything wrong with Vinetta at all. I think you just don't have your facts straight. I'd better talk to Mr. Kent.

1. Was it a good idea for Miss Patel to have a conference with Vinetta's mother if she felt Vinetta could be doing better work?
2. What went wrong with Miss Patel's conference?
3. What could she have done to back up her statements to Mrs. Kolsky?
4. Is there any way to make sure parents know their children have homework assignments? How can you be sure parents actually see the test papers you return?

You may want to record information about a student in an anecdotal report—an objective, detailed account of a student's behavior. Your reasons for selecting particular students to observe may vary. You may choose a student who is different in some way, perhaps in achievement level, relationships with other children, or ethnic origin. You may want to observe a student who is being recommended for an award or one who is being considered for disciplinary action. A concerned parent may request that you collect data on a student's progress, or perhaps you simply want to learn about typical behavior patterns by observing any student.

Be accurate and objective in recording your observations. Don't let your feelings affect what you select to record or how you write your observations. Write the date and time of each observation, and try to include everything that happens, both good and bad. It is better if the student doesn't realize what you are doing, so that she or he will continue to act naturally. Choose a child to study and complete Activity 4.2, an anecdotal report.

All the official records a school has concerning a student are generally kept in a cumulative record file in the school office. This file contains health and attendance records, comments by school personnel, and standardized test scores. As a student teacher, you will probably be allowed to see this information, but remember that it is confidential.

ACTIVITY 4.2   *Anecdotal Report*

Name of child selected:

Reason(s) for selection:

Types of information you are seeking:

Begin your anecdotal records below with your first entry. Be sure to include the date, time, and location of the observed behavior. If there is not enough room on the bottom of this page, use the back of the page to finish the first record. Continue with other entries on separate sheets of paper. Staple them, in order, to this cover sheet.

CASE STUDY 4.8

To Look or Not to Look

Three student teachers—Miss Luke, Mr. Feinstein, and Mrs. Tsai—are talking while waiting for their seminar to begin. They have been student teachers for four weeks.

Miss Luke: Do you know what cumulative records are?

Mr. Feinstein: I think they are some records in the office files that nobody ever looks at.

Mrs. Tsai: They *are* files that are kept in the office, but I've looked at the ones on my students. My cooperating teacher took me right down on the first day I got my classes and told me where they were and that he expected me to read them all the first week. Some of them are really eye-openers, I'll tell you!

Miss Luke: What do you mean?

Mrs. Tsai: I really learned a lot about my students, and I knew just how to treat them right from the beginning. Linda's file said that one time they caught her stealing a CD player, so I don't trust her for a minute. Anytime anything disappears, I feel sure Linda had something to do with it. And Tad. They said all through the grades that Tad has been a discipline problem, and they're surely right. He's always causing trouble.

Mr. Feinstein: I'm not sure it's right to read all that personal information about your students. Doesn't that influence how you feel about them?

Mrs. Tsai: Sure, it influences how I feel. But this way I know right away all I need to know about the students instead of waiting until the end of the semester to find out.

Miss Luke: I'm not going to look at my students' cumulative records. I want to make up my own mind about them and not go by what other teachers have said.

Mr. Feinstein: But suppose there's something really important in there? Something we *should* know about? Maybe one of the students had psychological testing or something and the psychologist made recommendations about how he or she learns best. Wouldn't that be helpful?

Mrs. Tsai: Definitely! It said in one of the records that Chad's parents had been divorced a couple of years ago and he had a real emotional problem with that. The teacher suggested that we all be patient with him and consider his feelings.

Miss Luke: I'm just not sure if it's a good idea to read all those records. It still might do more harm than good.

1. How do you feel about reading your students' cumulative records? If you feel you should read them, should you look at them as soon as you meet the students or at some later time?
2. How could the information in cumulative records be helpful? How could it be misused?
3. What is the purpose of keeping cumulative records?
4. Do you think Mrs. Tsai is able to treat Linda and Tad objectively? Would she have arrived at the same conclusions about these two students if she hadn't read their files? Do students tend to live up to our expectations of them?
5. Who is allowed to read cumulative records? Do you know what the law says about this?
6. Did Mrs. Tsai breach confidentiality when she gave out personal information about her students to her peers? How could she have discussed this issue without violating confidentiality?

In regard to examining students' cumulative records, it is a good policy to give yourself enough time to evaluate the students for yourself, then look at the records to learn more about them. When you read the files, keep in mind that test scores do not always accurately reflect a student's capability. Also, be sure to look for factual information and specific situations. Avoid being swayed by unsupported generalizations and statements of opinion previous teachers may have made. Using cumulative records wisely can help you understand your students better and help you plan appropriate learning activities for those with special needs.

The Family Educational Rights and Privacy Act of 1974 (PL 93-380) governs the control of students' records. Students over 18 years old or parents of students under 18 may examine these records—they have access to all teachers' comments (except notes of teachers or administrators for personal use), test scores, and special reports in the file. On the other hand, the law forbids anyone else except those directly involved in the students' education to see the records without written consent.

SUPERVISION OF STUDENTS

You are likely to share your cooperating teacher's assigned supervisory responsibilities, such as performing cafeteria, hall, or bus duty, or supervising study hall. Each school has its own policies regarding supervision of students waiting for buses, moving through hallways, eating in the cafeteria, and working in study halls. Observe your cooperating teacher closely, and learn the ground rules for these situations so that you can handle them properly.

A nutritious and relaxing lunch is important for helping students make it through the afternoon. Routine procedures are usually followed, so students know where to sit and what rules are in effect. If you are helping to supervise students in the cafeteria, you need to know what to do if any one of these situations arises: the noise level gets too high, a student drops a tray, a slow eater doesn't finish in time, a student loses a lunch box or bag, a student has forgotten his or her lunch money, students want to trade food, or someone offers you a sandwich. If there is no policy concerning such matters, keep in mind that students need to eat a nourishing lunch in an atmosphere that enables them to digest it!

You may have hall or bus duty. Hall duty simply means that, when students change classes, teachers are stationed in school corridors to keep an orderly flow of traffic, direct new students, and help with problems. In some schools, bus duty is handled by each student's homeroom teacher; in other schools, students assemble in a central location, where they are supervised by one or more teachers. If you must assist your cooperating teacher in supervising groups of students from different classes, you might suggest ideas for passing the time constructively. You may ask students to bring library books to read, or you can read to them, show videos, lead singing, or let them play guessing games.

You may need to supervise a study hall during a period when students do not have a scheduled class. The study hall provides a place for students to study during free periods, and you will be expected to maintain a quiet, orderly environment. Students will sometimes ask for help with assignments. If your school has formal study halls, find out what rules the students are expected to obey and your responsibilities as supervisor.

CLASSROOM ENVIRONMENT

As a student teacher, you will take some responsibility for the appearance and comfort of your classroom from the early days of your experience. By the time you take over full teaching responsibilities, the appearance and comfort of the classroom will, in most cases, be completely your responsibility. Naturally, in many matters you will follow the procedures established by your cooperating teacher. In some areas, however, you may want to try variations, with the teacher's approval.

Neatness and Cleanliness

Although in years past teachers were expected to sweep and mop their classrooms, chances are good that you will not be expected to perform these duties!

You may need to know how to summon the custodian for assistance, however, and how to handle emergency situations (e.g., spilled paint, milk, or sand) yourself. Be sure you know where cleaning materials are located. In schools where custodians work during class hours, be sure to develop a good relationship with them. Let them know that you value their help and that their work contributes to your effectiveness. Even if the custodians work only after hours, showing appreciation for a well-cleaned room is likely to pay dividends in the care your room receives.

Students should cooperate in keeping the classroom neat and orderly. They can be responsible for keeping the floor clear of trash and putting away supplies. Be sure there are designated places for storing all supplies and that these places are easily accessible.

Control of Temperature, Ventilation, and Lighting

Proper temperature, ventilation, and lighting in a classroom promote comfort and the ability to concentrate. Students are easily distracted when a classroom is too hot, too cold, or too stuffy, or when the lighting is too dim or there is a glare on work surfaces. The students focus on their discomfort rather than on their schoolwork. They may become drowsy from excess heat or insufficient ventilation, or they may develop headaches and eyestrain from inappropriate lighting. It is your responsibility to adjust these factors or to see that they are adjusted by the proper person. If your room has an uncomfortable temperature or poor ventilation, you may need to adjust thermostats, windows, or vents, or you may need to ask the custodian to make appropriate changes. You can handle lighting problems yourself by turning on more lights, rearranging students' seats, and adjusting blinds or curtains to provide enough light without glare.

CASE STUDY 4.9

Not Attuned to the Students

Ms. Jordan, a student teacher who tends to feel cold much of the time, entered her empty classroom at 7:45 one morning, took off her coat, shivered, and turned up the room's thermostat. This was the first day she had full responsibility for the classroom, and she didn't want to be uncomfortable all day. At 8:00, the students poured into the room. The body heat of 30 extra people, plus the higher thermostat setting, resulted in a very warm room. Ms. Jordan, who enjoyed the warmth, at first failed to notice how lethargic the class seemed as she began her day. As time passed, however, the signs were unmistakable. Students were inattentive, and many seemed to be drowsy.

"What is the matter with you?" Ms. Jordan snapped irritably. "Did you stay up all night watching television?"

"No! No!" came a chorus of answers.

"Then what is wrong?" Ms. Jordan asked again.

A boy in the back of the room finally replied, "It's too hot in here to work."

"That's ridiculous!" Ms. Jordan responded. "I'm perfectly comfortable. Now pay attention."

It was Ms. Jordan who was not paying attention. She was seeing the signs of an overheated room but doing nothing about them. Furthermore, she failed to pay attention to the fact that, because of her own tendency to feel cold, she could be comfortable when the students were not, despite a direct verbal cue.

1. Do you tend to feel extremely hot or cold? How may this affect your ability to keep your classroom at a comfortable temperature for your students?
2. What clues in the students' behavior may help you determine if the classroom is comfortable for them?

Bulletin Boards and Displays

Bulletin boards and displays can add much to the attractiveness of a classroom; however, they should not be limited to this function. The best bulletin boards and displays are both attractive and informative. They add color and interest to the room while conveying useful information in a content area or providing motivation to study a particular topic.

All bulletin boards and displays must be carefully constructed to maintain their effectiveness. Inaccurate data, material inappropriate for the age group, sloppy drawing and lettering, or faded or torn background material make them undesirable rather than helpful additions to the classroom. Even carefully executed displays lose their effectiveness if they are left up too long. Thanksgiving turkeys are out of place in January, even if the display has an excellent instructional focus.

You can make effective bulletin boards and displays for your classroom by following a few simple guidelines:

1. Choose material appropriate to your students' learning and maturity levels.
2. Make sure all the information is accurate.
3. Choose a central theme for a focus.
4. Organize the materials carefully to show their relationship to the central theme.
5. Choose a pleasing color scheme.

6. Do not use faded or torn background material.
7. Use a variety of materials, such as construction paper, crepe paper, yarn, cloth, and cardboard to give the displays texture. Consider use of three-dimensional effects.
8. Change your bulletin boards and displays regularly. They become faded as time passes and cease to generate interest. Never leave seasonal displays up past their time of relevance.
9. Make some bulletin boards manipulative. Students at lower grade levels particularly enjoy such boards. Examples are boards that require activities such as matching synonyms with yarn strips and opening cardboard doors for answers to riddles.
10. Involve students in planning bulletin boards, and display their work.

Bulletin boards and displays can be great learning experiences because they help make concepts more concrete. They can provide even more learning opportunities if you let the students construct the displays themselves or assist you in the construction. It is also easier to keep fresh displays in the classroom when you have the students' assistance.

Bulletin boards and displays should include examples of students' work. Don't put up only the best work; put up any work of which an individual can be proud, even if it lacks the precision of more advanced students' offerings. On the other hand, do not display especially poor work in an effort to embarrass a student into doing better work. This practice is psychologically unsound.

Use bulletin boards and displays as teaching tools that enhance the attractiveness of your classroom. Keep a file of good ideas as you observe your cooperating teacher and other teachers and as you read professional materials. This file will prove valuable when you have your own classroom.

Learning Centers

Learning centers are areas of the classroom set aside for developing and reinforcing skills and concepts. They usually consist of materials and directions to help students meet class objectives, a choice of activities, and a way for students to check their work. At centers, students are active participants in learning as they work independently or in small groups to complete various tasks. Well-designed centers are visually appealing, attract students' interest, and arouse their imagination. You can develop learning centers for any grade level or subject. Here are some possibilities.

Dramatic Play Center. Young children imitate adult behaviors as they gather at centers resembling familiar settings, such as the kitchen at home, a grocery store, a fast-food restaurant, a bank, or the post office. Literacy items, such as calendars, pencils and pads, and printed forms, encourage children to learn reading and writing as they play.

Math Center.   Manipulatives allow students to experiment and calculate as they complete math tasks. Graph paper, plastic coins and paper money, and pie-shaped fractional parts help students form math concepts.

Listening Center.   Equipped with headsets, tapes, and tape recorder, the listening center lets younger children listen to story tapes as they turn pages in a corresponding book. Older students may listen to dramatic presentations, narrations from literature, or classical music.

Writing Center.   A writing center should offer a wide array of writing materials—paper, clipboards, blank books, colorful folders, and choices of pens and pencils. Steps in the writing process may be posted above the center, and books placed nearby can serve as models for students to write their own books.

Computer Center.   Independently or in pairs, students may work at computer centers on simulations, math or science games, or printing a class newspaper. They may use the computer as a resource for locating information and writing research reports.

Publishing Center.   The publishing center should be near the writing and computer centers, or it may actually be a combination of the two. Materials should be available for students to copy edited versions of their best writing selections and make them into bound books for the class library.

Reading Center.   At the reading center students should find a variety of reading materials and a comfortable, relaxing setting for free reading. This center might include posters announcing new books, a file of books recommended by students, and book-related displays.

Thematic Center.   Thematic centers contain task cards and resource materials for carrying out projects and activities related to themes. Students contribute their own materials and ideas as they conduct investigations and develop projects.

Arts and Crafts Center.   This center allows students to use their imaginations to create, design, and experiment with different media. Here, the process is often more important than the product!

Science Center.   Students conduct experiments, make observations, record data, and seek solutions to problems at science centers. Science centers often deal with real-world problems, such as recycling and protecting the environment.

If you are using task cards or assignment sheets at centers, you must give clear directions for activities so that students can understand what to do without assistance. A task card might include the topic, materials to use, directions for the task, and instructions for what to do when finished. (See the sample task card in Figure 4–2.) You may need to provide accompanying cassette tapes for younger children or older students with reading disabilities.

Make routines for "center time" clear from the outset. Students need to know when they can use the centers, how many people are allowed to use a center simultaneously, how to care for materials, when assignments from centers are due, and what they should do when center activities are completed.

You may have one or more centers set up in your room at any given time. They can be set up on tables, in large containers such as refrigerator boxes, on the floor or carpet, in corners, behind bookshelves, or behind folding screens. Your ingenuity is the only limiting factor.

Setting up centers with computers presents some special problems. The computers need to be

1. convenient to electrical outlets.
2. located in a place that is relatively dust-free. (Dust can be lethal to disk drives.)
3. positioned so that glare on the screens is minimized.
4. positioned so that the screens are not visible to the part of the class that is not working on the computers. (Students are easily distracted by graphics on the screens.)

Learning centers have been prevalent at the elementary level for a long time, and in recent years applications have been made with excellent results at the secondary level. Don't write off the idea without trying it. You may be amazed at the results. Activity 4.3 involves creating a learning center.

Seating Arrangements

Few classrooms today have stationary furniture. The moveable furniture in your classroom represents another opportunity—flexible arrangements for varied purposes. You may want one arrangement for whole-class instruction, another for small-group instruction, and still another when students are working on individual projects. An instructional group that

FIGURE 4–2
Task Card for Reading Center

Free Reading

Select a book from the school or class library that interests you. Find a comfortable place to read the book and complete it in a reasonable time.

When you finish reading the book, take a 5- by 8-inch index card located at the center. On the unlined side of the card, draw an illustration for the book. On the lined side write the following:

Author (last name first)

Title

Type of book (fiction, nonfiction, biography, etc.)

One or two sentences that summarize the book

Your reaction to the book

Your recommendation—do you think your friends would like it?

When you have written this information, file the card by the author's last name in the card file box. Then you may choose another book, or go to another center.

requires a dry-erase board can cluster around the board for that lesson, then disperse when another learning activity begins. Chairs can be turned to face a film shown on a side wall, a follow-up discussion using a dry-erase board on a different side wall, and a demonstration at the front of the room, all within the space of a single class.

With all this mobility, there are other considerations about seating that you must not overlook. Students with certain disabilities must be seated in the most advantageous positions possible. For example, students who have hearing difficulties should usually be seated near you; those who are nearsighted may need to be seated close to boardwork, displays, and demonstrations; and so on. Potentially disruptive students should also be seated where they are less likely to cause trouble; this may mean seating them near you or making sure that certain students do not sit beside each other. Activity 4.4 gives you a chance to work on seating arrangements in one of your classes.

CASE STUDY 4.10

Arbitrary Seating Arrangements

When Miss Gomez first came into the seventh-grade business mathematics class to which she was assigned as a student teacher, the students seemed to be arranged in no logical order. Miss Gomez thought, "I'll never learn all their names! I'll put them in alphabetical order."

The next day as students took their new seats and began working, problems seemed to be developing. Li wasn't doing any work. When Miss Gomez asked what the problem was, Li looked at her blankly. Mae raised her hand and explained that Li didn't know enough English to work independently, so Mae always sat close by to interpret.

Miss Gomez noticed that Susie kept getting out of her seat to look at the words on the board. When Miss Gomez asked her to stay in her seat, Susie replied that she couldn't see the board from where she was sitting.

In the back of the room three boys wearing black T-shirts and sporting the same style haircuts started disrupting the class with laughter and coarse talk. As she approached the boys, Miss Gomez realized that alphabetical seating wasn't working. Obviously, her cooperating teacher had reasons for her seating arrangement.

1. What should Miss Gomez do now?
2. How could you prevent a similar situation from arising in your classroom?
3. What are some reasons for placing special students in certain locations within the classroom?

Another concern, particularly for teachers of younger children, is making sure each child has a chair and desk of suitable size. The children in a single grade will vary greatly in size, and one desk size will not be comfortable for all of them. If necessary, swap with other teachers to get a desk appropriate for each student.

The days of nothing but straight rows and alphabetical seating seem to be behind us. The future for teachers and students is much more flexible. Use this flexibility for your benefit and that of your students.

DISCUSSION QUESTIONS

1. Observe the groups that have been set up in your class. Can you see the reason for each type of grouping? Do you think it would be helpful to have additional groups? How might grouping be used to better advantage? If there are no groups now, can you see any reasons for forming them? If so, how would you do this?

2. Do you see any indications that students are discouraged by group placement? If so, how could you try to correct this situation?

3. Did you waste time today during the classes you taught? What did you spend time doing that wasn't really important to achieving your goals?

4. Why is it extremely important for teachers to be accurate and objective in the material they include in a student's cumulative record? What might happen if a teacher makes careless, negative generalizations about a student?

5. What special reports and records does your school require? What is your responsibility for keeping these records?

6. What is the school's grading system? Is there any provision for giving information to a student's parents about effort, attitude, or interest? Is it important for parents to know this information?

7. Why is control of the classroom's temperature, ventilation, and lighting an important responsibility? Do you have this responsibility?

8. What purposes do bulletin boards serve? How often should you change them? What role might students play in the design and composition of bulletin boards?

9. How could learning centers enhance instruction in your classroom?

10. Analyze the seating arrangements in your room. Could they be improved? If so, how?

11. Is your classroom highly structured or very flexible? What aspects of your classroom reflect structure or flexibility?

12. Can you recognize ways in which your cooperating teacher is integrating the curriculum? If so, how well are they working? If not, how could some subjects be integrated?

SELECTED REFERENCES

Bodine, R., & Crawford, D. (1998). *The handbook of conflict resolution education.* San Francisco, CA: National Institute for Dispute Resolution.

Burns, P. C., & Roe, B. D. (1991). *Reading activities for today's elementary schools.* Lanham, MD: University Press of America.

Carlsson-Paige, N., & Levin, D. (1998). *Before push comes to shove.* St. Paul, MN: Redleaf.

Coelho, E. (1994). *Learning together in the multicultural classroom.* Markham, Ont., Canada: Pippin.

Cooperative learning. (1989, December/1990, January). *Educational Leadership, 47.* Entire issue.

Eisele, B. (1991). *Managing the whole language classroom.* Cypress, CA: Creative Teaching Press.

Ellis, S., & Whalen, W. (1990). *Cooperative learning: Getting started.* New York: Scholastic.

Fogarty, R. (1998, May). The intelligence-friendly classroom. *Phi Delta Kappan, 79,* 655–657.

Foster-Harrison, E., & Adams-Bullock, A. (1998). *Creating an inviting classroom environment.* Bloomington, IN: Phi Delta Kappa.

Furtwengler, Carol. (1992, April). How to observe cooperative learning classrooms. *Educational Leadership, 49,* 59–62.

Houle, G. B. (1987). *Learning centers for young children* (3rd ed.). West Greenwich, RI: Consortium.

Johnson, D., Johnson, R., Stevahn, L., & Hodne, P. (1997, October). The three C's of safe schools. *Educational Leadership, 55,* 8–13.

Kohn, A. (1996, September). What to look for in a classroom. *Educational Leadership, 54*(1), 54–55.

Lindblad, A. (1994, May–June). You can avoid the traps of cooperative learning. *Clearing House, 67,* 291–293.

Manning, M. L., & Lucking, R. (1993, September–October). Cooperative learning and multicultural classrooms. *Clearing House, 67,* 12–15.

Pike, K., Compain, R., & Mumper, J. (1994). *Connections: An integrated approach to literacy.* New York: Harper-Collins.

Roy, P., & Hoch, J. (1994, March). Cooperative learning: A principal's perspective. *Principal, 73,* 27–29.

Slavin, R. E. (1990). *Cooperative learning: Theory, research, and practice.* Englewood Cliffs, NJ: Prentice-Hall.

Slavin, R. E. (1991, February). Synthesis of research on cooperative learning. *Educational Leadership, 48,* 72–82.

Thompson, G. (1994). *Teaching through themes.* New York: Scholastic.

Yellin, D., & Blake, M. E. (1994). *Integrating language arts.* New York: HarperCollins.

ACTIVITY 4.3   *Learning Center Idea*

Decide upon an idea for a learning center in one of the subjects that you teach. Fill out the following form about this idea.

Subject area:

Objective(s) of the center:

Materials and equipment needed:

Sketch the center below, indicating the placement of the center (on a table, in a container, behind a set of shelves or screen, etc.), locations of the different materials to be used in the center (on a pegboard, in folders, in boxes, etc.), and any decorations that will be used to make the center attractive.

ACTIVITY 4.4   *Seating Arrangements*

Draw a seating chart for use with one of your classes during whole-group instruction. Circle the names of students with special needs who should have special consideration in seating arrangements. In the space below your seating chart, explain the reasons for the particular placements of these students.

Discipline

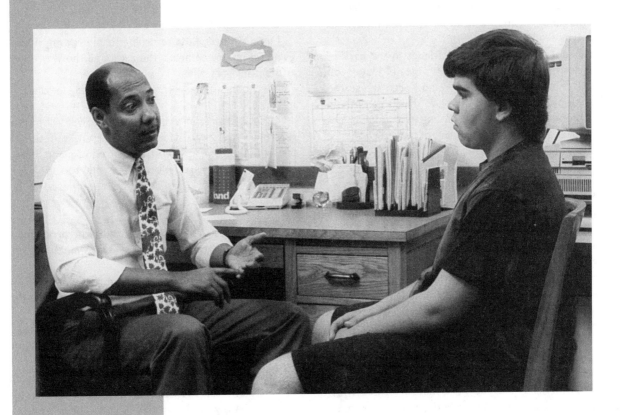

Out of Control!

In a science class, Mrs. Goldberg was teaching a unit on reptiles, and Miss Young, a student teacher, was helping her. For the culminating activity, the children were to bring some specimens to class. Maria had brought an unusual lizard, and Frank had brought a frog. Manuel had contributed a garter snake he had found near his house. These animals were placed in separate cages in the back of the room, on a counter that the students called their "zoo." Most of the students were curious about the reptiles and liked watching them. A few boys and girls, however, seemed timid about approaching the cages and avoided looking in their direction. The day before the reptiles were to be taken home, Mrs. Goldberg was called to the office for an emergency meeting with a parent. Miss Young was in charge.

Manuel (whispering to some friends in the back of the room): Hey, Mrs. Goldberg's gone. Have you noticed the way Benjy and Tony and Karen are scared to death of those animals? Let's give the three of them a real good scare. When Miss Young isn't looking, let's sneak over and let the animals out of their cages.

Rachel (also in a whisper): Yeah, let's each get one of the cages on a signal and let them all out at once.

Jake: What a blast! Let's do it!

Miss Young (trying to introduce a lesson on pronouns): Quiet down in the back of the room. There's no need for any talking. Do you have your English books out yet? Turn to page 79.

Manuel, Rachel, and Jake (mumbling): Yeah, sure, we're with you. (The three send secret messages to one another with their eyes, waiting for the right opportunity.)

Miss Young: All of you get on with your work. Try to have this finished before Mrs. Goldberg returns. (She bends down to help a student who is having trouble with a sentence.)

Manuel, Rachel, and Jake (in a mutual, excited whisper): Now! (They sneak quickly and quietly to the cages, unfasten the hooks, open the doors, and return to their seats. A few children who notice begin to giggle.)

Dottie: Oh, no! The frog's loose. He's hopping over to the window.

Allen: Look out. Here comes the snake!

Benjy: I'm getting out of here! (He runs for the door and makes a quick exit down the hall.)

Miss Young: What's happening? Oh, no! Who let those animals out? Put them back. Manuel, get your snake back in its cage. Somebody catch that frog. (The lizard is hiding under a leaf in the cage; the snake is crawling toward a dark spot in the corner of the room.)

By now, several of the children are screaming and standing on their desks. Miss Young, who is terrified of snakes, is now speechless and can only stand rooted to the spot. Some of the children are grinning at each other as they stand around the snake, watching it glide across the room.

Mrs. Goldberg (just returning to the room): What's going on in here? I heard the racket all the way down at the principal's office.

Miss Young (in a weak voice): Somebody let the animals out.

Mrs. Goldberg (in a firm voice): All right. All of you return to your seats. Manuel, put the snake back and fasten the cage. Cathy, you catch the frog; and, Mark, close the lizard's cage before it gets out, too. Now get on with your work. I believe you're supposed to be studying pronouns.

1. Could Miss Young have anticipated the problem? If so, how? Were there any preventive measures she might have taken?
2. What are some ways Miss Young might have handled the situation when she first noticed that the reptiles were out of the cages?
3. Can you think of a way Miss Young could have regained control of the class before Mrs. Goldberg returned?
4. Do you think Mrs. Goldberg got the class under control when she returned and spoke to the students? Why or why not?

ISSUES IN DISCIPLINE

In every classroom, students occasionally misbehave. How to deal with them can be a problem for you. Consider the following situations. None of the answers is necessarily right; in fact, you might be able to come up with a better solution. In some cases, you might choose more than one answer. Consider what the circumstances might be and the probable consequences of each alternative. After you read this chapter, reconsider your answers.

1. Billy sticks out his tongue at you and gives you a smart answer. What do you do?

   a. Paddle him.
   b. Tell him to shut up and sit down.
   c. Ignore his behavior this time.
   d. Speak to him calmly, explaining why you cannot tolerate this kind of behavior.
   e. Punish him by making him stay in at recess.
   f. Laugh at him. He really was sort of cute.

2. Chrissy throws an eraser at Tammy and hits her on the head. What do you do?

   a. Check to see if Tammy is hurt. If not, ignore the situation.
   b. Let Tammy throw an eraser at Chrissy and hit *her* on the head.
   c. Warn Chrissy that, if she does it again, she'll have to miss lunch for one week.
   d. Make an example of Chrissy. Scold her severely in front of the class, and make her stand in the corner for an hour.
   e. Stop what you are doing. Quietly point out that throwing things can be dangerous and that this behavior is unacceptable.
   f. Go on with your lesson as if nothing happened.

3. Two students are talking and giggling in the back of the room while you are trying to conduct a discussion. What do you do?

   a. Move closer to the students, pause, and look at them significantly.
   b. Call on one of them to answer a question you have just asked.
   c. Stop and wait as long as necessary until everyone is quiet.
   d. Call them by name, and ask them to pay attention.
   e. Say in a loud and angry voice, "Your talking is disturbing to the rest of the class. I want you to stop this minute. If I hear one more word out of either of you, I'll send you both to the office."

   f. Wait until after class; then talk to the students, and explain that their talking was very disturbing.

4. Carol is eating potato chips during reading group. You ask her to stop, and she defiantly tells you "No." What do you do?

   a. Try to take the bag away from her by force.
   b. Tell her that if she is going to eat potato chips in front of the other students, she will have to bring enough for everyone.
   c. Tell her that if she'll put the potato chips away now, she can eat them during recess.
   d. Ask her to return to her seat until she is finished.
   e. Insist that she stop eating. Warn her that she will be punished if she does not stop right now. Continue until you win your point.
   f. Drop the request for the moment. Get the children interested in an exciting part of the story, and then quietly ask Carol to put the chips away for now.

5. Judy and Jerry are passing notes during math class. What do you do?

   a. Pick up the notes from their desks, and read the notes aloud to the class.
   b. Pick up the notes from their desks, tear them into shreds, and drop them into the wastebasket.
   c. In front of the class, say sarcastically, "Judy and Jerry seem to know all there is to know about math, since they aren't paying attention." Then send them to the board, and give them a difficult problem to work in front of the other students.
   d. Assign Jerry and Judy 10 extra problems for homework, and threaten to do the same to anyone else who doesn't pay attention.
   e. Walk toward their desks; look at them intently until they understand they are not to write notes anymore; then continue your lesson.
   f. Have them stay after school and pick up all the scraps of paper in the room.

To deal with situations such as these, you should begin by understanding what discipline is and what it is not. Discipline is controlled behavior. It is also your ability to get attention when you need it. It does not call for an absolutely quiet and rigidly controlled class, although some degree of order is implied. There is often quiet, purposeful talking in a well-disciplined classroom, with students moving freely about as they work on projects.

Discipline problems may be *real* or *perceived* (Thompson, 1994). Problems are real when students infringe on the freedom of the teacher to teach and the freedom of other students to learn. For example, the teacher should be able to speak without interruption in order to teach, and students should be able to listen attentively without distractions caused by other students. When students' behavior interferes with these freedoms, discipline problems exist. If a student is merely inattentive but isn't interfering with others, there is no real discipline problem, but you may need to deal with this student's lack of attention at a later time. Teachers vary in their tolerance for students' talk and movement. By simply learning to accept reasonable activity as students work independently or cooperatively, you may find that many perceived discipline problems don't really exist.

Teachers often consider discipline their number one problem. Why is it so difficult to establish and maintain classroom control? The answer probably lies partly in the complexity of the causes of discipline problems. You must consider the students' personalities and backgrounds, the type of learning situation in which they are involved, and the distractions that may interfere with their concentration. Disciplining students is also difficult because, in most cases, you must decide what to do on the spot, and you cannot always anticipate the consequences of your actions. Modeling courtesy and respect in your interactions with students guides them toward appropriate relationships with others.

Even though effective classroom discipline may be difficult to achieve, you must have it to accomplish any of your objectives. Without it, too much time is wasted, your lessons are likely to break down, and students lose opportunities to learn. Also, without discipline, you may not survive as a teacher. Burnout is often the result of ineffective discipline.

CAUSES OF DISCIPLINE PROBLEMS

All behavior has a cause or a purpose. Discovering and understanding the cause of an undesirable behavior may help you prevent its recurrence. Unfortunately, many causes are complex and difficult to analyze.

Who or what might cause discipline problems? Maybe society, maybe something in the classroom environment, maybe the students themselves—or maybe you! Let's look at some of the causes.

Society may need to shoulder part of the blame. At one time, teachers were highly respected and their word was law, but this is rarely the case anymore. Parents today seem to be more permissive toward their children and may challenge the teacher's authority. Law enforcement agencies do not always support the

schools in dealing with juvenile offenders. There is little you can do about society's changing attitudes toward the teaching profession, except to show through your actions that you are worthy of respect.

You *can* do something about your classroom environment, however. When there are so many other things to think about, it's easy to forget such apparently obvious factors as lighting, temperature control, room arrangement, and distracting elements. Analyze your classroom. Is there something in the room you could change that might reduce the number of discipline problems?

Without realizing it, you may be responsible for some of the discipline problems that arise. Can you answer all of these questions affirmatively?

1. Is my lesson well planned and purposeful?
2. Am I meeting the interests and needs of the students? Are they motivated to learn?
3. Are the students actively involved in learning?
4. Is the material at an appropriate level of difficulty, and do I have reasonable expectations for each student?
5. Do the students understand exactly how I expect them to behave and know the consequences of misbehavior?
6. Am I fair and consistent with discipline, and do I carry out my promises?

Being able to answer "Yes" to each of these questions will go a long way toward preventing discipline problems.

Students bring with them such a bewildering array of emotional, physical, and social problems that it's no wonder they sometimes misbehave. Sometimes you may be able to help students solve problems or accept what's troubling them. Sometimes just knowing that you care makes a difference to them. Students whose personal problems no longer interfere with their concentration are less likely to cause problems for you.

Students may misbehave to get the attention they crave and aren't getting elsewhere, but giving attention to undesirable behavior only encourages it. As adolescents move toward adult independence, many take risks to see how far they can go, until their behavior becomes unacceptable and you must do something about it. Older students may be uncooperative because they resent being in school and attend only because the law requires them to be there until they reach a certain age.

Dreikurs believes that students are social beings who want to be accepted. When they misbehave, they believe that their actions will get them the recognition they crave. These students usually progress through four stages, or mistaken goals: (1) *attention getting*, often in the form of disruption, wanting special favors and extra services, and irrelevant questioning; (2) *power seeking*, through arguing, lying, contradicting, and showing hostility; (3) *revenge seeking*, by hurting others through vicious or violent acts; and (4) *displaying inadequacy*, through withdrawal based on feelings of helplessness and failure. Dreikurs advises teachers to confront such a student: express the mistaken goal, discuss the faulty logic involved, and get the student to think about the reason for the behavior. He claims that this opens communication and allows the teacher to take constructive actions that will ultimately change the student's behavior (Charles, 1989).

Discipline problems may result from misunderstanding the traditions and behaviors of students from diverse cultures. For example, in many cultures children cooperate and work together at home, but in our schools, they are often expected to work individually, especially on tests. Thus, the teacher may regard children as cheating or disruptive when they are simply following their natural inclinations to help each other on such tasks. Providing cooperative learning activities helps these students adjust to the school's expectations.

Some students are at times simply unable to control their behavior. Students with Attention Deficit Hyperactivity Disorder (ADHD) are fidgety, easily distracted, inattentive, and often quite disruptive in class. Although medication may help, you can also reduce disruptions by assigning their most difficult work early in the day, giving explicit instructions, providing active involvement, assigning short tasks, and seating these students close to you.

Your situation as a student teacher or practicum student is slightly different from that of the classroom teacher. No matter who is doing the teaching, the standards of discipline set by the regular teacher usually prevail (see Activity 5.1). The students realize that even if you're in charge of this lesson, they will ultimately have to answer to their regular teacher. Lacking the experience of a regular teacher, you may fail to notice small incidents that could lead to trouble in time to stop problems from occurring. You may also overlook occasional infractions because you want the students to like you, but they will take advantage of you when they discover they can get away with misbehaving.

PREVENTION OF DISCIPLINE PROBLEMS

Learning how to prevent discipline problems is one secret of classroom control. A *reactive* approach to discipline fails to anticipate problems and offers no well-thought-out plan for responding to situations. Thus, discipline strategies vary from one case to another and may often be inappropriate. On the other hand, a *proactive* approach requires forethought. It involves anticipation and preparation, and it relies on consistent behavior by the teacher and consistent consequences for violations (Ban, 1994). Proactive discipline can be learned, and four models of discipline appear later in this chapter. Some problems may develop regardless of precautions, but you may be able to prevent minor skirmishes from erupting into full-fledged battles.

Relationships with Students

Your relationship with the students is of primary importance. They are amazingly perceptive and know how you feel about them. Here are some tips:

Learn Students' Names. Learn names and use them as soon as you can. Use a seating chart or name tags to help you. Calling students by name gets their attention quickly. Expect them to say Mr., Mrs., Ms., or Miss before your name when addressing you, to maintain a respectful relationship.

Check Seating Arrangements. See if you might eliminate some centers of disturbance by relocating a few students. Observe those who are likely to initiate trouble and avoid seating them near each other.

Avoid Confrontations with Students in Front of Their Peers. It's better to discuss problems rationally later, during a one-to-one conference. Whenever you can, try to help students work out their problems without having to send them to an outside source.

Ignore Insignificant Infractions. Overlook minor misbehavior, such as rumpling paper and passing notes, rather than disrupt the entire class by calling attention to these incidents. You may want to deal with such matters later, on an individual basis.

Stay in Control. Remain calm when faced with discipline problems. If you yell and become excited, students will probably take advantage of you, because they will sense that you are beginning to lose control.

Be Fair, Firm, and Consistent. It doesn't take students long to figure out what kind of disciplinarian you are. You need to be firm from the first day if you expect to have good classroom control.

Set Up a Reward System. Provide incentives or rewards for good behavior at the elementary school level, such as participating in a popcorn party at the end of the week, getting to help the teacher, being class leader, gaining extra time for free reading, being excused from homework, and getting to work with friends. Avoid giving stickers or candy for completion of routine work.

Give Students Choices Whenever Possible. All students should be able to make some choices of their own—what books to read, projects to complete, interests to pursue, friends to work with, and behavior patterns to follow. The students should know and be prepared to live with the consequences of their choices. They should be granted privileges as long as they behave appropriately; if they abuse a privilege, you may need to take it away.

Encourage Students to Solve Their Own Problems. Instead of arbitrating conflicts yourself, turn some problems over to students and let them find solutions, perhaps during group or class meetings. In so doing, you help them develop responsibility and problem-solving skills. You may be familiar with some *conflict resolution* strategies that help students deal with conflicts peaceably and avoid violence (see Chapter 4).

Involve Students in Making Rules. When students participate in setting rules and understand why these rules are necessary, they are likely to feel responsible for their actions. You will probably continue many of the policies already in effect in your classroom, but you may negotiate some rules of your own to take care of problems that seem to be arising. Don't create too many rules, however, or you'll have trouble enforcing them all. Make sure that both rules and consequences are explicit; avoid vague requests such as "behave" or "cooperate" because students may not know what you mean. After rules have been established, help your students evaluate their effectiveness. If a rule is frequently violated, perhaps the rule is unnecessary, or if a penalty seems unfair, perhaps there is a more appropriate consequence.

Presentation of Lessons

If you follow these suggestions, your lessons should give little cause for misbehavior: Make sure the classroom is as comfortable and free from distractions as you can make it. Get everyone's attention before you begin, and be sure that desks or tables are cleared of everything except what the students will need during the lesson. Be well prepared, and maintain good eye contact with students during a lesson. Know your lesson well enough that you don't have to read from the manual while you teach. Watch for students who may have trouble understanding the work, and be ready to

help them over their hurdles; otherwise, their frustration can erupt as behavior problems. Be ready to switch to another method if one strategy isn't working, as in the incident below.

CASE STUDY 5.1

Restructuring the Situation

Mrs. Keen was teaching an American history lesson to her general curriculum students. It was the last period of the day, and the students were tired and restless. Mrs. Keen tried to involve her students in a discussion about the Pilgrims. When she called on Kirk, usually a good student, he told her he hadn't heard the question. Randy didn't know the answer either, but he whispered a few words to his neighbors that made them laugh. Mrs. Keen looked at Susan, who was watching Dennis try to balance his pencil on an eraser. Susan wouldn't know the answer either. As Mrs. Keen surveyed her class, she realized that no one seemed the least bit interested in what happened to the Pilgrims.

Mrs. Keen racked her brain for a way to get the students to respond. She suddenly thought of simulating this event, of having each person in the room become involved in the story by acting it out. She stopped her lesson, told the students that for the rest of the afternoon they were going to do something different, and began explaining the procedure. The class gradually got caught up in acting out the landing of the Pilgrims and their attempts to survive in a cold and primitive new world.

Mrs. Keen was perceptive enough to realize that if her students were to get anything out of the lesson, she would have to change her tactics at once. Her change of pace worked, and she added simulation to her repertoire of teaching techniques.

Start and end your lessons promptly and make transitions from one lesson to another quickly and smoothly. In discussion lessons, let only one student answer at a time to prevent the confusion that results when students call out answers. Keep your lessons interesting and fast-paced. Be enthusiastic, and the students will catch your enthusiasm. Get them actively involved in your lessons and keep them motivated, because highly motivated students seldom cause discipline problems. Have more than enough material for the entire class period. In case you run short, keep ideas in mind for filling in the remaining minutes productively. (See "Filler, or Sponge, Activities" in Chapter 4.)

ACTIVITY 5.1   *Observation Sheet for Discipline*

Carefully observe your cooperating teacher for discipline strategies. Note nonverbal behavior, preventive actions, and disciplinary techniques.

Discipline strategies:

Most effective strategies:

Least effective strategies:

Conclusions about strategies I may want to use with this class:

Give directions clearly and precisely. Reinforce important directions by writing them on the chalkboard. Be sure the students know what choices they have when they finish their work. If they don't know what to do next, they may become disruptive. Be patient with slow learners. If necessary, explain things more than once so that everyone understands. Put things in simple words for young children.

Your teaching style makes a difference in how students respond to you. Move around the room, and use nonverbal communication to interact with various students as you teach. Call on students who seem inattentive to get them to stay with you.

The volume of your voice can set the noise level of the class. If you raise your voice to be heard, the students will only get noisier. If you lower your voice, they will become quiet to hear what you have to say. Be sure, however, that you can be heard in the back of the room and that you speak distinctly. After a week of teaching classes, try Activity 5.2.

Reacting to Danger Signals

If you're alert to impending trouble, you can often stop problems just as they start. Boredom, daydreaming, restlessness, and long periods of inactivity breed discipline problems. Danger signals include a paper wad shot across the room, a half-smothered giggle, or a quick exchange of glances between students.

When you sense trouble brewing, nip it in the bud. Try these ideas:

1. Change your tactics fast. Switch to a different approach, read a story, play a rhythm game, or discuss an event in which students share an interest.
2. Use nonverbal communication to arrest the problem. Catch and hold the instigator's eye. Pause in midsentence and look intently at the potential troublemakers. Shake your head slowly to indicate disapproval.
3. Remind the students of a privilege or reward that will be the consequence of good behavior, while looking in the direction of the potential problem.
4. Move closer to the source of trouble. Indicate that you are aware of what's going on.
5. Speak more softly and slowly. You will get the students' attention for the moment, as they try to figure out why you shifted your speech.
6. Catch them off guard by saying something like, "I surely hope no one in here is thinking about throwing a pencil" or "Did I tell you what is going to happen this Friday?"
7. Use humor. Laugh with the students and occasionally at yourself. A good laugh reduces tension. Laugh off a minor incident instead of mak-

ing a big deal of it. For example, to a student who has just thrown a paper airplane, say "Billy, I'll bet the Air Force could use you to help design airplanes. Now let's get back to work."
8. Call on students you believe are about to cause a problem to answer a question. Or simply insert a student's name in midsentence to bring attention back to the lesson; for example, "The next question, Johnny, is number seven."
9. Confiscate distracting materials, especially toys or food, that are diverting students' attention.

FOR YOUR PORTFOLIO

Describe an occasion when you used discipline effectively, or discuss how you were able to improve a student's behavior by applying certain techniques (or do both).

MODELS OF DISCIPLINE

Several models of discipline have emerged that might guide you in forming your own beliefs. We will discuss four of these models briefly and illustrate their correct and incorrect use. Refer to these models as you do Activity 5.3.

Reality Therapy Model (Glasser)

According to Glasser (1985), students misbehave because they are unsuccessful in fulfilling their needs for belonging, power, freedom, and fun. Teachers, therefore, should structure schoolwork so that it helps satisfy these needs in order for students to make the effort to learn. Teachers should also guide students in making wise choices in their behavior.

Students must also accept responsibility by assuming control over their behavior. When they make good choices resulting in good behavior, they are successful. If they choose inappropriate behavior, the teacher accepts no excuses and the student must take the consequences.

CASE STUDY 5.2

A Joint Endeavor

Mrs. Burks likes an orderly, quiet classroom with each student in her or his seat. She constantly has to remind Yvonne, a gregarious student, to stay in her seat, stop talking, and finish her work.

Mrs. Burks: Yvonne, you're out of your seat again. I've told you not to leave it without permission. Why do you keep getting up?

Yvonne: I get so tired of sitting still—I just *need* to get up sometimes.

Mrs. Burks: Let me think. . . . Would it help if you could work with other students sometimes on group projects?

Yvonne: I think it would be a lot easier if I could talk about my work to my friends sometimes. Could we do that?

Mrs. Burks: I'll try to work something out, but you must agree to do your share of the work if we plan some group activities. You can't just talk and move around unless you are working on your project. Do you understand?

Yvonne: Yes. I'll really try.

Mrs. Burks: I'll give group work a try, but remember that I hold you responsible for working cooperatively with your group.

Although she is reluctant to do so, Mrs. Burks modifies her class structure in order to make it more satisfying for Yvonne, as well as for other students with similar tendencies. At the same time, she expects the students to do their part in working cooperatively to achieve learning goals.

CASE STUDY 5.3

The Teacher's Authority

Dennis constantly shows off to the other students, rarely does his work, and is always jumping up to do or say something.

Mr. Olsen: Dennis, come up to my desk. I want to talk to you.

Dennis: What did I do now?

Mr. Olsen: You know perfectly well. You were about to throw that paper wad toward the trash can.

Dennis: Oh, that. Well, I had to get rid of it somehow—and I'm usually a pretty good shot.

Mr. Olsen: That's beside the point. I expect you to sit in your seat and do your work. Is that clear?

Dennis: Yes, Mr. Olsen.

Mr. Olsen: Go back to your seat and stay there until the end of class.

This encounter resolved nothing. Mr. Olsen was unwilling to consider any changes in structuring his

class and did not help Dennis take responsibility for his actions. Dennis will probably continue his inappropriate behavior.

Effective Momentum Management (Kounin)

Kounin advocates smooth lesson transitions and effective teaching strategies to deter behavior problems. Teachers should achieve *momentum* by pacing instruction so that the lesson's objectives are met without distractions from students. Teachers must keep their lessons moving along without interrupting themselves with *dangles* (leaving a lesson hanging while tending to something else) or *flip flops* (changing back and forth from one subject to another). They must keep their students alert by calling on them randomly and occasionally calling for unison responses. They should become skilled at *overlapping,* the ability to handle two or more students or groups at one time. Teachers should be *withit,* using their sixth sense to react quickly and accurately to disturbances.

One aspect of Kounin's discipline theory is the *ripple effect*—the effect of a disciplinary measure on the rest of the class. Students learn how to behave by observing your reactions to other students, particularly class leaders. You can make good use of this ripple effect if you know how. When you correct someone, clearly identify who the student is, what he or she is doing, and what should be done instead. Vague generalizations have little effect. For instance, say "Cathy, stop playing with those cards, and finish your spelling paper." Simply saying "Class, get busy" makes little difference in students' behavior.

CASE STUDY 5.4

Being Withit

Mr. Wiseman had taught algebra for 14 years and knew pretty well what to expect of his students. They rarely tried to take advantage of him because he supposedly had eyes in the back of his head. One day he was writing an equation on the board for the students to work during class. The class was quiet as he began writing, but as he continued, he heard some whispers and movement in one corner of the room, where Karen was usually the instigator of any trouble. As he turned around, Edna jumped up from her seat and demanded angrily, "All right, whoever has my calculator had better give it back." Two or three students got out of their

ACTIVITY 5.2   *Self-Analysis of Discipline Techniques*

After your first week of teaching classes, analyze the effectiveness of your discipline techniques. Identify each strategy and rate it on a scale of 1 (worst) to 5 (best). (You may want to repeat this activity periodically.)

TECHNIQUE	RATING

Briefly summarize your most and least effective techniques.

What are some other techniques you might want to use?

ACTIVITY 5.3   *Case Study of a Student with Behavior Problems*

As you observe a class, identify one student who appears to have behavior problems. Notice how the teacher handles each situation with this student. Study the models of discipline and decide which techniques might be useful for improving the student's behavior. With your cooperating teacher's approval, try some of the techniques when you begin teaching. Analyze the results.

Thumbnail sketch of case study:

Techniques the teacher uses:

Techniques I want to try (based on models of discipline):

Effectiveness of my techniques and future recommendations:

seats to help her look for her calculator. Mr. Wiseman looked directly at Karen, who was stealthily passing the calculator to Paul. Mr. Wiseman said, "Karen, return the calculator to Edna. Class, get to work on these problems." The students settled down to work.

Mr. Wiseman handled the situation well. He anticipated trouble when he first heard the whispering and turned quickly to intervene at the onset of the problem. By knowing his students, he was able to locate the source of the trouble, correct the problem, and get the students back on task with only a small interruption. The students respected him for knowing who the culprit was and dispensing with the problem quickly.

CASE STUDY 5.5

Not Being Withit

In the class next door, Mr. Dole was preoccupied with assembling a science experiment, while the students waited with nothing to do. He heard some commotion in the classroom but hoped it would subside without his intervention. He continued connecting a hose to a pump, but eventually the hubbub became so loud that he looked up. Mike and Bonnie were throwing an eraser to each other, and Alex was running between them trying to intercept it. Students were shouting encouragement, and one or two others were moving into the game. Mr. Dole couldn't understand how things had gotten out of hand in such a short time. He tried to yell over the noise, but only a few students heard his voice, and they ignored him. He frantically flipped the light switch, threatened the students with expulsion, and eventually got them back into their seats. He told Bonnie, Mike, and Alex to go to the principal's office, even though they protested that playing Catch the Eraser hadn't been their idea. He told the rest of the class that there would be no experiment and that they should read Chapter 4 for a test the next day.

Mr. Dole made a number of mistakes. He was unprepared when the class started, and he left his students with nothing to do. He ignored the first signs of trouble when he could still have prevented a major disruption. He was unable to deal with more than one issue at a time. In his panic to restore order, he made a threat that he had no intention of carrying out. He wasn't sure how many students were really at fault, so he chose the three who were participating in the game and punished them by sending them to the principal's office. In effect, he punished the rest of the class as well

by assigning a test for the next day. The students were resentful and felt they had been unfairly treated.

Assertive Discipline (Canter and Canter)

The Canters advocate assertive discipline to establish effective classroom control. Assertive discipline is based on the concept that teachers have the right to teach and to expect students to behave. At the beginning of the school year, teachers establish rules for behavior along with logical consequences for both proper and improper behavior. They communicate these expectations clearly to the students. Good behavior brings positive consequences, such as material rewards, special privileges or awards, personal attention from the teacher, and positive notes to parents. Failure to behave well, after warnings have been given, results in negative consequences, such as losing privileges or preferred activities, remaining after school, being sent to the principal's office, or being given time-out (isolation). Teachers need to get support from parents and administrators.

CASE STUDY 5.6

Playing by the Rules

It was raining, and Mr. Arrow's students were staying inside for recess. They had requested free time and were well aware of the rules for behavior. Mr. Arrow had suggested that the students might like to go to the reading corner, play one of the games, or work on their mural. As Mr. Arrow was talking with a group of children, he noticed that Ken had snatched Dottie's lunch box and begun to run around the room with it. Dottie started to chase him but soon realized she couldn't catch him. She whined, "Give me back my lunch box." Ken taunted her: "You'll have to catch me first."

At that point, Mr. Arrow said firmly, "Ken, come here." When Ken reached him, Mr. Arrow continued, looking Ken directly in the eye. "Ken, I don't like what you have done. You know the rules in here. There is to be no running in the classroom. Also, you are not to take something that belongs to someone else. You have broken both of these rules. I want you to return Dottie's lunch box. Then I want you to sit in that chair by the counter until recess is over." Ken reluctantly did as Mr. Arrow told him.

Mr. Arrow had set limits for behavior early in the year. Students were well aware of them and the consequences of exceeding them. Occasionally, a student slipped, and Mr. Arrow asserted himself, as in the case of Ken. He spoke to Ken firmly, maintained eye contact, explained the inappropriate behavior, and followed through with a reasonable consequence.

CASE STUDY 5.7

Anything Goes

Mr. Wilson, a new teacher, knew that classroom control was important, but felt it was even more important for the students to like him. Wanting to be a pal to his students, he overlooked many relatively minor incidents at the beginning of the year. He finally realized that he had to enforce some rules or he would lose control of the class altogether. He told the students, "You'd better settle down now" and "Please get quiet." These requests didn't seem to make any difference.

The next time the noise level rose, Mr. Wilson threatened to send all the students to detention hall. They were confused by this unusual behavior and responded with complaints of unfairness and pleas for another chance. Hating to lose the friendship of his students, Mr. Wilson gave in to their requests and withdrew his threat.

A similar situation occurred the next day, so Mr. Wilson told the students to put their heads down on their desks for 10 minutes. After a minute or two, some students began looking up. They said they thought they'd been punished long enough, so Mr. Wilson let them keep their heads up.

Mr. Wilson's students took advantage of his nonassertiveness by misbehaving in class. His requests for good behavior were vague and unclear, so the students ignored him. They soon realized they could talk him out of any threats he made. They liked Mr. Wilson, but had little respect for him because of his inability to set and enforce limits for behavior.

Behavior Modification

All discipline deals with modifying behavior in some way, but behavior modification is a specific model of discipline based on B. F. Skinner's ideas. The basic premise is that all behavior is shaped by what happens to the students following an action. In this model, reinforcement is used systematically to change students' behavior. Students who perform well are given reinforcers, or rewards. The rewards may be words of approval, awards, grades, or even such tangible items as raisins or candy. Students who perform badly receive no reinforcers; their behavior is ignored.

CASE STUDY 5.8

Catching More Flies with Honey

Mr. Sahai had studied behavior modification in a psychology course and decided to put it into action. He introduced the plan to his class, announcing that points would be awarded to the class for good behavior. He displayed a poster showing the maximum number of points that could be earned for each accomplishment. For instance, if everyone was seated and ready to work when the bell rang for class to start, the class would earn 10 points. If Mr. Sahai didn't have to correct anyone's behavior during an entire class period, the class would earn 15 points. He continued with other examples and explained that the number of points would be totaled at the end of each week. Mr. Sahai then showed the class another chart, indicating the number of points required to earn certain privileges.

The students were very responsive to this plan. They cared more about behaving well when they were rewarded for doing so. The only problem was that Jon kept calling out during class, and Mr. Sahai sometimes had to correct him. No points were earned during these classes. The other students decided to take matters into their own hands and make Jon stop interrupting. This peer pressure changed Jon's behavior so that the class was soon earning the full number of points.

Mr. Sahai's experiment with behavior modification was successful. He had carefully thought out his plan and made the rules clear to the class. He kept careful records and never forgot to let students choose their rewards. Students soon began to enjoy working for points that earned them rewards. They responded more actively in class; they liked the quieter, more businesslike atmosphere; and they respected Mr. Sahai for thinking of this plan. By exerting peer pressure, the students helped their teacher control the misbehavior of individual students.

CASE STUDY 5.9

Catching Fewer Flies with Vinegar

Mr. Wynne decided that it was time to crack down on his class. He was tired of the myriad interruptions and the inattentiveness of his students. He believed in giving them fair warning, so he told them that beginning Monday morning, he was going to expect them to behave themselves, or else!

The students came to school Monday in their usual carefree way, entirely forgetting Mr. Wynne's threat. Mr. Wynne remembered, however, and wasted no time in carrying out his intentions. "Bobby, stop talking and sit down," he snapped. Bobby looked bewildered. He was only talking to Terry while he put his jacket away. "Anyone who talks in here before the bell rings will have to come straight back to the room after lunch," Mr. Wynne said. The students looked at each other in confusion. Until now, they had always been permitted to talk before school started. Mr. Wynne continued, "We're going to run a tight ship from now on. I don't want to hear a sound in this room."

Some students resented Mr. Wynne's treatment and thought he was being unfair. He had not even discussed with them the new rules of conduct he was imposing. Although they were afraid not to comply with his demands, the students no longer cared about the quality of the work they turned in to him. Mr. Wynne had tried to improve his classroom control through threats and punishments, but he had failed to gain the willing cooperation and respect of his students.

These models are teacher-directed. Although teachers may need to manage and enforce appropriate behavior on occasion, ultimately students must learn to monitor and control their own actions. We'll look next at some ways that students can become responsible for developing their own appropriate social behaviors.

DEVELOPING STUDENTS' SELF-DISCIPLINE

As long as students rely on you to control their behavior, they are likely to lapse into poor behavior if you do not constantly direct their actions. The objective of good discipline, according to Marshall (1998, p. 14), "is to increase self-responsibility, social awareness, and social responsibility." Rewards and punishments, or consequences, usually last only as long as they are in effect (Kohn, 1994). These are *extrinsic* motivators and do not change underlying attitudes and behaviors. Although rewards usually work better than threats and punishments, Kohn claims that they are both strategies teachers use to manipulate behavior. The child who finishes work in order to get a sticker or a piece of candy soon works only for the reward, instead of thinking creatively, exploring ideas, and taking risks.

As an alternative to rewards and punishments, Kohn (1993, 1994, 1996) recommends creating a classroom community where there is trust, where responsibility is shared, and where students make choices and actively participate in decision making. As part of the community, students feel valued and respected; they care about one another. They feel safe, both physically and emotionally. Because these students care about others, they are better at conflict resolution and there is little need for such disciplinary measures as rewards and punishments.

Students are often unaccustomed to being responsible for their own behavior because teachers have usually told them what to do and what not to do. Creating a democratic class community may take some time and patience, but your efforts will pay off in terms of building rapport with your students, gaining their respect, and decreasing disruptions. Begin by teaching them to be responsible for their actions by forming groups where they direct some of their own activities, expecting them to perform classroom duties, encouraging them to keep records of their progress, having them evaluate their own progress, and setting up a tutoring program where they guide other students' learning. Start with small tasks and work up to larger ones as students demonstrate readiness to assume more responsibility. Help them identify and set goals for themselves; then encourage them to find ways to reach their goals. If you show students that you believe they are capable of directing many of their own activities, they are likely to live up to your expectations.

FOR YOUR PORTFOLIO

Write your philosophy of discipline. State your goals and the techniques you would use and those you would avoid.

DISCIPLINARY MEASURES

As a student, you may have wondered why some teachers seemed to be aware of everything that went on in the classroom, even when they didn't appear to be looking. This is a knack good teachers develop, a sort of sixth sense that enables them to pick up the vibrations from their classes so that they usually know what's happening. You can acquire this ability if you develop sensitivity to sounds, movements, voices, and behavior patterns within your classroom.

Teachers with "eyes in the back of their heads" are usually good disciplinarians. In fact, it is difficult to observe the techniques they use because their methods are subtle and unobtrusive. A quiet nod, the mention of a student's name, or a warning glance usually suffices. Don't worry if you haven't yet mastered this technique—it often takes years of practice.

Even these master disciplinarians occasionally have problems that require more attention, as you probably will also. When problems do develop, consider several factors before taking action. Keep in mind the purpose of disciplinary action: to maintain or restore order by helping the student control his or her behavior, not to seek revenge for violation of the rules. You should also consider the reason for misbehavior and the personal circumstances of the misbehaving student. Appropriate disciplinary measures vary according to the student's grade level, special needs, degree of motivation for learning, ability level, and personality. As you can see, there is no single solution for any problem.

Before deciding what to do, consider your school's policy regarding discipline. Check with your cooperating teacher to find out what types of disciplinary action are permitted if a student misbehaves. Can you keep students after school, or do bus schedules prohibit this? Can you deny a student recess, or is a certain amount of free time compulsory? Is there a detention hall, and do you have the option of sending a student there? What do you do if a student doesn't have a hall pass, talks back in class, or destroys school property?

In cases of persistent inappropriate behavior or major infractions, you need to know what to do. You may need to keep dated, explicit records of incidents, which may be used for referrals or for decisions about placing students in an alternative school. You need to know when parents should be contacted and when suspension or expulsion is a consequence. Your cooperating teacher has the responsibility for contacts with parents in most cases and, along with the administration, for any decisions about suspension or expulsion.

Knowing Some Options

Although you attempt to instill a sense of social responsibility and create a community, you may sometimes reach a point at which you must discipline a class or an individual student. You may want to ask the advice of your cooperating teacher before choosing one of the following, but here are some potentially appropriate consequences for specific types of misbehavior:

1. If a student tries to be the class clown . . .

   a. Explain that there are times when that kind of behavior is appreciated, but it is not appropriate during class.
   b. Give the clown special assignments to show your confidence in her or his ability to assume responsibility.
   c. Praise the clown for completion of serious work, but ignore the clowning.
   d. If the behavior persists, isolate the clown temporarily.

Remember that the purpose of discipline is to restore order by helping students regain control of their behavior.

2. If students talk at inappropriate times . . .

   a. Ignore the interruption, if possible.
   b. Change the seating arrangement. Some students may encourage those who sit near them to talk during class.
   c. Give students a few minutes of free time to get talking out of their systems.
   d. Stop your lesson and wait until everything quiets down.

3. If students litter or mess things up . . .

   a. Provide time for them to clean up their desks and work areas.
   b. Provide incentives for neat work.
   c. Brainstorm all the ways to make the room neater, cleaner, and more attractive.
   d. Let students be messy sometimes; then give them a chance to clean up.
   e. Confiscate articles left carelessly around the room. Return them at the end of the week.
   f. Use creative dramatics. Turn young children into robots, and see how quickly they can run around and put everything in its place.

4. If students push, shove, and make noise when forming lines . . .

   a. Appoint a different leader each week who is responsible for maintaining a disciplined line.
   b. Dismiss one row or group at a time. Choose the best-behaved group first.
   c. Have students line up according to some plan, such as alphabetical order, height, or color of clothing.

5. If a student tattles . . .

   a. Explain that you don't want to hear personal information about another student (gossiping), but only news of rules that have been broken or of someone who has been hurt (reporting).
   b. Ask the tattler to write down the information for you to read at the end of the day, because you do not have time to listen. Writing should discourage him or her.
   c. If there are several tattlers in your class, ask them to save all their tales to tell on Friday afternoon. By then, they will probably consider the matters too trivial to share.
   d. Role-play a tattletale incident so students can understand why this behavior is undesirable.

Testing the Technique

Some common disciplinary practices are considered generally effective; some are considered good or bad depending on the circumstances; others are thought to be inappropriate. Do Activity 5.4 to analyze the effectiveness of your strategies.

FOR YOUR PORTFOLIO

Make a copy of the discipline plan you create for Activity 5.4.

Effective Techniques

Reinforcers.   Both verbal and nonverbal reinforcers are effective for encouraging good behavior and discouraging improper conduct.

Restitution.   A student who takes or destroys something should be expected to return or restore it. If this is impossible, the student should compensate for the loss in some other way.

Role Playing.   Students appreciate the feelings of other students and see incidents in a new light when they role play (see Chapter 7).

Contracts.   The use of contracts works well for intermediate and secondary students. Contracts are agreements that deal with specified behaviors, tasks, responsibilities, and rewards. They give the effect of a legal commitment and are signed by both the teacher and the student.

Group Discussions.   Guided, open discussions are good ways to handle disputes and discipline problems. Students feel involved and responsible for carrying out their own recommendations.

Gripe Box.   A suggestion box or gripe box allows students to express dissatisfaction. After reading the students' notes, you might want to make some changes. Select one or two gripes for students to discuss in class in order to resolve the complaint.

Nonverbal Signals.   Effective use of nonverbal signals and body language is one of the best forms of discipline. Examples are a frown, a smile, a nod, movement toward a student, an intent look, a raised hand, and a wink.

Time-Out.   Time-out can be used to remove a student who is highly distracting to the rest of the class or who is acting in such a way that she or he could harm others. The teacher isolates the student from the rest of the class for a period of time until the student cools off and regains control. The isolation area should be secluded, quiet, and dull.

Appeal to Reason.   Explaining why good behavior is necessary often persuades students to act well. You might say, "Be careful with the equipment so we don't break anything" or "Work quickly so we'll have time to plan our party."

Approval of Behavior.   This method generally works well in elementary school. The teacher notices students who are "ready to begin," are "sitting up nicely," or "have their books open to the right page." Other students follow suit because they also want recognition.

Grounding.   This technique is effective for a student who can't work well or can't cooperate at an interest center. The student must return to his or her seat to work until ready to rejoin the group.

Matching the Penalty to the Offense.   A consequence should relate to the offense so that the student can see the reason for it.

Attention-Getting Signals.   Agree on a signal to get instant attention, such as raising your arm, ringing a bell, or saying "Freeze!"

Writing It Out.   When a student misbehaves, ask the student to write what happened, why it happened, and how the situation could be handled better next time.

Borderline Techniques

Planned Ignoring.   This technique may work for a while. Sometimes if you ignore a problem, it will go away; but at other times it only becomes worse, until you are forced to deal with it.

Apologies.   If apologies are genuine, they are effective. If you force students to say words they don't mean, you are only teaching them to lie. Their apologies mean nothing.

Removal of Students from the Classroom. Although you may be tempted to remove a student who is out of control, try to settle the matter yourself, since you and your cooperating teacher probably know the situation better than anyone else.

Merits and Demerits.   This system consists of awarding or taking away points for certain kinds of behavior. This technique may work well if it is care-fully structured and used on a temporary basis. Students should eventually learn to control their own behavior, however, rather than rely on outside incentives.

Remaining after School.   Keeping a student after school, either in your own room or in detention hall, may have some value as a penalty for misbehavior. Unless some educational experience is planned for this time, however, this method will waste time for both you and the student. Remaining after school can also interfere with bus schedules or worthwhile extracurricular activities.

Denial of Privileges.   A denied privilege is usually an effective penalty. It can have a negative effect, however, if a student is being denied something which he or she really needs. For instance, a hyperactive child who is denied recess probably needs this outlet for surplus energy.

Scoldings.   An occasional reprimand is often necessary, but a bitter harangue has a negative effect on the whole class. Avoid nagging, constant faultfinding, and long discourses on behavior.

Personal Conferences.   A one-to-one conference often clears up problems and helps the student and teacher understand each other. Privacy is necessary for a free exchange of views and for keeping a matter confidential. The teacher must listen carefully to the student's views. Conferences are ineffective when the teacher simply makes accusations and the student is unresponsive, and they can be destructive if they deteriorate into arguments.

Inappropriate Techniques

Additional Classwork or Homework.   This practice generally results in the student's disliking the subject.

Ridicule or Sarcasm.   Students who are embarrassed or humiliated by their teachers may suffer serious psychological damage.

Grade Reduction.   Grades for academic achievement should not be affected by behavior.

Obsolete Punishments.   Punishments like wearing a dunce cap, holding a book at arm's length, standing with the nose in a circle drawn on the board, and writing sentences are techniques that may deter students from certain kinds of behavior, but they do nothing to rehabilitate the student or solve the problem.

ACTIVITY 5.4   **Discipline Plan**

As you can see, there are a multitude of disciplinary theories and practices. Reflect on your observations of effective disciplinarians, the techniques and various programs given in this chapter, and what works for you. Then create a discipline plan that you would like to implement when you have your own classroom. Consider the following: How will I prevent discipline problems from occurring? What choices am I willing to give students? How can I establish a classroom community? How can I enable students to use effective conflict-resolution strategies? How do I feel about rewards and punishments? To find more information about methods of discipline that you might want to use, refer to the website *prenhall.com/methods-cluster,* "Topic 3: Discipline/ Classroom Management."

Threats.   It's usually better to act than to threaten. If you do make threats, be prepared to follow through. Generally, threats cause students to become upset and suspicious.

Corporal Punishment.   Corporal punishment rarely corrects a problem. Like threats, it usually has a negative effect on students and should be used only as a last resort, if ever. Improper use of corporal punishment can result in legal problems.

EVALUATING FOUR CASE STUDIES

The following case studies are based on actual situations. Read them, and evaluate the teacher's action in each case. Were other options available? How would you have handled these students?

CASE STUDY 5.10

The Last Straw

Jeff, a twelfth-grade student, came from a low-socioeconomic-level home where he was taught the value of a good education. His parents were interested in his progress and encouraged him to do well.

In industrial arts class, Jeff was a reasonably good student, but he often caused minor disruptions. He would distract other students by sticking his foot out to trip them, making wisecracks, laughing raucously at nothing, and occasionally defying his teacher, Mr. Hamlin. Mr. Hamlin put up with his behavior for several weeks. He knew that Jeff was basically a good student and did not feel that Jeff's interruptions warranted a confrontation.

One morning, Jeff decided he would go to the cosmetology class to get a haircut during industrial arts. When he told Mr. Hamlin he was going, Mr. Hamlin refused to give him permission. Jeff cursed at Mr. Hamlin and said that he was going to get his hair cut anyway. At this point, Mr. Hamlin realized he had been too lenient with Jeff. He knew something would have to be done, or there would be a total breakdown in discipline in his class. Mr. Hamlin took Jeff to the office, where the principal suspended him for his defiant and discourteous behavior.

Following his suspension, Jeff returned to school with his father. During a conference with the guidance counselor, Mr. Carlin, the entire situation was reviewed and correct standards of behavior were discussed. A contract was drawn up, which allowed Jeff to return to class as long as he acted like a gentleman. Mr. Carlin went over the contract with Jeff and his father in detail. If Jeff failed to live up to his commitment, he would be dropped from the class roll. Jeff seemed to

hold no malice toward his teacher or the counselor and willingly agreed to sign the contract, along with his father and Mr. Carlin. The counselor also requested that Jeff apologize to Mr. Hamlin and the rest of the class, but only if he felt he owed them an apology.

Mr. Hamlin later reported that Jeff had been much less disruptive in class and that he was behaving more maturely.

CASE STUDY 5.11

Moving toward Acceptable Behavior

Jill is a fifth-grader who lives with her mother and stepfather. She was abused by her father as a young child, and her stepfather has helped her make adjustments. Jill and her mother do not get along well. Both parents are beginning to lose patience with her.

At the beginning of the year, Jill threw temper tantrums when things didn't go her way. She nearly went into convulsions sometimes and had to be taken from the room. At other times, she was told to stand in the corner as punishment for her fits of temper. She hated standing in the corner, so the number of tantrums gradually decreased.

Jill was hostile toward the teacher, Mrs. Lynch, and the other children. She was loud and aggressive when she came to school in the morning. She called people names and frequently told lies. She was easily distracted and rushed through her work, not caring if it was done correctly. On the playground, she tried to get control of the ball and take it away from the other children. She had no remorse about hurting people, even when she caused them to bleed.

During the year, three things seemed to help Jill. First, Jill enjoyed getting the attention of the other students. She was beginning to discover that when she was nice to them, they would be friendly toward her. To win friends, she began to change her attention-getting strategies to more acceptable behavior patterns.

Jill's relationship with Mrs. Lynch also helped her. Mrs. Lynch and Jill talked frequently in private about why Jill acted as she did and how she might get along better with the other children. Jill began to trust Mrs. Lynch and stopped feeling that Mrs. Lynch was picking on her.

Jill was also helped by the school psychologist, with whom she met each week. The psychologist required her to earn points for satisfactory achievement. Jill's teachers had to sign a paper each time she earned a point. Jill then took the paper to the psychologist, who granted her a privilege if she had earned at least 16 points in a week.

Jill is still immature and demands attention in unacceptable ways, but her behavior is much better than it was at the beginning of the year.

CASE STUDY 5.12

Parental Restitution

Troy, a fifth grader, is a rather homely and unpopular boy whose parents have a lot of money. His mother places a great deal of importance on wealth and continually brags about recent trips and acquisitions. It seems to Troy that money can buy anything.

Troy wanted more than anything to be accepted by his friends. He decided to ask Sheila, the cutest girl in class, to "go with" him for $10 a week. This seemed like a lot of money to Sheila, but she was doubtful about the arrangement. She discussed Troy's proposition with her friends before deciding what to do. She really didn't want to be Troy's girl, even for the money. She finally agreed, however, and Troy brought $10 to school for her.

Until this time, Sheila had barely spoken to Troy, but now she occasionally sat with him during lunch and talked to him during the day. She allowed him to call her at night, but they never went anyplace together. This arrangement satisfied Troy. He boasted to his classmates about his new girlfriend. They were properly impressed, and Troy gained status among his peers.

After two or three weeks, Troy's teacher, Mrs. Hobson, became suspicious. She had observed the new relationship between Troy and Sheila and thought it was unusual. One day she saw Troy handing $10 to Sheila. She talked to the two quietly and found out about their arrangement.

Mrs. Hobson felt that the only thing to do was to bring both sets of parents to school and discuss the matter with them. During the conference, the parents agreed to talk to their children about ending the arrangement. Sheila's parents returned the money to Troy's parents, and the matter ended. Troy and Sheila resumed their original relationship. Troy did not seem depressed over losing Sheila's attention.

CASE STUDY 5.13

Peer Pressure Does the Trick

Dan came from a high-socioeconomic-level home and had the support of his family. He didn't believe in law enforcement, school regulations, or God. He was an excellent student academically, but had begun using drugs as a high school sophomore.

As a junior, Dan became even more hooked on drugs. His guidance counselor, Mrs. Tilton, was aware of Dan's dependence on drugs and talked to him about this problem on several occasions. Dan insisted that it was his right to use drugs and that no one could tell him what to do. He claimed that all the students used drugs, but Mrs. Tilton denied this. Mrs. Tilton warned him that drugs could eventually ruin him, but nothing she said made any difference. Dan continued to be cooperative and do well in his classes, but was beginning to go downhill by the end of the year.

Despite his heavy use of drugs, Dan won the history prize in his junior year. As he walked across the stage to receive his award, the students booed him. Because of his involvement with drugs, they had no respect for him. *[handwritten: yeah right!]*

For some reason, this rejection by his peers turned Dan around. He cared about his fellow students and their feelings toward him. He stopped using drugs and was elected president of the student body in his senior year. According to some, he was the best student body president the school ever had. He went on to the local university, where he carried a double major and made the Dean's List each semester.

DISCUSSION QUESTIONS

1. Which model of discipline do you think would have been effective in the vignette at the beginning of this chapter? Why?

2. Select one or two students who tend to be disruptive in class. Can you determine the causes? Is there anything you can do to change this disruptive behavior?

3. Analyze the models of discipline. Which model, if any, does your cooperating teacher use? Which model do you prefer? Can you put together parts of the different models and come up with a plan you think would work for you? Can you identify some basic concepts that appear to be true of all the models?

4. Watch your cooperating teacher carefully. How does she or he control behavior? Do the teacher's signals, warnings, nonverbal messages, or other subtle measures prevent discipline problems from arising? Which techniques seem most successful? Do all students respond the same way?

5. Develop a plan for helping your students acquire self-discipline. What reasonable responsibilities can you give them? Can you vary the responsibil-

ities to meet the capabilities of each student? How can you check students' progress toward developing self-discipline?

6. What kinds of verbal and nonverbal reinforcers do you use during the day? Do you reinforce each student's good behavior, or do you reserve reinforcers for just a few? How might you make better use of reinforcers to encourage good academic work and proper behavior?

SELECTED REFERENCES

Au, K. (1993). *Literacy instruction in multicultural settings.* Orlando, FL: Harcourt Brace.

Ban, J. (1994). A lesson plan approach for dealing with school discipline. *The Clearing House, 67,* (5), 257–260.

Canter, L. (1986). *Assertive Discipline, Phase I,* (Video recording). Santa Monica, CA: Canter and Associates.

Canter, M. (1987). *A model for effective discipline.* Bloomington, IN: Phi Delta Kappa Educational Foundation.

Charles, C. M. (1989). *Building classroom discipline* (3rd ed.). New York: Longman.

Dill, V. S.(1998). *A peaceable school.* Bloomington, IN: Phi Delta Kappa.

Glasser, W. (1985). *Control theory in the classroom.* New York: Perennial Library.

Hanny, R. (1994). Don't let them take you to the barn. *The Clearing House, 67* (5), 252–253.

Horne, A., Draper, K., & Sayger, T. (1994). Teaching children with behavior problems takes understanding, tools, and courage. *Contemporary Education, 65* (3), 122–127.

Kirby, E. & Kirby, S. (1994). Classroom discipline with attention deficit hyperactivity disorder children. *Contemporary Education, 65* (3), 142–144.

Kohn, A. (1993). Choices for children: Why and how to let students decide. *Phi Delta Kappan, 75*(1), 8–20.

Kohn, A. (1994, December). The risks of rewards. Urbana, IL: ERIC DIGEST (EDO-PS-94-14)

Kohn, A. (1996). *Beyond discipline: From compliance to community.* Alexandria, VA: Association for Supervision and Curriculum Development.

Kounin, J. S. (1977). Discipline and group management in classrooms. Huntington, NY: R. E. Krieger.

McDaniel, T. (1994). A back-to-basics approach to classroom discipline. *The Clearing House, 67* (5), 254–256.

Marshall, M. (1998). *Fostering social responsibility.* Bloomington, IN: Phi Delta Kappa.

Rogers, B. (1998). *"You know the fair rule" and much more.* Melbourne, Australia: ACER.

Scarlett, W. G. & Associates. (1998).*Trouble in the classroom.* San Francisco, CA: Jossey Bass.

Thompson, G. (1994). Discipline and the high school teacher. *The Clearing House, 67* (5), 261–265.

Wasicsko, M. M., & Ross, S. (1994). How to create discipline problems. *The Clearing House, 67*(5), 248–251.

Wolfgang, C. (1995). *Solving discipline problems* (3rd ed.). Boston: Allyn and Bacon.

Instructional Planning

Importance of Planning

Mr. Thomas is the cooperating teacher; Miss Alwood is his student teacher; Mrs. Marshall is the principal.

Mrs. Marshall: Miss Alwood, Mr. Thomas has called in sick today. A substitute has been called, but she won't be here for a couple of hours. I know that you have been checking the roll and leading opening exercises for some time now. That shouldn't be a problem. And Mr. Thomas said that you were supposed to teach the science class today. You can switch the times for the science class and the reading class, and the substitute will be here in time to teach the reading. Will that be all right with you?

Miss Alwood: Well, I guess so, but I was going to locate the materials for an experiment and run off some handouts for the science class while Mr. Thomas was teaching reading this morning. I guess I can postpone the experiment until tomorrow, though.

Mrs. Marshall: You mean that you waited until an hour before the lesson to locate your materials and make your handouts? What if you were unable to find what you needed here? What if the copier were broken?

Miss Alwood (staring at the floor): I didn't think about that. I just assumed that I would be able to find everything here because Mr. Thomas said he did that experiment last year with his class, and I know he has a big box of stuff for science experiments. I did bring a battery, because I thought his old one might have gone dead in a year.

Mrs. Marshall: How many other lessons did you have to prepare for today?

Miss Alwood: None. I don't take on another subject until next week.

Mrs. Marshall: What did you do after school yesterday?

Miss Alwood: I went shopping first. Then I went home, ate supper, and prepared a crossword puzzle for the class. After that, I watched some television. I was really tired from the day because the class was rowdy, so I just tried to relax.

Mrs. Marshall: Doesn't Mr. Thomas ask you to plan your lessons in advance?

Miss Alwood: Oh, yes. I gave him my plans for this whole week last Friday. He thought my experiment with electromagnets and having the students write a lab report were good ideas. He said my lesson on magnetism yesterday got my unit off to a good start. We brainstormed about the topic, and I made a web of what they already knew about it on the board. The students all copied the web on their papers. We are going to add to it as they learn new things about the topic.

Mrs. Marshall: Was that your whole lesson?

Miss Alwood: Yes.

Mrs. Marshall: Did it take the whole science period?

Miss Alwood: Well, it took most of it for some of the students, but some of them copied the web really fast. I had to watch them, because they bothered the ones who were still working. Mr. Thomas suggested that I have something prepared for those "fast finishers" to do while the others finish. Today I had a crossword puzzle with terms related to magnetism all ready for them. I just needed to run it and the lab report forms off this morning.

Mrs. Marshall: I'm glad you are taking Mr. Thomas's suggestions seriously, but I think that you need to prepare for your lessons further in advance. Your written plan will be useless if you don't locate the needed materials.

1. When should the preparation for Miss Alwood's science lesson have taken place?
2. Did Miss Alwood make a good impression on Mrs. Marshall? Why or why not?
3. What does this situation tell you about the importance of time management?

PLANNING FOR INSTRUCTION

Without planning for instruction, your teaching experiences are likely to turn into disasters. Planning offers organization and direction for your teaching efforts. It can help you make sure that you cover all important aspects of a lesson, while avoiding overemphasis on isolated points that interest you but do not merit extensive coverage. Planning can save you from not having enough to do in a lesson, especially if you practice overplanning. (*Overplanning* means planning extra related and purposeful activities that you don't expect to have time for, but have ready in case the rest of the lesson progresses rapidly and time is available.) See Chapter 4 for some suggested filler, or sponge, activities. Planning can also help you avoid trying to cover too much material at one time. As you look at the complexity of the concepts you plan to present in a lesson format, you may find that you have selected more material than the students can readily absorb at once and that certain complex concepts need much elaboration, rather than a hasty mention.

Good planning also enhances your poise and confidence, and, as a result, class control will tend to be positively affected. Since class control is a major problem for student teachers, this advantage alone should encourage planning.

Written plans allow you to consult your cooperating teacher and college supervisor about the likelihood of a successful teaching experience. They can give you valuable feedback, which may avert a teaching disaster brought on by inexperience. Some cooperating teachers and college supervisors *require* written plans. If yours don't, we highly recommend that you do them anyway, for your personal benefit. It will pay off.

There is a current emphasis in schools to teach in accordance with standards set by a variety of professional organizations or by state organizations. Standards have been developed by the National Council of Teachers of English and the International Reading Association (1996), the National Council of Teachers of Mathematics (1989; 1998), the National Research Council (1998), the American Association for the Advancement of Science (1993), the National Geographic Society (1994), the National Council for the Social Studies (1994), and the National Skills Standards Board (1998). States have also gotten into the act. Clark and Wasley (1999, p. 591) point out that "Forty-nine states have adopted some form of higher academic standards for school-age children," and that the standards of the national subject-matter organizations have influenced these state standards. Being familiar with the standards of the state in which you are teaching and the professional organizations related to your subject area or areas will enhance your ability to plan lessons.

When you are actually assigned to teach, it is vitally important that you plan for instruction, whether or not you actually write down the plans. Your instructional plans should always relate directly to the course of study for your class and should always build upon previous learning.

One good way to ease into your teaching experience is to work jointly with your cooperating teacher in planning a lesson, watch him or her teach the lesson in an early class, and then try it yourself in a later class. This arrangement gives you the benefit of seeing an experienced teacher move from plan to execution. Obviously, this procedure will only work in departmentalized settings where a teacher has several sections of the same course.

At first you will probably be assigned responsibility for single, isolated lessons. Later, as you progress, you will probably be assigned to teach entire units of instruction. These two planning tasks will be considered separately, in the order in which you are likely to encounter them, even though, obviously, lesson planning is an integral part of unit planning.

For information about planning for instruction, visit *http://www.prenhall.com/methods-cluster*, "Topic 17: Planning Instructional Objectives and Goals" and check out the web links on "Instructional Planning Guides" and "Planning Instruction."

Lesson Planning

Your lesson plans should be detailed enough that you or another person qualified to teach your grade or subject can teach from them with ease, yet brief enough that they do not become cumbersome. Usually, more detailed plans are needed at the beginning of your student teaching experience than at the end or after you become a regular classroom teacher. More detail gives an inexperienced person greater confidence and makes the inclusion of all important material more likely. Too much detail, however, can inhibit flexibility in a lesson. Do not, for example, plan to get one particular answer from students and build all your subsequent plans on this answer. That answer may not come. Plan to accommodate a variety of responses.

What belongs in a good lesson plan? Opinions vary, and each teacher generally has to evolve a planning scheme that fits his or her personality. Certain components appear almost universally, however, and you would do well to use these in initial planning activities. (See Figure 6–1.)

When you write objectives for a specific lesson you have been asked to teach, be sure to study the overall

FIGURE 6–1

Components of a Lesson Plan*

*See Appendix B for sample lesson plans.

1. Subject
2. Grade
3. Date (not always essential)
4. Time (useful for secondary teachers who teach more than one section of a subject and grade)
5. Objectives (be specific)
6. Content to be covered (be specific)
7. Materials and equipment needed
8. Activities and procedures with time allocations (to keep you from running out of time in the middle of something)
9. Alternative activities (in case a piece of audiovisual equipment won't work, a film doesn't arrive on time, or you overestimated how long other activities would take)
10. Method of evaluation (to determine if the students really learned the material)
11. Assignments (to provide practice on a taught skill, to prepare for a future lesson, or to achieve some very specific purpose)
12. Self-evaluation (Put this section in your written lesson plan, to be filled out after you teach the lesson.)
13. Supervisory feedback (Put this section in your written lesson plan, to be filled out after you have been critiqued by your cooperating teacher, your college supervisor, or both.)

objectives of the unit of which the lesson is a part, and check on the instruction that has previously taken place in that unit. Your chosen objectives should build upon previously taught material and lay a groundwork for future instruction, either by you or by your cooperating teacher. Be specific in your objectives. Don't use a vague objective, such as "To help them understand verbs better"; instead, say "To help the students understand and apply the concept of subject-verb agreement" or in more behavioral terms, "In 20 consecutive trials the student will demonstrate accurate use of subject-verb agreement," if you are looking for mastery learning.

In the content section of your plan, list the major concepts you plan to cover. Don't just write "Causes of the Civil War"; list specific causes. Consult resources other than the textbook when planning this part of the lesson.

On your list of materials, include *everything* you will need. If you need a transparency marker and a blank transparency for the overhead projector, list them. You can use this list to help you accumulate all necessary materials before the lesson begins, so you won't have to disrupt your lesson while you search the room for an appropriate pen for writing on transparencies.

In the activities and procedures section, you may wish to list questions you plan to raise, motivational techniques you plan to use, what you plan to do, and what you are going to ask the students to do. Consult your college methods textbooks when you plan this part of your lesson. Vary activities. Students become bored with lessons that require just one type of response. Plan to have students do some combination of listening, watching, reading, speaking, and writing in each lesson. Don't forget to develop background for the lesson before you begin the new material, and model for the students the skill or strategy you want them to acquire. When you *model* a skill or strategy for students, you demonstrate its use for the students, including an oral explanation of your thought processes related to the activity.

By estimating how much time each activity should take, you minimize the risk of finishing an hour lesson in 20 minutes or of getting only halfway through a 30-minute lesson before the time has elapsed. At first, of course, your time estimates may not be extremely accurate, but the very act of keeping up with them in each lesson helps you learn how to judge time needs better. A common problem for student teachers is finishing all the planned material early and being forced to improvise. This will not be a problem for you if you plan some good alternative activities to use in such an eventuality, or in case a projector bulb burns out and there is not another one in the school, or if some other unforeseen difficulty occurs.

You should always consider how to determine whether or not your students have learned the lesson material. You can evaluate through oral or written questions, observation of students' performance, or some other means, but you *must* evaluate. Planning future lessons depends upon whether or not students learned the material in the current lesson.

The assignments you give students for independent work should be carefully planned to meet a specific purpose. One assignment might be designed to offer further practice in a skill just taught, to help fix it in the students' minds. Another assignment might be designed to prepare the students for a future lesson. Any materials that students are assigned to read independently must be chosen carefully. Students will be unable to complete independent assignments in materials that are too difficult for them to read; for this reason, differentiated reading assignments may be necessary.

After you have taught the lesson, you should evaluate your effectiveness much as you evaluated lessons you observed others teach. When you recognize weaknesses, consider how you would teach the lesson differently if you taught it a second time. Those of you in departmentalized settings who are assigned to two sections of the same class may even have a chance to try out your ideas for improvement later in the day. If you do, remember to evaluate the second presentation also. When you receive feedback from your cooperating teacher and your college supervisor about your lesson, compare their comments with your self-evaluation. If you noticed the same things they did, your evaluation skills are probably good. If they mention many things you missed, you may need to work at evaluating your performance more critically and objectively.

Complete the Lesson Plan Outline in Activity 6.1 for one lesson that you plan to teach this term. You may wish to photocopy the blank form to use with other observations for your own benefit or at the request of your cooperating teacher or college supervisor. Although this is only one possible lesson plan form, completing it can help you determine important components for your lesson that would need to be included on any form you might use for future lessons.

Once you have presented the lesson specified in Activity 6.1, complete Activity 6.2 to help you analyze it.

FOR YOUR PORTFOLIO

Include in your portfolio one completed lesson plan and an analysis of this lesson. Choose a lesson that shows some of your best accomplishments.

Thematic Unit Planning

After you have achieved some success at planning individual lessons, your cooperating teacher will probably move you into planning thematic units. Such planning involves developing coordinated sets of lessons built around central themes. In the elementary school, a thematic unit plan frequently cuts across disciplines and includes activities in language arts, mathematics, social studies, science, art, music, and other areas. An example of this type of unit might be one on the "Westward Movement." Although this unit has basically a social studies theme, the teacher can incorporate language arts instruction through reference reading, oral and written reports, and class discussions; mathematics instruction in figuring distances and calculating amounts of needed supplies and prices of supplies in those days to discover the cost of a journey; science and health instruction through comparing disease remedies used then with those used today; art in illustrating modes of transportation, clothing, or other features of the times and in constructing dioramas and models; music instruction through singing and playing songs of the time; and even home economics instruction by making recipes of that era (which also requires mathematics skills) and performing sewing tasks appropriate to the times, such as quilting and making samplers. When thematic units are thoroughly integrated across the curriculum, in a natural, holistic way, the approach is often referred to as *theme studies*. Because not all curricular areas will fit a particular theme study, connections should not be forced. Integration should be meaningful and natural. Secondary-level thematic units, especially in social studies and literature classes, may cut across disciplines, but this is not as common as at the elementary level.

Most thematic units at the secondary level and many at the elementary level are based upon major topics within single disciplines. A mathematics class, for example, may have a unit on measurement, incorporating a multitude of mathematical concepts and skills. You should review your methods textbooks for types of thematic units appropriate to your grade and/or discipline.

Different situations require different types of units; that is, there is no one form for all units. Different reference books promote different formats, some of which are harder and some easier to use in a particular situation. You should examine these options and pick the one that best fits *your* situation.

Despite the variations in form suggested for unit preparation, there are certain important considerations you should not overlook when preparing any unit. They are described on pages 133–134.

ACTIVITY 6.1 Lesson Plan Form

Name: _____ Subject: _____

Grade level: _____ Date: _____ Time: _____

Objectives (Be specific.):

Content to be covered (Be specific.):

Materials and equipment needed (Indicate sources.):

Activities and procedures (Include time allocations.):
Introductory activities:

Developmental activities:

Concluding activities:

Alternative activities—emergency fillers:

Method of evaluation:

Assignments—homework or in-class supervised study:

Self-evaluation:

Supervisory feedback:

ACTIVITY 6.2 **Personal Lesson Analysis Form**

Name: _____ Date: _____

Class: _____

Area 1 Did the students seem to grasp how the lesson was tied to previous learning? _____ Did the motivational activities seem to arouse students' interest? _____ Why do you think they did or did not accomplish their goal? _____

_____

_____

Area 2 Were the purpose and relevance of the lesson made clear to the students? _____ Why or why not? _____

_____

_____

How might they have been better clarified? _____

_____

_____

Area 3 Were your procedures effective for presenting the content? _____ Might some other procedures have been more effective? _____ Why do you think so?_____

_____

_____

Area 4 Were the lesson materials appropriate and effective? _____ Would other materials have been more effective? _____ Why do you think so?_____

_____

_____

Area 5 Was your teaching style effective with this particular group and for this particular lesson? _____ Why do you think so? _____

_____

_____

Area 6 Did you have adequate knowledge of the subject matter? _____ Was enough outside knowledge brought into the lesson? _____ If not, what else might have been included? _____

_____

_____

Was content effectively related to the students' lives? _____ If not, how might this have been accomplished? _____

_____

_____

Area 7   Were adequate provisions made for individual differences? _____ If so, how? _____ If not, what steps might have been taken to improve the situation? _____

_____

_____

Area 8   Were disciplinary techniques appropriate and effective? _____ Why do you think so? _____

_____

_____

If they were inappropriate or ineffective, what techniques might have been better? _____

_____

_____

Area 9   Did your personal qualities advance the lesson effectively? _____ Why do you think so? _____

_____

_____

Might changes in this area be helpful to future lessons? _____ How? _____

_____

_____

Area 10 Was the conclusion of the lesson effective? _____ Why or why not? _____

_____

_____

If not, what might have been done to improve it? _____

_____

_____

Area 11 Were your evaluation techniques appropriate and effective? _____ Why do you think so? _____

_____

_____

If not, what techniques might have been better? _____

_____

_____

Make your unit plan fit into the class's overall course of study. If you are allowed to pick your own unit theme, examine the course of study and pick a theme that fits into the long-term plans for the class. Whether you pick the theme or your cooperating teacher does, check to see how your unit fits into the overall instructional plan. Find out from your cooperating teacher the prior learning upon which your unit can build. Check on the relationships between your unit and the previous and succeeding units. Decide what things you must include to ensure students' success in succeeding units.

Find out from your cooperating teacher the time allotment for your unit, and make your plans conform to this allotment. You will probably not be able to include every aspect of your chosen topic within the given time frame. You must decide, either independently or in conjunction with the students, which aspects to include.

Consider carefully the students who will be studying the unit. Find out their backgrounds of experience in relation to the theme, their general levels of achievement in school or in your subject area (or both), their levels of interest in the unit theme, their reading levels, their attitudes toward school and the subject area or areas involved, their study habits and ability to work independently or engage in group work, and their special talents. Plan all your activities with these characteristics in mind. It may be useful to actually write down a profile of your class, including all these characteristics, to refer to as you develop objectives, teaching methods, activities, and evaluation methods.

After you have learned how to plan individual lessons, you may be asked to plan a unit.

Collect ideas for the thematic unit from a variety of sources: students' textbooks, your college textbooks, professional journals, local resources (businesses and individuals), resource units on file in your school or college media center, and, of course, your cooperating teacher. Make lists of helpful books, periodicals, websites, audiovisual aids, and resource people for future reference. One caution is in order here: do not lecture straight from your old college notes. Remember that your students are not yet ready for material as advanced as the material in your college classes. Use the college notes as background material, and work in information from them only as it is directly applicable and appropriate for your particular students.

Draft your objectives for the thematic unit according to the content you want to cover and the students with whom you will be working. You may wish to refer to your methods textbooks to refresh your memory on writing clear objectives. Include both cognitive and affective objectives when appropriate.

Organize the procedures section of your unit plan to include the unit introduction, the body of the unit, and culminating activities:

1. The introductory part of the unit should connect this unit with prior learning or backgrounds of experience, determine the needs of the students and their strengths in this area of study (through pretests or informal discussions), and arouse interest in the topic and motivate students to study it. Methods and activities for this part of the unit should be of high interest; frequently, they should vary from the usual classroom routine. When a theme studies approach is used, the students often have much input in the choice of the theme. This results in a high level of motivation because of their sense of "ownership" of the topic.

2. The body of the unit should address the teaching of each objective, matching teaching procedures and student activities, including assignments, to objectives. Include evaluative measures as needed. With a theme studies approach, the students will have some choice of activities and assignments, once again promoting motivation.

3. Culminating activities for the unit should tie together all the previous learning. Frequently, culminating activities include practical applications of the concepts acquired in the unit, interrelating the various concepts. Teachers and students may choose these activities together. Overall evaluative measures may be a part of the culminating activities.

Vary your planned activities. This will help keep the students' attention and can help your unit progress more smoothly, because certain activities suit certain types of learning better than others. Consider audiovisual aids, field trips, resource people, class discussions, library research activities, computer searches, simulations and dramatizations, construction activities, oral and written reports, games, demonstrations, and creative applications. Be sure, however, that all activities relate directly to unit objectives.

CASE STUDY 6.1

Failure to Follow Through

Jerry Clement was planning a unit on law enforcement. Jerry's cooperating teacher, Mrs. Granger, knew an excellent resource person, Mr. McDonald, whom Jerry might use in the course of his unit. She told Jerry about Mr. McDonald and, to her surprise, discovered that Jerry was a friend of his. She strongly suggested that Jerry ask Mr. McDonald to come to the class and share his knowledge with the students. Jerry seemed to think this was a good idea, but he never actually contacted Mr. McDonald. At the end of the term, Jerry was surprised that his cooperating teacher rated him lower than he would have liked on use of community resources.

1. Do you believe that having a resource person speak to the class would have enhanced Jerry's unit? Why or why not?
2. If you had been Jerry, what would you have done if you decided that having Mr. McDonald would not add substantially to your unit?

Decide on the different forms of evaluation you intend to use during the course of the unit, to be sure you haven't overrelied on a single type. Consider the use of formal and informal written tests, oral or performance tests, observation of students' performance in activities and discussions, evaluation of daily in-class and homework assignments, conferences with individual pupils, and portfolios of work, among other evaluation methods.

Estimate the time needed for the various instructional procedures and student activities, and make tentative decisions about daily coverage. Make adjustments if your plans do not fit the allotted time.

Consult your cooperating teacher about the plan you have constructed. If it meets with the teacher's approval, you are ready to make detailed daily lesson

---

A. Topic and overall time allotment
B. Students' characteristics and backgrounds
C. Resources and materials
D. Unit objectives
E. Unit procedures
   1. Introduction
   2. Body
   3. Culminating activities
F. Evaluation

FIGURE 6–2
Unit Plan Outline*

*See Appendix B for sample unit plans.

plans based on your unit plan. Figure 6–2 shows a brief outline to use in unit planning.

If you remember that a unit of work is a series of interrelated lessons clustered around a central theme, then you will probably plan a good unit. Poor units are characterized by lack of continuity and interrelatedness and by irrelevant activities.

Complete Activity 6.3 as you plan your first thematic unit. You may wish to photocopy this activity form and use it for other units as well.

FOR YOUR PORTFOLIO

Choose the best unit that you have planned and taught for inclusion in your portfolio.

PLANNING FOR EVALUATION

You will need to check students' progress through various means—observation, informal techniques, and formal tests—as you teach. These evaluative activities will help you to decide whether or not learning is taking place.

Teaching without evaluation is like taking a trip without checking the map to see that you are going in the right direction. Periodic assessment enables you to observe students' progress and then make adjustments in your instruction that enable students to achieve instructional goals.

Evaluation is an important component of any instructional plan, but it is not an easy task. You will want to know: How do I find out how well my students

ACTIVITY 6.3   *Thematic Unit Planning Form*

Unit topic:

Overall time allotment:

Students' characteristics that need to be considered in teaching this unit:

List of resources and materials:

Unit objectives:

Unit procedures:

     Introduction:

     Body (list of lessons—*not* complete lesson plans, activities, and assignments):

     Culminating activities:

Evaluation:

are learning? What kinds of tests should I give? How often should I give them? How difficult should the questions be? What happens if everyone fails, or if everyone gets a perfect score? What can I learn from the test results that will help me plan instruction? How can I measure different types of learning, and how can I be sure that my assessment techniques are appropriate for measuring each student's ability in various situations? You probably know some of the answers to these questions from courses in evaluation and measurement, from your own experiences as a student, and from observations of your cooperating teacher. In this section, you should find the answers to other questions.

CASE STUDY 6.2

Difficulty of Evaluation

Mr. Todd has been a student teacher in eighth grade for 4 weeks and has become aware that evaluating students' progress is more difficult than he expected. Instead of simply averaging test scores, Mr. Todd finds that he should probably consider a number of other factors as well. Five students in particular puzzle Mr. Todd.

Amy is alert, interested, outgoing, and talkative. She always has her hand up to answer questions, even though she sometimes can't answer correctly. Despite her eagerness and enthusiasm during class, however, Amy makes very low grades on tests. Her written work is below average for the class.

George appears bored during class, often gazes out the window, and seldom participates in class discussions. He makes average grades on tests. Mr. Todd notices, however, that George shows spurts of interest and creativity when the class works on special projects. He appears to be a natural leader during group work and can analyze and solve problems remarkably well.

Julie Beth is a straight-A student. She rarely participates in class discussions and seems very nervous when called on to respond in class. Her homework is meticulous, but she never shows any interest in class activities other than what is required for getting good grades.

Barry is a careful, thorough worker. He pays close attention to details and conscientiously and systematically completes all assignments. He is never able to finish a test within the time limits, however, so his test scores are low.

Carol races through her work so that she can read her library books. She catches on quickly to new material and readily grasps difficult concepts. Her work is sloppy and careless, however, and she seldom turns in her homework. Her test scores are average.

1. From the information given, what do you believe are the learning strengths and weaknesses of each student?
2. For which students, if any, do you think test scores accurately reflect ability?
3. What factors should a teacher consider when evaluating students?
4. How can evaluation help a teacher plan appropriate instruction to meet individual needs?

Informal Evaluation Techniques

As a student teacher or practicum student, you will usually evaluate students' progress informally, although you may occasionally give a major examination covering a unit. The most useful information you are likely to get is from day-to-day observations, samples of students' work, and short quizzes for checking students' understanding of the material you are presenting.

Observation.   You have many opportunities to observe students in different situations, both academic (during class) and social (before and after class or during extracurricular activities). If you observe purposefully, perhaps by using the Observation Guide in Activity 6.4, you can find out a lot about how students learn. You can determine which students are self-motivated, easily distracted, uninterested, quick to learn, or capable of better work. You'll find that some possess leadership qualities while others prefer to be part of a group, and that some are naturally attentive and eager to learn while others appear bored and uninterested. As you systematically observe your students, you are acquiring information that will help you plan lessons and activities to meet the wide range of individual differences within any class.

Teacher-Made Quizzes.   You need to consider certain factors when planning your testing program. After identifying the objectives and content to be covered in a test, make sure your test distributes the emphasis appropriately over the content. For example, if most instructional time has been spent on identifying main ideas in novels, be sure the greater part of the test asks questions about main ideas in novels, not about interpreting the mood projected by the authors. After assigning relative importance to the topics to be tested, you must decide what type of test items to use—for example, completion, short-answer, essay, true-false, matching, or multiple-choice. Completion, true-false, multiple-choice, and short-answer items are often used for short assessments. Essay items are best for major examinations that require students to organize and present a careful discussion.

A review quiz can be part of a lesson plan. The quiz may be oral, or it may be a short written one of perhaps three to five questions, limited to the material taught in the immediate lesson. The quiz should be varied, with true-false and short-answer items. The main purpose of such a quiz is to see what concepts each student has not grasped or perhaps has misunderstood. It may be marked by the students and then checked by you.

A longer test may be appropriate periodically. It may have 20 to 25 true-false, multiple-choice, and short-answer questions. Such a test should be duplicated, rather than written on the board or dictated.

A unit test covers a larger block of teaching and may require most of a class period to complete. You will want to have several parts, including short essay items. You should prepare a standard answer sheet before marking the test, so that you will be consistent in your grading.

Some teachers give midterms and final examinations to cover a half or whole semester of instruction. You may want to assign points to each part of the examination in terms of its percentage of the whole test. These percentages should reflect the importance of the material covered to the class objectives.

Completion items are often used to measure knowledge of names, dates, terms, and other simple associations. Choose only important concepts, and make sure only one response correctly completes the statement. Short-answer items are similar in format to completion items.

True-false items should cover only important content, not trivial items. Avoid use of words, such as *all* and *never,* that may give clues to correct answers. Avoid negative statements, since students often miss such items through misreading them, rather than because they don't know the answer. To discourage guessing, a true-false test may call for inclusion of a reason for any item marked "false."

Matching items are often used to test knowledge of definitions or identification of objects presented graphically or pictorially. To help eliminate guessing, present extra possible response items.

Multiple-choice items should be in the form of questions involving complete ideas. The four or five possible responses should be grammatically and logically consistent and similar in length, and correct responses should appear in all positions over the course of the test (for example, not invariably as the third choice or the last choice).

Essay items should be phrased carefully, specifically defining the expectations for each answer. Directions must be thorough and specific as to the number of points or percentage weight to be assigned to each question. The answer key should contain the essential components of the answer, and you should score papers against these components.

Traditional types of test questions are not always suitable for evaluating certain types of knowledge. For example, it is better to judge a student's writing competence by evaluating actual writing samples than by asking objective questions about, for example, placement of commas and spelling of words. Also, when evaluating higher-order thinking skills, teachers should design open-ended test questions that allow students to give various solutions or interpretations.

Some guidelines for administering informal tests are:

1. Make sure that your test is based on the material you have taught.
2. Ask "fair" questions. Avoid using misleading, ambiguous questions or questions that relate to insignificant material.
3. Make sure that students have the materials they need for taking the test (sharpened pencils with erasers, enough paper, and so forth).
4. Give clear instructions, and make sure that students understand what they are to do. You may need to do an example with the students before they begin.
5. Be certain that students understand the purpose of the test.
6. Let students know your expectations regarding neatness and correct spelling and punctuation.
7. Space students so that they will not be tempted to cheat.
8. Walk quietly around the room while the students are taking the test, and make sure they are following directions.
9. Make sure that students understand your grading policy.
10. Make a scoring key on one copy of the test you are giving.
11. When grading papers, always give students the benefit of the doubt.
12. Return tests promptly, and go over them with the students so that they can learn from their mistakes.
13. Make sure that students understand the meanings of their scores in terms of letter grades and percentages of total grades.
14. Do not change a grade unless you have made an error in grading the test.

ACTIVITY 6.4   **Observation Guide**

This observation guide will help you make systematic observations of students, which will help you plan learning experiences. You may wish to make copies of this observation guide for all your students, or you may prefer to make copies only for selected students.

Student's Name _____

Key:

_____ 1. Volunteers to answer questions posed to class   A—Always occurs

_____ 2. Listens carefully during class time; follows directions   B—Often occurs

_____ 3. Asks questions about what is not understood   C—Occasionally occurs

_____ 4. Completes homework assignments   D—Seldom occurs

_____ 5. Participates in voluntary projects   E—Never occurs

_____ 6. Likes to help others and share activities with them

_____ 7. Projects a good self-image

_____ 8. Attends regularly

_____ 9. Performs well on quizzes

_____ 10. Uses resource materials well

If all of your students made perfect or nearly perfect scores on the test, it means that either you taught very well, the students were very bright or studied very hard, the test was too easy, or some combination of these factors existed. If nearly all the students did poorly on the test, it may mean that they didn't understand the material, they didn't study, or the test was too difficult. If the problem seems to be that they didn't learn the material, you may need to reteach it. Your cooperating teacher can advise you on these matters.

Rubrics.   Rubrics are essentially scoring guides that identify the characteristics of students' work at different levels of quality. For example, a rubric would list the characteristics of a high-quality paper or presentation; then it would list the characteristics of each succeeding lower level of quality. For example, a high-quality research paper might be designated as one in which the writer defines the topic in an exemplary fashion, presents an abundance of relevant information, includes information from several sources (possibly a designated number of sources) in a completely integrated fashion, presents thorough documentation, organizes the material well, and uses correct mechanics (syntax, spelling, etc.). A medium-quality paper might be one in which the writer defines the topic adequately, presents some relevant information, includes information from several sources with some attempt at integration, presents documentation that is minimally adequate, has a recognizable organizational pattern, and generally uses correct mechanics. Lower levels would be similarly described, allowing you to evaluate the research paper in a holistic manner.

If you give each characteristic in a scoring rubric (for example, definition of topic or presentation of relevant information) a numerical value (excellent = 5, very good = 4, average = 3, low = 2, very low = 1), analytic scoring can be achieved, and you can generate a numerical score by adding the ratings for all characteristics. Different characteristics may be weighted differently by multiplying each score by the percentage of the total score that you want it to represent.

Computer Applications to Testing.   Computers can be useful in assessing students' progress, but school systems vary in the availability of computers and software designed for assessment and test analysis. If computers are available for your students to use, you may assess their knowledge of skills by observing their completion of class-related computer activities or by giving tests on the computer.

If a computer is available for your use, you may wish to use it for test construction and analysis of grades. Even if you are not a good typist, you can use a word processor for preparing your tests because you can readily make corrections. Word-processing programs allow you to edit test questions and move items from one section of the test to another easily and efficiently. "Authoring" software designed to assist your test construction may also be available at your school, as may computer programs to help you average grades, analyze the difficulty of individual test items, and keep records of students' scores.

Formal Tests

Most school systems administer formal standardized tests only once or twice a year, so you may not have an opportunity to give one to your students. Nevertheless, you should be able to interpret the scores and understand the place of formal tests in measuring students' progress.

Norms are averages of test scores of students in the norming population. They are ordinarily applied to formal or standardized tests.

Group achievement tests serve the purpose of telling the teacher how the *class*, not an individual class member, is performing in comparison with other groups of students. The most important score is the class average, which helps the teacher determine whether the class is performing about the same as, better than, or worse than students elsewhere.

Standardized tests report norms in several ways:

1. *Grade equivalents*—The grade level for which a given score is a real or estimated average. Scores are expressed in terms of grade and month of grade, such as 4.8 for fourth grade, eighth month.
2. *Percentile rank*—Expression of a test score in terms of its position within a group of 100 scores. The percentile rank of a score is the percentage of scores equal to or lower than the given score in some reference group.
3. *Stanine*—One of the steps in a nine-point scale of standard scores. The stanine scale has values from 1 to 9, with a mean (average) of 5.

Table 6–1 summarizes the types of tests that are appropriate for different assessment purposes.

TABLE 6–1	**Purpose**	**Appropriate Types of Tests**
Guide for Selecting Tests	To check short-term progress	Short, objective written quizzes; oral questioning sessions; computer drill and practice
	To check depth of understanding of a subject	Thought-provoking essay questions
	To evaluate writing ability	Writing samples (evaluated using rubrics), essay questions, journals
	To assess problem-solving and thinking skills	Observation of performance, open-ended test questions
	To evaluate learning over an extended time period	Typed or word-processed examinations with a variety of questions (such as essay, true-false, multiple-choice, and completion)
	To assess skill mastery	Short-answer or completion questions, computer practice
	To get a quick estimate of reading ability or level	Observation of oral reading performance and answers to oral comprehension questions
	To compare achievement with that of students across the nation	Standardized achievement tests

Portfolio Assessment

Many educators believe that test scores alone do not accurately reflect what students can do. One popular alternative that many have embraced is portfolio assessment. Portfolios are collections of varied, representative samples of students' work over a period of time or examples of the students' best work in specific areas. Although informal tests can be part of a portfolio, work samples—such as drafts of students' writing or audiotapes of oral reading—are more likely to be present. The following items are among those that may be included: writing samples, project reports, lists of books read, tape recordings of oral reading, students' self-appraisals, semantic maps, checklists, illustrations, selected daily work, informal quizzes, teacher's notes on observations, literature logs (responses to reading), content area journals, pictures of project results, videotapes of presentations, multimedia presentations on disk, parents' comments, reflective analysis of portfolio contents, and a table of contents that shows the organization of the material.

At the secondary level, portfolios can be designed specifically for each subject. The following are examples of things that may be included in different areas.

- *Art*—Collages; prints; portraits; still lifes; sketches from rough draft to finished form; photographs of sculptures, weaving, and other three-

dimensional pieces; printouts of websites that have been designed; and analyses of various art processes students have used.
- *Science*—Reports on the progress of experiments, drawings (diagrams and charts), biographies of scientists, labeled earth samples, statistical data for projects, journals of direct observations of phenomena, videotapes of experiments or presentations, multimedia presentations on disk.
- *Composition*—Initial and all other drafts through publication of articles and stories, note cards, letters, poems, and essays.

If you decide to use portfolios, you need to explain to the students what you are doing and why. Students need to understand that, instead of simply averaging test and daily work grades, you will be asking for their help in evaluating samples of their work. Together with the students, you should establish guidelines for the types of material to include. In most cases, selections should relate to instructional goals and represent the students' work processes and best work; otherwise, portfolios can become stuffed with all sorts of materials that may have little value for analysis. Make sure that students date each piece of work so that you and they can see the progress they are making. You should plan to have individual conferences with

FIGURE 6–3
Key Concepts for Using Portfolio Assessment

Portfolio inclusions relate to instructional goals.

Students engage in reflective and critical thinking as they select and review their work.

Both teacher and students select material for inclusion in portfolios.

Periodically, the teacher and students have conferences about portfolios, noting changes and progress, discovering insights, and seeking new directions for growth and learning.

Portfolios combine instruction and assessment by looking at the learning process as well as the product.

Portfolios are accessible to students at any time; they are working folders.

Students and teachers become partners in learning as they cooperatively assess students' work.

students about their portfolios periodically to discuss the items and assess progress.

Although you may require students to include certain samples of their work, letting them select most items for their portfolios is a worthwhile activity. Making decisions about what to include and how to organize the contents causes students to use critical thinking skills, reflect on the merits of their work, and evaluate their progress. In fact, you may ask them to write on cards or large stick-on notes why they selected particular pieces to include. When they do this, they must justify their selections, and you will see what they value about their work.

You may additionally want to place in students' folders some of your observations, such as anecdotal notes about their contributions during class discussions. You may also want to include checklists about such areas as their progress toward achieving literacy or their participation in a social studies unit. Some key ideas for using portfolios are given in Figure 6–3.

Portfolio assessment requires additional time and effort, but it can be extremely informative about how and what your students are learning. Portfolios are also useful for conferences with parents because you can show examples of what students are actually doing in class. Additionally, portfolios provide you with supporting information when you fill out report cards. You may want to try portfolio assessment for just one 6-week period to see how it goes. (See Activity 6.5 for using portfolio assessment.) If the system works well, you may want to continue using it. You and the students, along with your cooperating teacher, must decide what happens to the portfolios when you leave. Your cooperating teacher may want either to keep them, pass them along to next year's teacher, give them to the students to keep, or send them home to parents.

DISCUSSION QUESTIONS

1. What are some different lesson plan forms you might use? What are advantages and disadvantages of each form?
2. Are units more effective in your teaching situation when they cut across disciplines or when they are chosen from content within a single discipline? Why do you think so? Is there a place for both types of units?
3. How would you modify the observation guide (Activity 6.4) to fit your particular class or classes?
4. What types of tests would be appropriate for the following situations?

   a. To see if a group of third-graders can divide words into syllables
   b. To discover the reasoning powers of high school students in relation to foreign policy
   c. To assess the knowledge gained during a 6-week unit on plant life
   d. To find out how your class compares with the national average on mathematical computation
   e. To assess the creative writing abilities of students
   f. To check understanding of last night's homework assignment, which was to read part of a chapter from the textbook

5. How might test scores indicate which students are or are not working up to their ability?
6. How does evaluation enable a teacher to plan better instruction?
7. In the grade or subject you teach, what items would be appropriate to include in an assessment portfolio? How would you guide students in selecting which items to include?

SELECTED REFERENCES

American Association for the Advancement of Science. (1993). *Project 2061: Benchmarks for Science Literacy.* Washington, DC: Author.

Anthony, R. J., Johnson, T. D., Mickelson, N. I., & Preece, A. (1991). *Evaluating literacy.* Portsmouth, NH: Heinemann.

Batzle, J. (1992). *Portfolio assessment and evaluation.* Cypress, CA: Creative Teaching.

Beane, J. A. (1995, April). Curriculum integration and the disciplines of knowledge. *Phi Delta Kappan, 76* 616–622.

Charbonneau, M. P., & Reider, B. E. (1995). *The integrated elementary classroom.* Boston: Allyn and Bacon.

Clark, R. W., & Wasley, P. (1999, April). Renewing schools and smarter kids: Promises for democracy. *Phi Delta Kappan, 90,* 590–596.

DeFina, A. A. (1992). *Portfolio assessment.* New York: Scholastic.

Farr, R. (1992, September). Putting it all together: Solving the reading assessment puzzle. *The Reading Teacher, 46,* 26–37.

Farr, R., & Tone, B. (1994). *Portfolio and performance assessment.* Fort Worth, TX: Harcourt Brace.

Frank, M. (1994). *Using writing portfolios to enhance instruction and assessment.* Nashville, TN: Incentive.

Gamberg, R., Kwak, W., Hutchings, M., Altheim, J., & Edwards, G. (1988). *Learning and loving it: Theme studies in the classroom.* Portsmouth, NH: Heinemann.

Glazer, S. M. (1994, August/September). How you can use tests and portfolios, too. *Teaching K–8, 25,* 152, 154.

Glazer, S., & Brown, C. (1993). *Portfolios and beyond: Collaborative assessment in reading and writing.* Norwood, MA: Christopher-Gordon.

Grady, E. (1992). *The portfolio approach to assessment.* Bloomington, IN: Phi Delta Kappa.

Harp, B. (Ed.). (1994). *Assessment and evaluation for student centered learning* (2nd ed.). Norwood, MA: Christopher-Gordon.

Jasmine, J. (1993). *Portfolios and other assessments.* Huntington Beach, CA: Teacher Created Materials.

Johnston, P. H. (1992). *Constructive evaluation of literate activity.* New York: Longman.

Lipson, M. Y., Valencia, S. W., Wixon, K. K., & Peters, C. W. (1993, April). Integration and thematic teaching: Integration to improve teaching and learning. *Language Arts, 70,* 252–263.

McCarthy, R. (1994, May/June). Assessing the whole student. *Instructor Special Supplement, 18.*

National Council for the Social Studies. (1994). *Expectations of excellence: Curriculum standards for social studies.* Washington, DC: Author.

National Council of Teachers of English/International Reading Association. (1996). *Standards for the English language arts.* Urbana, IL: Author.

National Council of Teachers of Mathematics. (1989). *Curriculum and evaluation standards for school mathematics.* Reston, VA: Author.

National Council of Teachers of Mathematics. (1998). *Principles and standards for school mathematics: Discussion draft.* Reston, VA: Author.

National Geographic Society. (1994). *Geography for life: The national geography standards.* Washington, DC: Author.

National Research Council. (1998). *National science education standards.* Washington, DC: National Academy Press.

National Skills Standards Board. (1998). *Occupational skills standards projects.* Washington, DC: Author.

O'Neil, J. (1994, August). Making assessment meaningful. *ASCD Update, 36,* 1, 4–5.

Panaritis, P. (1995, April). Beyond brainstorming: Planning a successful interdisciplinary program. *Phi Delta Kappan, 76,* 623–628.

Peters, T., Schubeck, K., & Hopkins, K. (1995, April). A thematic approach: Theory and practice at the Aleknagik School. *Phi Delta Kappan, 76,* 633–636.

Valencia, S. (1990, January). A portfolio approach to classroom reading assessment: The whys, whats, and hows. *The Reading Teacher, 43,* 338–340.

Valencia, S., Hiebert, E., & Afflerbach, P. (Eds.). (1994). *Authentic reading assessment: Practices and possibilities.* Newark, DE: International Reading Association.

Wepner, S. B. (1992, April). Using technology with content area units. *The Reading Teacher, 45,* 644–645.

Wepner, S. B. (1992, November). Technology and thematic units: A primary example. *The Reading Teacher, 46,* 260–263.

Wepner, S. B. (1993, February). Technology and thematic units: An elementary example on Japan. *The Reading Teacher, 46,* 442–445.

ACTIVITY 6.5   *Summary Sheet for Portfolio Assessment*

Complete this summary sheet for your conferences with your students. You will probably want to make enough photocopies of this page for all your students.

Grade: _____   Subject: _____   Date: _____

List of items in portfolio:

Student's assessment of portfolio items:

Teacher's assessment of portfolio items:

Conclusions and recommendations:

Student's signature _____

Language, Thinking, and Learning across the Curriculum

Making Sense of Text

Mr. Viera, a student teacher, had led his students in a unit on the Holocaust. He had involved them in planning and implementing the unit by finding out what they already knew and what they wanted to know, by helping them to locate resources, and by discussing events during that time period. The students found several books related to the Holocaust, and one student brought some sample identification cards from the Holocaust Memorial Museum in Washington, D.C. It was time to turn to the text and ask students to read the chapter dealing with the Holocaust.

Despite Mr. Viera's careful introduction, many of the students had trouble comprehending the text. Some found it difficult, and others were completely confused.

Mr. Viera (attempting to clear up the problems): What can you do when you try to make sense out of what's in the textbook?

Beth: I just keep reading till I get to the end. I don't know what else to do.

Mr. Viera: But if you don't understand what you are reading, isn't there something you can do about it?

Juanita: Sometimes I go back and read the parts I don't understand over again slowly until I get it.

Mr. Viera: Good idea! Let's write some of your ideas on a chart so you can refer to them as you read. (He begins recording students' ideas.) Does anyone else do something while you're reading if you don't understand?

Clay: I sort of predict what I think is going to happen and then read on to see if I got it right.

Jamie: I try to put it in my own words. The textbook has big words, and I try to put it in easy words.

Mr. Viera: That's called paraphrasing, and it's a good strategy to use. We're going to have a test covering this chapter on Friday. What are some things you can do to help you study?

Carl: I like to write down the important names and dates so that I can remember them.

Steve: And sometimes I say things out loud to myself to help me concentrate.

Mr. Viera: These are good ideas. Anyone else?

Mateo: There's a glossary in the back of the book. I can look up words there if I don't know what they mean.

Veronica: The headings and subheadings help me get my thoughts straight. They sort of give the main idea of what's coming.

Carol: Sometimes I study with Betsy. She asks me questions and I ask her questions so we know if we understand it.

Mr. Viera: That works, as long as you stay focused on the subject. There's something else that you should all do.

Jon: We can think about what we already learned about the Holocaust, like how we pretended to write our experiences in journals and how we acted out how the prisoners must have felt. And we can think about the books and pictures we found.

Mr. Viera: That's one of the most important things to do. Think about what you already know and use that knowledge as you read more about the subject. You've come up with a pretty good list, and we can add to it if we think of something else later. First, you need to know whether you understand it or not; then, if you don't understand, you need to find some strategies like the ones you just listed. When you read, always be sure you're getting the meaning. If the text isn't making sense to you, do something about it!

1. How was Mr. Viera's questioning useful for his students? Was he right to take time to discuss reading and study strategies?

2. Do you think all the students will begin to apply these strategies after this lesson? If not, what else could Mr. Viera do to make sure students use them?

3. What were some of the ideas he used during the presentation of the unit? Were these good teaching strategies?

4. What are some options that you have as the teacher if the text is indeed too difficult or confusing for the students to read?

RELATIONSHIPS AMONG LANGUAGE, THINKING, AND LEARNING

Language and thinking are intricately related. People use language to think; without using words and sentences, it is virtually impossible to think, and it is certainly impossible to express complex or abstract ideas. By improving skill in language use, teachers develop an important tool for higher-order thinking. Study skills, such as those involving location and organization of information, retention, interpretation, and metacognition, involve the use of higher-order thinking skills and effective use of language. Study skills promote the effective learning of content presented in classes. Therefore, all the areas focused on in this chapter promote effective learning.

LANGUAGE ARTS

Language skills are vital to your students' success in all curricular areas. If you are an elementary grade teacher, you may have a special period devoted to language arts instruction, during which you will teach listening, speaking, reading, and writing. Secondary English teachers will also be expected to include these language arts in their instruction. Simply focusing on language skills in a separate period is not sufficient for their complete assimilation, however. Language is used daily in all classes. Elementary teachers should help students apply language skills throughout the day as the students read to complete assignments, give and listen to oral reports, participate in discus-

sions, and complete written assignments. Secondary teachers of content areas other than English should try to reinforce language skills as they are needed for assignments.

Reading Proficiency and School Assignments

Students are expected to learn much content from their textbooks and other supplementary printed materials. Often, however, the textbooks chosen for use in particular classes are too difficult for many of the students to handle with ease. It is important for you to be aware of the difficulty of the materials the students are asked to read and to provide appropriate alternative materials for students who cannot handle the standard assignments.

Reading assignments may be adjusted for students who are unable to read the text or other assignments by providing those students with easier texts or materials that cover the same topics or by writing explanations of key concepts at easier reading levels for their use. It is also possible for you or a good reader from the class to tape the assignments and make the tapes available to poor readers to listen to as they "read" the assignments. By following along in their books as they listen, they should pick up some of the key terms and add them to their sight vocabularies, easing the reading of further assignments in this subject area. If you delegate the taping to students, be sure to check the materials before you release them for use by their classmates. Poorly prepared materials can do more harm than good. Using videos or other

Teachers should be prepared to help students apply their language skills as they read and complete written and oral assignments.

media, manipulatives, and activities such as creative dramatics and simulations also helps students who have difficulty in reading assignments.

If you want to promote comprehension of the reading material that you assign, give students purposes for the reading. Purpose questions help students focus on important information and promote comprehension and retention of the material, but remember that good purposes will be of no value if assignments are too difficult for the students to handle. Another way to help students set purposes for reading is to ask them for predictions about what the material will say or to have them decide upon questions that they hope the material will answer for them.

You can also enhance reading comprehension by building background for reading material that you are about to assign. Class discussions, films or videotapes, pictures, computer simulations, and class demonstrations can all provide background concepts that will make the reading assignment easier to understand. Introduction of new vocabulary terms related to the concepts at this point can help students acquire the information in the assignment more readily. This approach works because vocabulary terms are labels for the concepts that are presented, and knowing the proper labels makes discussion of the concepts easier.

Writing across the Curriculum

Writing is also a skill that is used in every area of the curriculum. In English and language arts classes, students are taught how to write effectively, but in all classes writing provides an effective technique for learning. You should take advantage of this technique in your classes. Although you will focus on composition and mechanics of writing if you are an English teacher, you may employ some writing assignments that are primarily designed to help students learn other things that you are teaching. If you teach another subject, you may occasionally ignore split infinitives and comma splices in favor of focusing exclusively on the student's message. Of course, if the message is obscured by poor mechanics, a teachable moment for this skill area exists. Students will not succeed in many future endeavors if their writing skills are not sufficient for clear communication.

Ways to use writing as a tool for learning in different curricular areas include having students write summaries of class lectures, which can sometimes be shared with the class and revised as needed; explanations of new concepts presented in the textbook or in class; descriptions of processes being studied; reactions to curricular material; and descriptions of applications for ideas presented in class. The following list shows some ways for students to apply writing skills in various areas of the curriculum.

- *Literature*—Writing imaginative newspaper accounts of happenings in a novel, character sketches of major characters, diary entries that a character might have written.
- *Science*—Recording the results of an experiment, composing an essay about the impact of a scientific discovery on society, tracing the development of an area of technology over a period of time.
- *Social studies*—Producing imaginary letters from one historical character to another, writing reactions to the actions of a historical character, writing explanations about the causes of historical events.
- *Physical education*—Writing directions for a sports activity or an exercise, writing about the benefits of an exercise program.
- *Art and music*—Writing descriptions of techniques or reactions to paintings, sculptures, and compositions.
- *Home economics*—Writing case studies related to child care techniques or nutritional practices, writing about advantages and disadvantages of certain home management practices.

There is no area in which writing opportunities are not available, and these activities can help students organize their knowledge, as well as clarify their feelings, about many topics. Having students write about their studies gives you a chance to see each student's current level of understanding of the topics and allows you to plan instruction to overcome misconceptions. The writing activities also make students more aware of what they already know and what they need to find out. Personal journals, which may be read by others only at the invitation of the students who produced them, may allow students to explore their feelings and clarify their personal beliefs.

Consider possible writing activities as you plan each lesson. Think about possible benefits of each activity, and choose judiciously. These activities—if they are handled well—can offer dividends in initial learning and retention and may even improve attitudes toward the area of study. Complete Activity 7.1 to help you analyze your use of writing in your classes.

Literature across the Curriculum

Literature is often relegated to English class, especially in secondary schools. Many teachers have found, however, that literature can enrich other curricular areas as well. Integrating literature across the curriculum can be accomplished more easily in self-contained classroom situations than in departmentalized settings, but it can provide rewarding results for teachers in departmentalized settings if they work together as a team.

ACTIVITY 7.1   *Writing across the Curriculum*

Place a checkmark (✓) before the writing activities that you have used or intend to use in your class or classes. After you have tried each activity, place a plus (+) after the activity if it worked well or a minus (−) after the activity if it was not successful in meeting your goals.

_____   Summaries of class lectures _____
_____   Summaries of textbook readings _____
_____   Summaries of outside reading assignments _____
_____   Explanations of new concepts _____
_____   Descriptions of processes being studied _____
_____   Reactions to material presented in the texbook or in class _____
_____   Applications of ideas presented in class or in the textbook _____
_____   Newspaper accounts based on material read _____
_____   Character sketches of real or fictional characters _____
_____   Diary entries that real or fictional characters might have written _____
_____   Results of experiments _____
_____   Explanation of impact on society of a scientific discovery or political action _____
_____   Account of the development of an area of technology over a period of time _____
_____   Imaginary letters from one historical or fictional character to another _____
_____   Written reactions to the actions of one historical or fictional character _____
_____   Written explanations about the causes of historical events _____
_____   Written directions for a game or other activity _____
_____   Explanation of benefits of an exercise program or particular diet _____
_____   Written description of an artistic technique _____
_____   Written reactions to works of art _____
_____   Case studies _____
_____   Personal journals _____
_____   Other _____
_____   Please describe:

_____   Other _____
_____   Please describe:

_____   Other _____
_____   Please describe:

Social studies classes are a natural place to use literature to enrich the curriculum. Both fiction and nonfiction selections set in specific historical periods can make these times come alive for readers. Many stories in books, for example, are set during wars, and they can help the students see, in a way that history textbooks cannot, how these wars affected the people's lives. Similarly, stories in books that are set in particular geographic regions can add to the understanding of material presented in a geography text. Books are also available that clarify lifestyles and occupations for students. Biographies of important historical figures can make these people's contributions to civilization clearer, and books about people from diverse cultures can help students to understand themselves and others better.

Literature can also help students in science classes understand scientific concepts and obtain insight into the lives of inventors and innovators. Finding out the painstaking experimentation behind many scientific discoveries can put textbook information in perspective. Reading books that focus upon a single aspect of science, such as the solar system, also can be helpful to students, since material in textbooks has often been condensed so much that its clarity has suffered. A book on a single topic has the space to elaborate on and flesh out spare textbook discussions. Books that contain experiments for the students to perform allow hands-on experiences that promote motivation and understanding of concepts. Many books for young children highlight the cycles of the seasons and life cycles of plants and animals. Many books focus on conservation and the environment.

In physical education classes students may read books about the sports that they are playing or biographies of sports personalities. Both factual how-to-play books and fictional and factual stories about sports can add interest and motivation to these classes.

Even in mathematics classes, literature can be useful. Books are available for young children that emphasize counting, concepts of numbers, telling time, understanding calendars, learning about measurements, and comprehending concepts of size. Older students may enjoy and learn from mathematical puzzle books, such as these two books by Martin Gardner: *The Unexpected Hanging and Other Mathematical Diversions* (University of Chicago Press, 1991) and *My Best Mathematical and Logic Puzzles* (Dover, 1994).

Applications of literature in English classes are numerous. Literature can be used to study genres, characterization, plots, settings, themes, and writing styles. It can be used to promote literary appreciation, or it can serve as a stimulus for writing. Comparisons and contrasts of literature selections can reveal information about genres, cultures, and points of view, among other things. An English class without literature would be unthinkable, but many uses of literature may not be included in English classes, if the teacher fails to examine the many possibilities that exist. Activity 7.2 gives you a chance to assess your use of literature in the class or classes that you teach.

Constructivism

Constructivism means that learners construct their own knowledge instead of reproducing someone else's knowledge (Zahorik, 1995). They create understanding as they try to make sense of their experiences. For example, two students may get different meanings from reading the same selection or from participating in the same event because of differences in their prior experiences and attitudes. People's knowledge and understanding can also change over time as they learn more, have more experiences, and understand at deeper levels.

Constructivist teaching emphasizes thinking, understanding, and self-control over behavior. Many of the teaching strategies you have learned and will continue to use are likely to be constructivist, as are many of the ideas presented in this chapter. Some characteristics of constructivist teaching and their classroom applications appear in Figure 7–1.

Think about your own beliefs regarding teaching practices. Then complete Activity 7.3 to see if you are a constructivist.

FOR YOUR PORTFOLIO

After completing Activity 7.3, write a summary of the teaching practices that you plan to use. Begin with a statement of your philosophy about instruction.

HIGHER-ORDER THINKING SKILLS

The current interest in higher-order thinking skills in education is making many teachers aware of the need to help students learn how to think, not just recall information. Thought processes, including learning how to learn, are far more useful for dealing with life than knowledge of facts. In and of themselves, facts have little value, but a person trained in the use of thinking skills can act on knowledge of facts to solve problems, make decisions, and generate new ideas. For additional information on higher-order thinking skills, refer to *http://www.prenhall.com/methods cluster*, "Topic 7: Instructional Strategies," on the

Constructivism	Class Applications
Activate prior knowledge. Relate new knowledge to what is known.	Brainstorm what students know. Create timelines of events.
Focus on the whole, the "big picture." Identify major concepts, not fragments.	Demonstrate square dancing as a whole; don't focus on only one movement at a time.
"Scaffold," or provide support. Build on prior knowledge. Withdraw support gradually.	Model a skill by thinking aloud. Use manipulatives, models, explanations.
Understand concepts. Enable students to explore new content and share views.	Compare a book with its film. Hold debates, role-play, do simulations, make displays.
Use knowledge in authentic, interesting, holistic, long-term, and social ways.	Solve "real-world" problems. Create a quilt or totem based on family traditions.
Reflect on knowledge. Know what you know and how you know it (metacognition).	Write in journals. Do role playing and simulations. Teach someone what you know.

Internet. Knowledge-level skills, such as recognition and recall, are not included in this discussion.

Although you may occasionally want to do some puzzles or problem solving for specific purposes, you should usually integrate thinking skills with subjects across the curriculum instead of teaching them in isolation. Thinking skills then become a natural part of learning. Students not only learn information in each content area, but they also learn how to think about what they are learning.

A Framework

Higher-order thinking skills can be organized in many ways, but the framework for thinking skills in this handbook is relatively simple. It looks like this:

Higher-Order Thinking Skills
Inferential thinking

      Making inferences

      Generalizing and drawing conclusions

      Observing relationships

Critical thinking

      Analysis

      Evaluation

Creative thinking

      Synthesis

      Fluency and flexibility

      Imagination

      Originality

Combinations of thinking skills

      Problem solving

      Decision making

Before looking at ways to implement instruction in thinking skills, you need to understand the meanings of some of these terms.

In *inferential thinking,* the learner must put together clues in order to understand information that is not directly stated, but is implied. *Generalizing* is the process of grasping an overall meaning or purpose from limited information, and *drawing conclusions* is making decisions based on evidence. *Observing relationships* is the mental ability to perceive similar or dissimilar features of ideas or objects. These relationships may be in the form of (1) *classifications* (systematic ways of categorizing), (2) *comparisons and contrasts* (awareness of similarities and differences), or (3) *cause and effect* (observance of the relationships between actions and their consequences).

Critical thinking is the process of mentally acting on something that already exists by interpreting, analyzing, or evaluating it in some way. *Analysis* is the act of breaking down a whole into its parts and studying the relationships of the parts, and *evaluation* is the process of questioning and making judgments based on existing information.

ACTIVITY 7.2   *Literature across the Curriculum*

List four literature selections related to a class or several classes that you are teaching. Note how the use of each of these selections could enrich the teaching of your class or classes.

1. Class:

   SELECTION   USEFULNESS

2. Class:

   SELECTION   USEFULNESS

3. Class:

   SELECTION   USEFULNESS

4. Class:

   SELECTION   USEFULNESS

ACTIVITY 7.3   **Aptitude for Constructivist Teaching**

Respond to each of the following statements by writing *true* or *false*.

I believe . . .

_____   1. Children can and should help each other learn.

_____   2. Children are capable of making reasonable decisions and taking responsibility for much of their own learning.

_____   3. Role playing and simulation can help students understand processes and content.

_____   4. Students should be involved in authentic (real-world) activities whenever possible.

_____   5. Reflection is an important aspect of learning.

_____   6. Learning often occurs through discovery.

_____   7. Modeling by the teacher is an effective way for students to understand various skills and processes.

_____   8. When introducing new material, the teacher should activate students' prior knowledge.

_____   9. Learners should compare their understanding with that of others.

_____ 10. Students should be able to regulate their own behaviors.

_____ 11. More than one interpretation is possible when students discuss issues or literature.

_____ 12. Teachers should provide opportunities for students to be original and creative in their thinking.

_____ 13. Students should see the whole picture first before perfecting each skill that makes up the whole.

_____ 14. Students learn through active involvement, such as hands-on experiences and manipulatives.

_____ 15. Journal writing is a good way for students to reflect and to make them aware of what they know.

_____ 16. One way that students learn is through critiquing, or rethinking and thus strengthening their positions.

_____ 17. Problem solving is a useful strategy because it enables students to apply their knowledge to find solutions to actual problems.

_____ 18. Teachers should provide scaffolding, or support, for students until they are able to work on their own.

Count the number of responses marked "true." If it exceeds the number of responses marked "false," you are leaning toward constructivist teaching.

Unlike inferential and critical thinking, which are reactions to existing ideas, *creative thinking* leads to the development of new and unusual ideas or products. *Synthesis*, like inventiveness, is the process of combining simple ideas or elements into larger concepts or products. In school, synthesis often occurs when students write stories or poems, collaborate on projects, find different solutions to problems, or express ideas or emotions in art. *Fluency* is the ability to generate many ideas, and *flexibility* is the ability to create ideas that fit into many different systems or categories. *Imagination* is an ability that enables the learner to create mental pictures or patterns of things that are not actually present, and *originality* is the ability to produce unique responses.

Some thinking processes, such as *problem solving* and *decision making*, are actually complex combinations of various types of thinking skills. Problem solving consists of several steps, including the following:

1. Identifying a problem
2. Obtaining information related to the problem
3. Forming hypotheses
4. Testing the hypotheses and forming a conclusion
5. Applying the solution and evaluating its effectiveness

Decision making is similar to problem solving, but it involves the following steps:

1. Identifying a goal
2. Collecting relevant data
3. Recognizing obstacles to reaching the goal
4. Identifying alternatives
5. Analyzing and ranking alternatives
6. Choosing the best alternative

You can integrate thinking skills with your teaching in every area of the curriculum from kindergarten through twelfth grade, but be aware that young children are limited in their ability to think abstractly. Not until the age of 10 or 11 are children able to deal successfully with abstract thought and concepts beyond their experiences. Therefore, in the lower grades you should teach the rudiments of various thinking skills by having youngsters manipulate concrete objects or apply these skills to what they already know and understand. In the middle grades students are better prepared for learning higher-order thinking skills because they are now capable of some degree of abstract reasoning and can think outside the realm of personal experiences. By the time they are in high school, students are capable of analyzing situations in greater depth, creating more complex thoughts and products, solving problems logically,

making rational decisions, and evaluating concepts more critically.

If you consider thinking skills to be a high priority in your teaching, you should establish the kind of classroom climate that is conducive to developing them. In order to do this, you need to show respect for your students by accepting their ideas and tolerating their mistakes. Listen to them, help them find alternatives, and show them that there may not be a single correct answer for every situation. Give them time to work through real problems, and provide opportunities to experiment with ideas and materials. Encourage your students by providing constructive feedback, and build their confidence by enabling them to succeed with simple tasks. Perhaps most important of all, learn to think and create along with them so that they can sometimes see you struggle and make mistakes, but then try again and eventually reach a conclusion.

To develop thinking skills in your instruction, you need to structure activities and ask questions that cause students to think critically and creatively. On the next several pages you will find samples of activities for promoting thinking at different grade levels and in different content areas.

Inferential Thinking Activities

Two types of inferential thinking activities—classification and making inferences—are presented here with suggestions for using them. Try to think of other possibilities as you plan your lessons and units.

Classification.   Classification is the process of organizing items or concepts with similar features into categories. In classifying, you first scan the material to get a general impression, then select a characteristic common to more than one item, and finally group together items that share this feature. (Some items may fit logically into more than one category.) You repeat this process until you categorize all the items to be considered. Classifying is based on making comparisons and is one of several ways to see relationships and make meaningful connections.

Children who begin to classify at an early age might group concrete objects with common characteristics together, while slightly older children might categorize pictures that have been cut from magazines or catalogs. Still older students might classify words, concepts, literary works, or artistic masterpieces according to common features. At whatever level students are working, it is important for them to give reasons for their classifications. In order to clarify their thinking and justify their choices of categories, students need to explain the relationships they perceive.

Suppose you give an envelope of pictures of the following items to a group of second-graders and ask them to group the pictures that belong together. The children will probably consider many possibilities and find that some items could be placed in more than one category. Likely categories are given immediately following the items.

Items

set of drums	doll carriage
chalkboard	chair
television set	tape player
cheese	recipe book
toy box	roller skates
computer	lawn mower
stove	harmonica

Possible Classifications

Things with wheels—lawn mower, roller skates, doll carriage

Food-related items—cheese, stove, recipe book

Toys—doll carriage, set of drums, harmonica, toy box, roller skates, chalkboard

Household furnishings—stove, chair, television set, tape player, computer, toy box

Electrical things—television set, computer, tape player, stove

Music—set of drums, tape player, harmonica

Things for reading and writing—computer, recipe book, chalkboard

You can use classification skills as you teach subjects in any area of the curriculum. Some types of classification activities are:

- *Math*—Group objects, pictures, or line drawings by classifications of geometric shapes.
- *Science*—Classify animals according to various attributes.
- *Political science*—Categorize types of governments by salient features.
- *Music*—Classify musical recordings by such types as country, rock, classical, big band, and gospel.
- *Art*—Classify works of art according to their historical periods.
- *Literature*—Group literary works by genre, author's style, or some other characteristic.
- *Geography*—Classify cities by the continents where they are located.
- *History*—Make categories of great people through history (e.g., military leaders, philoso-

phers, artists, heads of state, scientists, and religious leaders).

Making Inferences. Making inferences calls for the ability to observe clues and use them to arrive at implied meanings. It involves thought processes that are similar to those used in drawing conclusions, making predictions, and making generalizations. When you read a murder mystery, you look for clues in order to determine who did it. If you want to know if someone likes you, you watch for behavioral clues, such as a wink or a smile. Frequently, the information you need is not clearly given, so you have to "read between the lines" and then make reasonable assumptions as to the full meaning. Making inferences is an important skill for critical reading and thinking, but students often have a great deal of difficulty learning to use it.

One technique you can use when teaching inferences is the "grab bag" approach, in which you give a bag of objects to a group of students. The objects can be readily available materials that you may have around your home. Students read the directions on the bag and create a story from the objects by making inferences about the objects' relationships to each other. You can use sets of pictures or sets of words and phrases, as well as sets of objects, to teach students to infer. An example follows.

Grab Bag Activity

Contents—An old wallet with three pennies, a "help wanted" ad asking for someone to deliver papers, a handwritten note that says "Do you know anybody who wants firewood for this winter?" and an ad from a catalog with a stereo system circled.

Directions—Someone has a problem. Can you figure out what the problem is from these clues?

Possible answer—A young person wants to earn money to buy a stereo system.

It is important for students to understand *how* they made inferences from the clues in order to transfer this thinking skill to other learning tasks. Students need to use the same thought processes for making inferences with word clues in reading as they used for making inferences from objects. Having students underline word clues in reading selections is a good way to help them make inferences in their reading.

Critical Thinking Activities

Critical thinking activities involve analysis and evaluation of information. Students need to consider the accuracy, timeliness, purpose, and appropriateness of information that they hear and read. Accuracy can be verified by checking other sources. Timeliness can often be determined by checking copyright dates. Deciding about appropriateness requires matching the information with what is needed for the reader's purposes. The purpose of material may be to inform, entertain, or persuade.

Material that is intended to persuade often includes *propaganda,* a form of persuasion that is intended to influence the audience, often by using exaggerations and emotional appeals. One way to develop critical thinking skills is teaching students to recognize propaganda. Both you and the students can enjoy this activity as you look for examples of propaganda, which are readily found in political promotions and product advertisements. If you are teaching during a political campaign, you can find brochures and newspaper articles to bring to class, or you may wish to videotape messages by the candidates and play them during class. In order to choose the best candidate, students should critically analyze material for evidence of misleading statements, biased or one-sided reports, false assumptions, avoidance of issues, exaggerated statements, and emotional appeals.

Advertising contains a great deal of propaganda, and you can obtain samples from newspapers, magazines, and television. Some types of propaganda are name calling (using negative words to produce an undesirable effect), transfer (associating a worthy concept or desirable person with a product), testimonial (having a person endorse a product), plain folks (identifying with ordinary people), and bandwagon (trying to get people to accept something because everyone else does).

Suggested propaganda-detection activities that will help stimulate students to think critically include having the students:

1. Distinguish between advertisements that simply make emotional appeals and those that give information.
2. Find examples of propaganda techniques, and make displays of them.
3. Look for examples of exaggerations, emotional appeals, and other propaganda techniques for a type of product or service in which the students are particularly interested (e.g., videotapes).
4. Compare ads for the same products, such as cereals or motorcycles, produced by different companies. Tell students to look for use of fact versus opinion, propaganda techniques, and emotional appeals.

Creative Thinking Activities

For the following activities, students need to use creative thinking skills. *Brainstorming* requires students to think fluently as they generate many ideas and flexibly as they think of divergent ideas. Their responses to brainstorming situations are often unique. In *simulation, role playing,* and *creative dramatics,* students need to use their imaginations to project themselves into situations that differ in some respect from their own experiences. You can use these and other creative activities to encourage children to use higher-order thinking skills.

Brainstorming. Brainstorming can be used to develop creative thinking at any grade level. Students are given a real or imaginary problem and asked to think of as many ways as they can to solve it. You will probably have to direct the activity yourself the first time you try it, but later a student can lead it.

Here's how it works. First, identify a *specific* problem, one that is limited in scope. Then divide the class into groups. Appoint a recorder for each group to write down the ideas. Brainstorming sessions should be brief. You may want to ask students to meet again the following day for additional "afterthoughts" and to select those ideas that are worth following up.

Before they start brainstorming, students must understand how the session will be conducted. Tell them to think of as many ideas as they can, including wild ones. They should build on the ideas of others, combining and modifying what other students suggest. A student can offer only one idea each time he or she speaks, and only one person can speak at a time. Most important of all, there must be no criticism of any ideas during the session. You may ask anyone who criticizes or ridicules someone's idea to leave the group, because such criticism destroys creative thinking.

You may want to use brainstorming to solve real problems, or you may want to use fantasy situations simply to promote creative thinking. Here are suggested topics for both types of brainstorming sessions:

Realistic Situations
1. What are some things we can do to make our classroom more attractive?
2. How can we become more considerate of Jorge? (Conduct session on a day when Jorge, a student with a disability, is absent.)
3. How can we prevent a group of ninth-grade bullies from picking on the seventh-graders?

Fantasy Situations
1. What would happen if we learned to create energy from sand?
2. In what ways are a steam engine and a chain saw alike?
3. How many ways could you change a bicycle to make it more fun to ride?

Simulation.   An interesting way to involve your students in real-life situations is through simulation activities. In simulations, a realistic situation is created in which students play various roles or act out scientific processes. It is "learning by doing." By acting out a situation, students come to understand what processes are involved and how problems are solved.

Simulation offers many advantages over textbook learning, but it has disadvantages, too. You will find that most students are enthusiastic about participating in simulations and are motivated to learn about the roles they are playing. They use high-level communication skills and think creatively. They need freedom to move around and negotiate with each other, though, so your classroom may become noisy and disorderly at times. Some students may remain on the fringe of the activity and not get the full benefit of the experience. The entire simulation can be a waste of time unless you direct the experience and the follow-up discussions skillfully.

If you decide to try simulations, your first problem will be to locate an activity appropriate for the students' age level, the time available, and the lesson topic. You may want to use computer simulations or commercial board games that require students to think about what they are learning. Simulations can provide opportunities for students to learn by discovery and to apply their knowledge to actual situations. Some classic computer simulations deal with flying an airplane, running a lemonade stand, investigating underwater ecology, and traveling on the Oregon Trail during pioneer days. Many more simulations are currently available. There are even online simulations. One called Westward HO! was inspired by the game Oregon Trail. The simulation involved collaboration on projects in a number of curricular areas in an integrated manner. There are a number of Oregon Trail sites on the Internet's World Wide Web (Coffey, 1996). Because World Wide Web sites change frequently, you may need to use a search engine such as Alta Vista to get an updated address.

Controversial issues are often the subject of simulation activities. Conducting a political campaign followed by a mock election is an excellent way for students to understand political maneuvering and strategic campaigning, especially during an election year. Other simulations can deal with zoning decisions, profits and losses, and ecology, to name but a few examples. Students discover why people hold certain values and attitudes as they play out the roles they have assumed. A site location simulation is described in Figure 7–2.

Creative Dramatics.   *Creative dramatics* is acting out a story or an event without a script or props. You can effectively use it in the classroom for interpreting literature and reenacting episodes from history. Students can become totally involved in creative dramatics through thinking, speaking, listening, movement, and imagination. Therefore, they are more likely to understand and remember what they portray than if they were merely to read from a textbook or listen to a lecture.

The procedure for creative dramatics is fairly simple. All you need is space. The students should become totally familiar with a story or historical event, including its sequence of action and the feelings of the characters. Sometimes students do additional research to learn more about the story. Then you choose students to play the parts. If there are not enough parts to go around, some parts can be invented (for example, extra members of a crowd or bystanders during a conversation involving only a few characters). The students improvise the dialogue as the story unfolds. After the play is over, help them evaluate the performance by asking them what was good about the presentation and what could be done to improve it. Usually, half the class participates while the other half is the audience, and then the play is performed again with students reversing roles.

Almost any historical event can be dramatized. Here are some good scenes to try:

A pioneer family's journey westward in a Conestoga wagon

The arrival of the missionaries in Hawaii

The Boston Tea Party

Some stories are better suited to dramatization than others, and in some cases you will want to dramatize just one or two scenes from a story. Most folktales move quickly, involve conflict, and have strong characterizations. Scenes from Shakespeare's plays are also good sources for classroom creative dramatics. These are some other good selections, ranging from primary to secondary levels:

Peddler and His Caps by Esphyr Slobodkina (New York: Scott, 1947)

The Pied Piper of Hamelin by Robert Browning (New York: Scroll, 1970)

Stone Soup by Marcia Brown (New York: Scribner, 1947)

Anne Frank: The Diary of a Young Girl by Anne Frank (New York: Doubleday, 1967)

To Kill a Mockingbird by Harper Lee (Philadelphia: Lippincott, 1960)

The Pearl by John Steinbeck (New York: Viking, 1953)

The Glass Menagerie by Tennessee Williams (New York: Random House, 1945)

The Speedwheel Bicycle Manufacturing Company wants to build a new plant. Members of the Site Selection Committee are meeting to select a desirable location. They are considering four sites. As members of the committee, discuss the advantages and disadvantages of each location, and reach a decision.

Criteria	City A	City B	City C	City D
General information	Population 90,000 Industrial part of a megalopolis	Population 450,000 State capital	Population 2,800 Isolated rural town	Population 25,000 Center of a generally rural area
Transportation facilities	On major tidal river, on major rail lines, near large metropolitan airport, no N–S interstate	On major railroad and interstate routes River running through city	On old E–W highway and railroad spur line Limited air service 30 miles away	On major N–S interstate and railroad freight line Small local airport
Tax situation	Extremely high taxes on individuals and industry	No state income tax Low municipal rates Adequate services	High, progressive state income tax Heavy industrial taxes	Low tax rates No state income tax Inadequate for services
Labor force	Heavily unionized Poor productivity Highly skilled Adequate supply	Unskilled or semiskilled Chiefly nonunion Short supply	Heavily unionized with coal mining background Unskilled to highly skilled Adequate supply	Large supply of unskilled and semiskilled Unions active
Utilities	Electricity, water adequate; low supply of gas; all expensive	Low rates Abundant supplies	Adequate supplies High rates	Low-priced electricity Adequate supplies of natural gas and water
Plant sites available	Existing old factory sites available No open land	Six well-developed industrial parks Land reasonably priced	Hilly forest land available No industrial park Expensive	Two industrial parks Reasonably priced
City management	Expects kickbacks from industry	Generally favorable to recruiting industry	Inactive in industrial recruiting	Selective recruiting of industry
School system	Meets state standards	Quality varies, but generally adequate	Good quality	Good quality but low funding
Cultural activities	Old buildings and outdated facilities None in city, but full range available in adjacent cities	New arts center Symphony orchestra Several universities	Limited facilities Nothing local Concert series and extension courses 30 miles away	University town Small orchestra Well-developed arts programs
Parks and recreation	Organized sports No local parks Eighty miles from ocean	Several city parks Lakes nearby	Good hunting, fishing Ski resort nearby	Lakes, waterfalls, and parks within an hour's drive, but not much locally

FIGURE 7–2
Site Location Simulation

Role Playing. A student can assume the role of another person—that is, engage in *role playing*—in order to understand the other's feelings and attitudes. Role playing that involves solving problems is sometimes called *sociodrama*. Role playing can develop communication skills and creative thinking processes and can clarify values.

In directing role-playing situations, you should observe certain guidelines. Encourage the players to speak distinctly and make their actions clear to the audience. Remind students who are not participating to be good listeners and not interrupt or carry on side conversations. When you choose students to play certain parts, assign roles that are unlike their own personalities; for instance, let a well-mannered student be a class bully.

Usually, in role playing, two or more characters become involved in a conflict. There should be plenty of action and dialogue. The characters are led to a point where they must choose from among several possible courses of action. After students play the situation, you should discuss what took place and whether or not the problem was solved.

Role playing helps students see emotional situations more objectively. In playing out a situation, they experience the emotions connected with it. Good subjects for role playing include conflicts on the playground, misuse of drugs, disobedience, and peer relationships. You can develop role-playing situations from real life or create imaginary circumstances. Here is an example:

Nick doesn't do his share—Mrs. Miller's ninth-grade class has been studying different systems of government. As a final project, the students have been divided into groups to make presentations. All students in each group will receive the same grade. Janie, Roger, Mel, Sandy, and Nick are investigating socialism. They agree to research certain aspects of socialism and combine their information into a final report. The day before the presentation is due, all the students are ready except Nick. When they ask him to do his part, he says he has a job after school and doesn't have time. The other four students are concerned that their presentation will be incomplete because Nick hasn't done his assignment. What courses of action are open to the four students? What is the best way to resolve this problem?

Combinations of Thinking Skills

Students solve problems and make decisions every day, but seldom do they approach problem solving and decision making logically or systematically. Both processes require the use of many different thinking skills, and examples of procedures and topics for each appear below.

Problem Solving. When introducing problem solving to your class, start by having the students identify a real problem. The following example for a fifth-grade class will help you understand the procedure.

Step 1: Identifying a Problem. The children brainstorm several problems to solve, including ways to improve the food in the cafeteria, get better playground equipment, and eliminate homework on weekends. After some discussion, the students agree to solve the problem of wanting to take an end-of-year field trip, even though no funds are available for transportation. They decide they want to go to the Space Center. They figure the approximate cost for hiring the school bus. The problem is that they need to find a way to get the money.

Step 2: Obtaining Information Related to the Problem. Once again, the students brainstorm. This time they generate many ideas for getting money, including various ways of asking for it and earning it.

Step 3: Forming Hypotheses. The students consider advantages and disadvantages of each option and check with people in authority about the merits of each alternative. They make a list of several possibilities, discuss the practicality of each one, and choose the three best ideas.

Step 4: Testing the Hypotheses and Forming a Conclusion. The three best possibilities are (1) asking the principal to take the money from a special fund, (2) earning the money individually by doing chores at home, and (3) earning the money through a class project—writing a school newspaper and selling it. The students make inquiries about the special fund and find that it is to be used only for schoolwide projects, and they find that the parents of several of the students will not pay them for doing chores. The students check about the newspaper and find that, although they will have to pay for the paper, the school office will reproduce copies of the newspaper. They decide that if they can sell 300 copies for 25 cents each, they can cover the cost of the paper and have enough money for the trip. Therefore, they decide that writing a school paper is their best option.

Step 5: Applying the Solution and Evaluating Its Effectiveness. The students begin writing the paper and advertising it. Because of their enthusiasm for the project, nearly everyone in the school wants a copy of the paper. When the paper is ready, the students sell 429 copies and have more than enough money for the trip. The solution was therefore satisfactory.

A similar process can be followed at almost any level, and it can be integrated into content areas. For primary grades you will want to use fairly simple problem situations with fewer options, such as rearranging the classroom to improve traffic patterns or finding ways to thank parent volunteers; but in the upper grades you will be able to deal with more complex situations.

You can use the following ideas for involving students in problem solving. Tell the students to:

1. Design an attractive display to fill a large empty space at the school entrance. (math, art)
2. Discover why plants die in the school library and correct the situation. (biology)
3. Survey the community to find volunteers and tutors. (social studies)
4. Find ways that the school can save money to alleviate the budget deficit. (math, business)
5. Find a solution to uneven heat distribution in the school. (physics)
6. Plan a physical fitness program for your school to raise the fitness of students to an acceptable level. (physical education)

You can also use hypothetical problem-solving situations, such as the following:

1. As community leaders, develop a plan to reduce unemployment in the area. (social studies)
2. As engineers, find practical alternatives for energy sources. (science)
3. As food service managers, plan a month of school cafeteria menus with food that is nutritious, delicious, attractive, and affordable. (health, home economics, business, math)
4. As curriculum designers, develop an annotated list of recommended reading for specific grade levels. (English, reading)
5. As directors of a cultural center, plan a series of concerts with famous performers that will offer a wide variety of good music to the citizens. (music)

Decision Making. Imagine that you have planned to work through the process of decision making, according to the steps given earlier, by helping your tenth-grade students decide on suitable careers. You might begin by discussing various career options and inviting a guidance counselor to answer questions about career opportunities. Then you could let individual students find out about educational requirements, prospects for employment, prospects for advancement, salaries, job satisfaction, and other information for their chosen fields. The students should realistically assess their likelihood of achieving success by examining such possible obstacles as financial resources, length of preparation time, access to specialized training, their current grade averages, geographical location, and parental sup-

port. They can find alternative ways of overcoming each potential obstacle.

Now imagine that Bob, one of your students, has chosen a business career and has identified some obstacles to reaching it, including lack of education and lack of financial resources. As he identifies alternatives, he considers overcoming financial problems by getting a scholarship, working part-time, or getting a loan. He can overcome his lack of education by going to college full-time or part-time, or by going to night school. In ranking his alternatives, he finds that the most practical solution for him is to go to college part-time, work part-time, and take out a small loan.

You might help Bob and the other students analyze their options more carefully by teaching them to make decision trees, a way of graphically organizing their alternatives. The students might list their alternatives and then place them on blank "trees" that you have given them, or they might want to create their own trees. Bob's tree might look something like the one in Figure 7–3.

Some ideas to use with your students follow. You can simplify or expand these ideas to serve different ages, and you can integrate them with various content areas.

1. Identify the best political system in which to live. (social studies)
2. Decide which novelist (or scientist, philosopher, artist, musician, etc.) made the greatest contribution to literature (or the related field of study). (literature or any other subject)
3. Calculate the best forms of transportation (or the best routes) to take to reach various destinations. (math, geography)
4. Decide which car would be the best purchase for you or your parents. (math, social studies)
5. Decide which region of the world has the best climate in which to live. (geography, science)
6. Identify the best form of energy to use. (science)
7. Decide on the best way to spend the $100 given to your class by the school. (math, social studies)
8. Identify the best language to use for worldwide communication. (language)

Complete Activity 7.4 to help you focus on your use of such activities.

FOR YOUR PORTFOLIO

On the basis of Activity 7.4, choose three or four of your most successful creative thinking activities, describe them in detail, and put them in your portfolio.

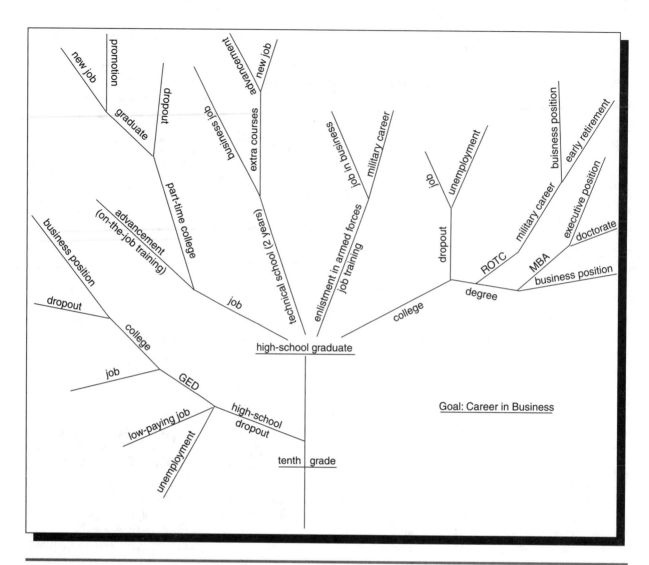

FIGURE 7–3
Decision Tree

Computer Applications. In some schools the computer is enhancing creative thinking instruction. For example, the computer allows art students to experiment with colors and shapes without fearing permanent errors, because change is easy. This situation promotes risk taking and problem solving and provides an environment for developing skills of divergent thinking, analysis, and criticism.

Videoconferencing has been used to connect students in Chicago, Los Angeles, and the Bronx for an environmental studies program. The students share information about pollution and recycling in their neighborhoods and then write scripts and plan an interactive theater production.

In New Jersey a school has had students create inventions and then develop multimedia presentations about them. Such activities promote problem solving skills (M. M. Smith, 1996).

STUDY SKILLS

Students at all levels and in all disciplines need to master a set of basic study skills that will enhance their ability to learn from content area materials. It is, of course, beyond the scope of this book to teach you *how* to teach study skills; the purpose of this discussion is to make you aware of *what* the important study skills are, so that you can help your students acquire them. Don't assume that students have learned these skills simply because they have been previously exposed to them. Check to see—through pretests, oral questions, and observation of classroom performance—if the students have actually acquired them. Many students have been exposed to the skills, but the exposure has not "taken." Many of Mr. Viera's students in the opening vignette may need several experiences with reading and study strategies before they can apply them successfully.

ACTIVITY 7.4   **Creative Thinking Activities**

Examine the following list of creative thinking activities. Place a checkmark (✓) by the ones you have used in your class. Place a plus (+) by the ones you intend to use. Under each activity you have used or intend to use, briefly explain how you applied or plan to apply it in your class or classes.

_____   Brainstorming

_____   Simulation

_____   Role playing

_____   Creative dramatics

_____   Problem solving

_____   Decision making

_____   Computer applications

CASE STUDY 7.1

Make No Assumptions

Ms. Jamison, the student teacher in a fifth-grade class, assigned each class member to write a report on a famous historical figure. First, class members were to check encyclopedia accounts, and then they were to seek additional information. Ricky was asked to report on James Otis.

Ricky: Ms. Jamison, James Otis isn't in the encyclopedia. I checked all three sets.

Ms. Jamison (puzzled): I'm sure you just overlooked his name, Ricky. I know it is there.

Ricky: No, it's not. I'm sure.

Ms. Jamison (suddenly realizing what she should do): Let's go to the encyclopedia together, and you can show me how you looked for his name.

Ricky (walking toward the reference books): Okay. Oh! I can't show you now. All the *J* encyclopedias are being used.

Ms. Jamison: Why did you look under *J*?

Ricky: His name starts with a *J*.

Ms. Jamison: It's his first name that starts with a *J*. In the encyclopedia, people's names are alphabetized according to their last names. That's why you couldn't find James Otis in the *J* encyclopedia. You should have looked for Otis in the *O* encyclopedia. Nobody is using the *O* encyclopedia now. Why don't you try it while I watch?

Ricky (picking up the encyclopedia): Okay. Let's see. Here it is—Otis, James! Thank you, Ms. Jamison.

1. What assumption had Ms. Jamison made about the students' research skills when she assigned the lesson? Was it valid?
2. What might you do before making an assignment like this one, to avoid a similar situation in your class?

Location Skills

Starting with the problem posed by Ms. Jamison's class, you should first consider the study skill of locating information. To carry out many routine assignments in content classes, students need to be able to locate information in trade books (nontextbook reading materials), textbooks, and reference books. They also need to be able to locate materials in the media center and be able to search electronic reference materials and Internet sites.

If students are to use trade books and textbooks to best advantage, you must ensure that they understand how to use prefaces and introductions, tables of contents, indexes, appendixes, glossaries, footnotes, and bibliographies. Many students do not even know the functions of these book parts; therefore, their chances of using them effectively to locate information are poor. Before some students can use indexes and glossaries effectively, they may need instruction in the prerequisite skill of alphabetizing. Most secondary students have mastered alphabetical order, which usually receives initial attention in first grade, but some will have difficulty with alphabetizing beyond the first letter of a word. For use of the glossary, they may also need instruction in use of guide words and pronunciation keys and in choosing the meaning that fits the context. Some students also need instruction in identifying key words under which to look when using the index or doing electronic searches. You need to assess the students' knowledge of the skills they need for using trade books and textbooks, as well as electronic sources, and offer information, instruction, and practice as necessary. Informal assessment will usually suffice. You can ask students to use each of the book parts and observe their performance, or you can ask them to explain the function of each part. Primary students will be concerned only with tables of contents and, by second or third grade, glossaries. Intermediate students should use all book parts, with the possible exception of the preface or introduction, and students in junior and senior high schools should use these parts as well. Students in classes with computers need to work with a variety of types of electronic searches.

Reference books call for a wide variety of skills. Knowledge of alphabetical order and the ability to use guide words are necessary with reference books, especially encyclopedias and dictionaries. Many secondary students still have trouble with guide words, although most have had repeated exposure to them since at least fourth grade. The ability to use cross references is particularly important for using an encyclopedia. Of course, for use of the dictionary, students need the same skills they need for use of a glossary, including the ability to use a pronunciation key and to choose the meaning that fits a particular context. To use printed encyclopedias, students must be able to determine which volume of a set contains the information they seek. (This is what Ricky could not do in Case Study 7.1.) Encyclopedia users must also be able to determine key words under which they can find related information. To use an atlas, students need to know how to interpret a map's legend and scale and how to locate directions on a map.

Reference books are often written at relatively high reading levels, considering the populations for which they are intended. Guard against assigning students to look up information in reference books with reading levels far above their abilities. Students will not learn from such assignments and are likely either to do nothing or merely copy from the reference book without understanding. These responses will not result in the learning outcomes you anticipated.

To teach or review library skills, you can plan cooperatively with the librarian or media specialist, whose familiarity with the media center may have made him or her aware of potential uses you have overlooked. Consider this resource person, as all support personnel in the school, an ally in your teaching endeavor.

FOR YOUR PORTFOLIO

Describe a way that you collaborated with the librarian or media specialist to provide resources or offer instruction.

Organizational Skills

Organizational skills are highly important to students working on reports for content area classes. These skills include outlining, summarizing, and organized note-taking. They are most easily taught in conjunction with an assignment on writing a report, since students can best see the need to learn them at such a time. These skills are usually not taught before the intermediate grades, but they ordinarily receive attention then. Still, many secondary students have not mastered these skills, perhaps because they were never taught in a functional setting. If you are teaching above the primary level, you need to assess students' mastery of these skills and help them acquire the skills if they have not yet done so. Primary teachers lay the groundwork for these skills, especially outlining, when they help students determine main ideas and supporting details. They lay the groundwork for note-taking and summarizing when they encourage students to paraphrase what they have just read.

Retention

A major goal of content area learning is retention of subject matter. Teaching students how to study so that they will retain what they read will be an important task for you. Here are some ways you can help students retain content. The codes indicate the appropriate levels: A = all levels, primary through secondary grades; I = intermediate grades; S = secondary grades.

1. Have class discussions covering all material you assign students to read. (A)
2. Encourage students to evaluate what they read. (A)
3. Give the students an opportunity to apply what they have read. (A)
4. Use audiovisual aids to illuminate concepts presented in the reading. (A)
5. Prepare students before they read by giving them background about the topic. (A)
6. Encourage students to picture in their minds what the author is trying to describe. (A)
7. Have students retell what they have read, in their own words, to you or a classmate soon after they finish reading. (A)
8. Always give students purposes for reading. Never just say, "Read pages 2 through 9 for tomorrow." Tell them what to look for as they read. (A)
9. Teach your students a study method, such as SQ3R (Robinson, 1961). (I, S)
10. Encourage students to analyze the author's organization. (I, S)
11. Have students take notes on the main points in the material. (I, S)
12. Have students write summaries of the material after they finish reading. (I, S)
13. Hold periodic classroom review sessions on material that has been read. (A)
14. Prepare study guides for students to use as they read the material. (I, S)
15. Have students use mnemonic devices. (I, S)
16. Give students immediate feedback on correctness of oral or written responses to the reading material. (A)
17. Encourage students to classify the ideas in their reading material. (A)

These techniques will bolster the students' retention.

Reading Rate

Another useful study skill your students need to acquire is the ability to adjust reading rate to fit the purpose for reading and the type of material. Many students have never had help in developing flexibility in reading rates. As a result, they frequently read everything at the same rate. Some employ a painstakingly slow rate that is inappropriate for reading light fiction, for locating isolated facts, or for seeking only general themes. Others use a rapid rate that is inappropriate for reading mathematics story problems, science experiments they must perform, or any type of intensive study material.

Make the students aware that a good reader uses many different reading rates and matches the rate to the purpose for reading and the nature of the material. Offer them opportunities to practice varying reading rates in the classroom; for example, have them scan for isolated details, skim for main ideas, and read slowly and carefully to solve a mathematics problem.

Interpreting Graphic Aids

The ability to interpret graphic aids in content materials is also vital. Students need to be able to interpret maps, graphs, tables, and illustrations in their textbooks, or they will not gain all they should from the content. Students tend to skip graphic aids, perhaps because their teachers have never explained the informative nature of these aids, or because they have never been shown *how* to interpret them. We have already mentioned the skills necessary for reading maps. When reading graphs, students must be able to decide what is being compared, the units of measure involved, how to extract specific information from the graph, and how to make overall generalizations based on the graph. When reading tables, students must be able to decide what type of information is included, the meanings of the columns and rows, and how to extract specific facts. Illustrations such as diagrams present problems because of their abstract nature, distortion of reality, and oversimplification. Students may think that a realistic illustration is just a decorative feature, when it really conveys information.

To help students understand the purpose and construction of graphic aids, ask them to create their own. They can make diagrams to compare the settings or characters in stories, charts or tables to summarize key points for a report, or graphs to identify their favorite breakfast cereals. By making their own graphic aids, students understand how these aids work and are likely to find it easier to interpret other graphic aids.

Metacognitive Skills

Metacognitive skills allow a person to monitor her or his intellectual functioning. They are important for comprehension and retention of content material. Metacognition includes awareness of what you already know, knowledge of when you have achieved understanding of new information, and realization of how you accomplished the understanding. You can help your students learn to monitor their comprehension of material presented in your classes.

In order to exercise metacognitive skills, students must become active learners, setting goals for their learning tasks, planning ways to meet their goals, monitoring their success in meeting their goals, and remedying the situation when they fail to meet the

goals. You can help them acquire techniques to do these things. Teaching them to relate new information to things that they already know, to preview material that they are about to read, to paraphrase ideas presented, to identify the organizational patterns in written materials, and to question themselves periodically will help them to monitor their comprehension effectively. In the opening vignette, Mr. Viera encouraged his students to brainstorm ways that helped them make sense of their reading.

You should teach students to expect their reading assignments to make sense and, if they cannot make sense out of the material, to attempt to find out why. They may ask themselves whether the words in the material are unfamiliar, the sentence structure is confusing, or some other problem exists. After the specific problem area has been determined, they should decide what reading skills need to be applied (for example, use of context clues) and apply the skills. Some ways to remedy the situation when material has not been understood are to read on and try to use subsequent context to help make sense of the material, to reread the material, and to use the glossary or a dictionary to clarify pronunciations or meanings of words.

You can help students learn to monitor their comprehension by modeling the monitoring skills for them. You can take a content passage and read it aloud to them, pausing to tell them how you are checking your own comprehension internally at frequent points in the reading. You should tell them what questions you are asking yourself about the material and how you can tell when you have found the answers. This technique is very powerful and effective, if used appropriately.

Study Habits

You may also find that your students have very poor study habits. They must learn that study should take place in an environment that is as distraction-free as possible (many may not have an entirely distraction-free place available), that they should gather their study tools (books, pens, pencils, paper) *before* they start to study, that they should budget their study time so that nothing is left out, and that they should set aside a time for study which they will not be constantly relinquishing to other activities. Those who do not have a good place to study at home should be encouraged to use school study periods as effectively as possible. Students who change classes should learn to gather all necessary study materials before they go to the study hall period, to have all homework assignments written down to take with them, and to concentrate on homework during the study period rather than visit with other students.

DISCUSSION QUESTIONS

1. Do you take a constructive approach to teaching? What are your reasons?
2. What can you do when there are students in your content classes who cannot read the assigned textbook? Would different techniques be better in different situations? Why or why not?
3. Choose a chapter from a textbook that you are using with students. What are some ways you could build the students' background for reading this material?
4. How can you incorporate writing instruction into your classroom instruction?
5. What opportunities do the students in your class have for developing higher-order thinking skills? How do you and your cooperating teacher react to students' efforts to think critically and creatively?
6. What can you do to provide a classroom environment that is more conducive to higher-order thinking? Would you need to make any changes in the room arrangement, scheduling of class work, types of activities, or assignments?
7. What critical or creative thinking activities are you willing to try in your classroom? What problems can you foresee in doing them? How could you prevent or minimize these problems?
8. What would happen to our society if there were no creativity? Which is more important, knowledge or creativity?
9. How can you help students develop metacognitive skills?
10. What is the most appropriate time to teach outlining, summarizing, and note-taking? Why do you think so? How would you begin?
11. How can you and the librarian or media specialist cooperate to ensure that students master important library skills?
12. How can inappropriate and inflexible reading rates inhibit students' learning? What can you do to change these habits?
13. What study methods might you use in your grade or discipline? Why would these methods be appropriate?
14. What kinds of graphic aids are most common in your content area or areas? How could you let students create their own graphic aids?

SELECTED REFERENCES

Allen, J. S. (1996, February). Potato barrels, animal traps, birth control, and unicorns: Re-visioning teaching and learning in English classes. *English Journal, 85,* 38–42.

Beyer, B. K. (1995). *Critical thinking.* Bloomington, IN: Phi Delta Kappa Educational Foundation.

Bone, A., & Busekist, S. (1996, February). Toward a whole partnership. *English Journal, 85,* 35–37.

Burns, P. C., Roe, B. D., & Ross, E. P. (1999). *Teaching reading in today's elementary schools.* Boston: Houghton Mifflin.

Coffey, J. (1996, May/June). Go west, young explorers! In Just for educators: Your own web guide. *Electronic Learning, 15,* 6.

Cunningham, P., & Allington, R. (1999). *Classrooms that work* (2nd ed.). New York: Longman.

Galda, L., & DeGroff, L. (1990, November). Across time and place: Books for social studies. *The Reading Teacher, 44,* 240–246.

Galda, L., DeGroff, L., & Walworth, M. (1990, December). Exploration and discovery: Books for a science curriculum. *The Reading Teacher, 44,* 316–325.

Harvey, S. (1998). *Nonfiction matters: Reading, writing, and research in grades 3–8.* York, ME: Stenhouse.

Greenlaw, M. J., Shepperson, G. M., & Nistler, R. J. (1992, March). A literature approach to teaching about the Middle Ages. *Language Arts, 69,* 200–204.

McCaslin, N. (1990). *Creative drama in the classroom* (5th ed.). White Plains, NY: Longman.

Moss, J. F. (1990). *Focus units in literature: A handbook for elementary school teachers.* Katonah, NY: Richard Owen.

100 best-bet websites across the curriculum. (1996, May/June). In Just for educators: Your guide to the web. *Electronic Learning, 15,* 2, 11–13, 15–16.

Raphael, T., & Au, K. (Eds.). (1998). *Literature-based instruction: Reshaping the curriculum.* Norwood, MA: Christopher-Gordon.

Robinson, F. P. (1961). *Effective study.* New York: Harper and Row.

Roe, B. D., Stoodt, B. D., & Burns, P. C. (2001). *Secondary school literacy instruction: The content areas.* Boston, MA: Houghton Mifflin.

Ross, E. P. (1994). *Using children's literature across the curriculum.* Bloomington, IN: Phi Delta Kappa Educational Foundation.

Ross, E. P. (1998). *Pathways to thinking.* Norwood, MA: Christopher-Gordon.

Routman, R. (1991). *Invitations.* Portsmouth, NH: Heinemann.

Short, K., & Burke, C. (1991). *Creating curriculum.* Portsmouth, NH: Heinemann.

Smith, F. (1998). *The book of learning and forgetting.* New York, NY: Teachers College Press.

Smith, M. M. (1996, May/June). The creative edge. *Electronic Learning, 15,* 47–54, 68.

Tompkins, G. E. (1998). *50 literacy strategies step by step.* Upper Saddle River, NJ: Merrill.

Walker-Dalhouse, D. (1992, February). Using African-American literature to increase ethnic understanding. *The Reading Teacher, 45,* 416–422.

Zahorik, J. A. (1995). *Constructivist teaching.* Bloomington, IN: Phi Delta Kappa Educational Foundation.

Instructional Resources

Making Use of Technology

Miss Dycus, a student teacher in a seventh-grade English class, was assigned to a classroom that had just received two multimedia computers from the school's Parent Teacher Association. The computers came bundled with AppleWorks software on the hard drive and 20 CD-ROMs. Mr. Tompkins, Miss Dycus's cooperating teacher, felt that two computers were not sufficient for curricular applications, so he had been using time on the computers as a reward for students who finished assignments early or made high scores on papers or exams.

When the students went to the computers to claim their reward time, they almost always chose the Flight Simulator or Game Empire CD-ROMs.

Miss Dycus felt that a valuable instructional resource was being wasted. She decided to try to remedy the situation, with her cooperating teacher's approval.

Miss Dycus: Mr. Tompkins, I'd like to try to get the students to make more use of the computer resources for their English assignments. Would you mind if I changed the ground rules for computer use when I take over responsibility for teaching the class?

Mr. Tompkins: No, I don't mind your experimentation, but I don't think you will get far with two computers and 30 students in a class.

Miss Dycus: I thought I would demonstrate the use of the multimedia encyclopedia, the almanac, the dictionary, the thesaurus, and the atlas, and then assign short cooperative papers that would require students to use these resources to find information.

Mr. Tompkins: How can you demonstrate to the whole class at the same time?

Miss Dycus: I can check out a projection device from our university media center. It sits on the overhead projector and connects to the computer. You can use it to show what is on the computer on a large screen.

Mr. Tompkins: That sounds useful, but there are only two computers for 30 students. They'll never get a chance to look up the information.

Miss Dycus: I'll put the students in groups of three. Each group will choose a topic from a list I compile related to the authors and works we will be studying this semester. Then each group will plan what types of information to include in its paper. The three students in each group will decide which reference sources they need to check for different purposes and submit the list to me. I'll check to see if they have made reasonable choices and give them a priority number for computer use. Five groups can use each computer, taking turns, according to the priority schedule that I post.

Mr. Tompkins: What about the ones not using the computer?

Miss Dycus: Oh, they will be brainstorming about the topic, outlining the paper, composing the paper, and revising the drafts. I'll put some other reference books in a resource corner for them to use, and I'll expect them to make use of their textbooks, as well. Synthesizing the information from all these sources should be a good experience and should keep everyone purposefully engaged. After the initial computer searches have been completed, students will be allowed to access the dictionary and thesaurus CD-ROMs if the computers are available, but I'll have printed dictionaries and thesauruses available for times when the computers are tied up.

Mr. Tompkins: Well, it sounds good, but the students may not apply themselves to the task. They may be distracted by the computer element.

Miss Dycus: I have an idea that would help avoid that. As a reward for the best paper, that group could get to use the word processor from AppleWorks to do a final draft for display in the classroom. If they don't have good typing skills, I could let them use the Typing Tutor CD-ROM to brush up on these skills.

Mr. Tompkins: I don't know if it will work, but I'm willing to let you try. It sounds good, but it sounds complicated, too.

Miss Dycus excitedly announced the plan when she started teaching the class. Some of the students grumbled about losing their game-playing time. Some were worried about using the computer, because they were afraid it was too hard. But some were excited about getting to try something new. Most of the students were at least mildly interested after the class demonstration of the CD-ROMs.

The students had done group work before, so the formation of the work groups and choosing of topics went smoothly. At first some of the groups had trouble using the CD-ROMs because they were not adept at reading the help messages. A Computer Club member was recruited from study hall to help with things that came up as the students worked on the computers, and then that part also began to move smoothly.

The whole process took longer than expected, however, and it was not completed before Miss Dycus had to leave. The papers had all been successfully written, but there was no time for the best paper to be word-processed at the end.

Mr. Tompkins told Miss Dycus that he thought he would continue the process when she left and let the students do that step as well. He did express concern at how much class time the project had taken, and he said he was not sure he would do it again.

1. Did Miss Dycus have a workable idea for use in the class?
2. How could she have made the experience more effective?
3. Was the result worth the time involved?
4. Would you try it?

INTRODUCTION TO INSTRUCTIONAL RESOURCES

People learn best the things that they experience. Much learning takes place through the vicarious (indirect) experiences of listening, reading, and viewing pictures and videos, but learning is likely to be more meaningful and lasting if it is supplemented with direct experiences.

You can find instructional resources in a wide variety of places. You can obtain audiovisual materials through the school, the public library, a college resource center, and local and state agencies. Industries, farms, and parks provide opportunities for field trips. People in various occupations can also serve as resources.

You may wish to make games and activities for teaching specific skills. The community is rich in resources to use in constructing such materials. For example, many home decorating and home supply stores give away scraps of materials that can be used for various purposes in the classroom. Newspapers may be a source of newsprint for murals and posters, and restaurants may provide place mats that have educational themes. If you use your imagination, you will find ways to take advantage of the resources that abound in your school and community.

Many audiovisual media are used in a variety of ways in schools today. If you are going to use audiovisual media effectively, you need to know *where* to obtain them, *when* to make use of them, *how* to use them, *why* they can enhance your lessons, and *which types* are most appropriate for your purposes.

Selecting Audiovisual Media

When you meet with your cooperating teacher, discuss what units, skills, and activities you will be expected to teach. Decide what materials you might want to use in connection with these teaching areas; then check to see what materials are available. Some materials may have to be reserved or ordered well in advance of the time you actually plan to use them.

One of the first things you should do is become acquainted with the school librarian or media specialist. Find out what resources are available in your school. Most school media centers have supplementary reading materials, newspapers and periodicals, reference books, maps and globes, files of photographs and slides, art prints, audiotapes, videotapes, transparencies, charts and posters, models and exhibits, computer software, and sometimes videodiscs.

After assessing the holdings of the school media center, you may wish to explore other possibilities. One place to look for additional materials is the school system's central office, which may have a file of resource materials. Another source is the public or regional library. You may be able to order videotapes or obtain computer software from the State Department of Education. In addition, don't overlook your university's resources.

Materials are also available from other places. The Public Documents Distribution Center (Pueblo, Colorado), various state departments and agencies, and businesses and industries will send you free or inexpensive materials. Locally, you can get maps and other printed materials from the Chamber of Commerce, banks, local industries, and the Department of Health.

If you still can't find what you need, you may want to make simple materials yourself, such as transparencies, slides, mounted pictures, or teaching games. You should protect some of these materials by laminating them or covering them with clear contact paper. A good way to begin a collection of teacher-made games and activities is to make some on the insides of file folders. Write the directions on the outside of each folder. You can then label and organize these activities according to learning objectives. (See Figure 8–1 for an example of a teacher-made language arts game.)

There are a number of factors to consider in selecting audiovisual materials to use with a particular lesson. Be sure you do not decide to use them simply to impress your cooperating teacher, fill up instructional time, or entertain the students. Consider these criteria in choosing materials:

1. *Relevance to the lesson*—Make sure the audiovisual material actually helps carry out the objectives of the lesson you are teaching. The material should be the most appropriate medium for your purpose, making the necessary points in the clearest possible manner. It should stimulate discussion and lead the way to further study.

2. *Appeal to students*—Be sure the material is suitable for the students' age level and that it will hold their attention. Students should have sufficient background information to appreciate the presentation.

3. *Quality of the materials*—Check your materials to make sure they are well designed and of high technical quality. The material should be accurate, current, and in good taste.

4. *Objectivity*—Examine your material for bias, propaganda, and controversy. If there is bias, help your students to see the other point of view. Point out misconceptions that arise as a result of propaganda techniques. If the material is controversial, be sure that each side receives equal emphasis. Free materials are often available to classroom teachers for the purpose of advertising a product or advancing a particular point of view. Be cautious about using these materials.

5. *Practical considerations*—Be sure you know how to operate the equipment you need for presenting

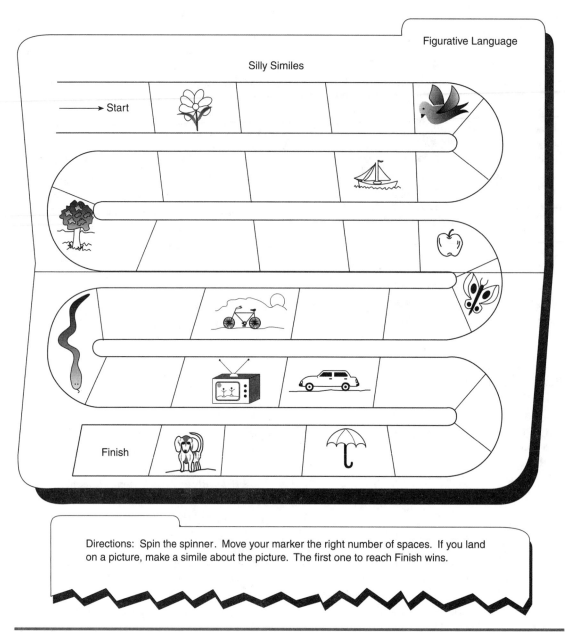

FIGURE 8–1
Teacher-Made Language Arts Game

your material. Check in advance to see that both materials and equipment will be available when you need them. Allow enough time to introduce the lesson, present the audiovisual material, and follow it up. Allow extra time in case something goes wrong. Prepare a suitable place for your presentation. Follow the checklist in Activity 8.1 to help you use audiovisual materials efficiently.

Choosing computer software requires a few more decisions than are necessary in choosing most other audiovisual materials. For example, choosing a cassette to play on a tape recorder is not likely to be a problem for teachers. However, choosing the correct software to use on a specific computer is more complicated. These additional considerations are necessary when you are choosing computer software for use in your classes:

1. *Make sure the software was designed to be used on the type of computer you have in your class.* If you have an IBM or IBM-compatible computer with a floppy disk drive, you will not be able to use a program on a floppy disk that was designed for a Macintosh

ACTIVITY 8.1   ***Checklist for Using Audiovisual Equipment***

PREPARATION

_____   Reserve or check out necessary materials and equipment.

_____   Preview material to make sure it is appropriate and in good condition.

_____   Prepare related materials for introduction or follow-up activities.

_____   If each student is to receive a copy of related materials, count the copies to make sure you have enough. Plan for efficient distribution.

_____   Arrange audience seats so that everyone can see.

_____   Consider the location of students with disabilities by placing those with visual or auditory difficulties near the front and providing places for students in wheelchairs.

_____   Check the room's temperature, ventilation, and lighting.

_____   Eliminate distractions as much as possible.

EQUIPMENT

_____   Practice operating equipment until you feel sure of yourself.

_____   Set equipment up in advance so that it is ready to use (check focus, position on screen, size of image, etc.).

_____   Have an extra bulb on hand, and know how to replace the old one.

_____   Get an extension cord or an adapter if you need one.

_____   Avoid having cords where the students will trip over them.

_____   Check the cleanliness of the lens and other vital parts of the equipment.

computer. The documentation accompanying the software will tell you with which computer or computers the program was designed to be used.

2. *Make sure the program is easy for your students to use.* Some programs contain useful information but are not user-friendly—they are hard to use, because of missing or inadequate instructions about how to enter information, how to progress through the program by moving from screen to screen, how to exit from the program, how to adjust the program's rate of presentation or level of difficulty, or where to obtain assistance when problems arise. If the programs are hard for *you* to use because of poor design, they will probably be hard for some of your students. Therefore, you should try programs out before using them for a class, even though reviews have indicated that they are just what you need. The reviewers may never have had a class like yours.

3. *Make sure the time available for use of the program is sufficient for all the students to complete the lesson.* Having only a small number of computers may make the use of some very good programs impractical on a whole-class or large-group scale.

4. *Check the program for sound effects.* Decide if they are likely to be disturbing to the part of the class not working on the program at the moment. If you think that they may be distracting, check to see if the sound can be turned down or even off. If you plan to turn the sound off, make sure the program is still effective without it. Maybe you can use the program with earphones for the students involved. Try to take all possibilities into account.

Effective Use of Audiovisual Media

Audiovisual media can be used for many purposes: introduction and orientation to a new area of study, representation of events and processes, and individualized learning experiences. They can arouse students' interest and curiosity as you introduce a new topic. A display of brightly colored photographs of wild animals, a recording of Renaissance madrigals, or a time-lapse video of a flower opening can be a stimulus for learning. Since students have become accustomed to acquiring ideas and information through television, an audiovisual presentation, such as a videotape or television program, can command their attention more effectively than a textbook or lecture. In addition, because students have become accustomed to playing video games in arcades and on home game machines and computers, computer programs may excite interest not generated by other classroom presentations.

You can use certain types of audiovisual media to individualize instruction according to the learner's style or special needs. If the same information is available in the classroom in different forms, learners can choose the forms that best suit their ways of learning. For instance, a student who has great difficulty with reading can listen to a tape about the African jungle. Another student who has trouble visualizing what is read might operate a videotape recorder and watch motion pictures of the jungle. A third student who is an excellent reader might prefer to read about the jungles of Africa in several reference books. Students with visual disabilities may need to use recordings or large-print materials. A student who learns best through active participation may best gain information about the African jungle or any other habitat through a computer simulation.

When you use audiovisual material, prepare carefully for your lesson by previewing the material and reading the accompanying study guide or lesson plan. Create a feeling of readiness and anticipation among the students by raising questions and telling them what they can expect to learn. Relate the audiovisual material to what they are studying; make it a part of your overall instructional plan. Explain any unfamiliar terms or concepts that will be used.

During the presentation, observe the students' reactions. There may be some points they do not seem to understand or some parts that do not hold their interest. You may be able to interrupt the presentation, but more likely you will need to address these matters during your follow-up discussion. You should take notes of your observations so that you can recall anything that needs to be mentioned later.

The follow-up activities are based on the audiovisual presentation but are not limited to it. In fact, the presentation may serve primarily as a taking-off point. Follow-up activities may consist of lively discussions, the application of concepts to real situations, or experiments, projects, and reports. Students may be divided into groups to pursue special interests, and the projects may continue over an extended period of time. Students' participation in follow-up activities is essential for learning to take place.

CASE STUDY 8.1

Breakdown of a Lesson

Mr. Ray, a student teacher, is introducing a unit on Scandinavia in a middle school social studies class by showing his students slides of the region. He has reserved the slides and projector, arranged the slides in the tray, and positioned the projector and is ready to begin. Mrs. Colby is the cooperating teacher.

Mr. Ray: Everybody sit down and be quiet. We're going to see some slides.

Students (shuffling to their seats and mumbling): Wonder what they're about. Probably something boring.

Mr. Ray: Hey, you guys. Keep quiet. Okay. Ellen, turn out the lights, please. Here we go. (Mr. Ray turns on the projector, and the students settle down. He begins explaining each slide. Suddenly the screen goes blank. Mr. Ray stares at the projector and wonders what happened.)

Mrs. Colby: I believe the bulb has burned out. Do you have another one?

Mr. Ray: I don't think so. Let me look. (Pause while students start whispering, poking each other, and laughing.) I can't find one. Do you think they'd have one at the resource center?

Mrs. Colby: They probably do, but the librarian is out today, and I doubt if the substitute would know where to find one.

Mr. Ray: Peter, would you go to the resource center for me and ask the substitute librarian if she can find a slide projector bulb? (Peter starts off in search of a bulb. By now the students are talking again, and some are getting out of their seats. Carmelita trips over the projector cord and falls against the filing cabinet.)

Mr. Ray (speaking in an excited, almost angry tone): All of you get back in your seats! Be quiet! Peter should be back soon.

Students: Oh, look! Carmelita hurt her mouth!

Carmelita (holding her hand to her mouth): It hurts!

Mr. Ray glances helplessly at Mrs. Colby, starts to say something, and then stops.

Mrs. Colby (speaking calmly and turning the lights back on): All of you get back to your seats now. Get out your math books and work on your assignment for tomorrow. (Students do as she says.)

Mrs. Colby: Let me see your mouth, Carmelita. I believe it will be okay if you go to the girls' room and put a cold, wet paper towel over it for a while. Kim, you go with her.

Peter (just returning to the room): She looked for a bulb but couldn't find one. She says we'd better wait and show the slides tomorrow when the regular librarian will be back.

Mr. Ray: Thank you, Peter. Class, I guess you might as well keep working on your math, and we'll do social studies tomorrow when we can see the slides.

1. Did Mr. Ray succeed in his objective of introducing his unit on Scandinavia? Could he have introduced the unit anyway, even if he couldn't show the slides?
2. Did Mr. Ray ever make clear to the students his purpose in showing the slides? If the slides had been shown, do you think the students would have gained much from them? What could Mr. Ray have done to create interest in the slides and make sure the students learned all they could from them?
3. What could Mr. Ray have done to prevent the class from becoming unruly?
4. How could Carmelita's accident have been prevented? How might Mr. Ray have handled the incident?
5. What would you do to avoid making the same kinds of mistakes Mr. Ray made?
6. Is there anything you think Mr. Ray did correctly? If so, what?

CASE STUDY 8.2

Salvaging a Lesson

Mr. Carson, a student teacher, is introducing a unit on Africa in a middle school social studies class by showing his students slides of the region. He has reserved the slides and projector, arranged the slides in the tray, and positioned the projector and is ready to begin. Miss Rios is the media specialist.

Mr. Carson: This afternoon we are going to see some slides. The slides are of scenes in Africa. We are going to begin studying a unit on Africa today. Africa is the second-largest continent and is made up of many different countries. As you watch the slides, I want you to notice the different kinds of land regions you can find in Africa. Also, pay attention to the natural resources that Africa has. Kim, will you please close the blinds? I believe we're ready to start. (Mr. Carson turns on the projector and begins discussing the slides, but suddenly the screen goes blank.)

Students: What happened?

Mr. Carson: I'm afraid the bulb has burned out. I tried to get a spare just in case, but there wasn't one. I'll try to get one by tomorrow.

Mike: Oh, good. No slides. Can we play a game?

Susan: Let's have free time.

Sally (jumping out of her seat): I think I know where there's an extra bulb. I'll go ask Miss Rios.

Mr. Carson: Never mind, Sally. I already checked with Miss Rios, and she doesn't have one. We'll have to do something else instead.

Anthony: I want to get my math homework done. Is it okay if I do that?

Mr. Carson: Wait a minute, everybody. We can still begin learning about Africa today even if we can't see the slides. We'll begin by finding Africa on the globe. Who can come up and show us where it is?

Sonya (raising her hand): I can see it from here. Let me show them.

Mr. Carson (after discussing the features of Africa on the globe and on a pull-down map): Africa has been in the news quite a bit lately, and I've been clipping some items from the newspapers. I'm going to divide you into groups of four and let each group take one clipping. I want you to read your clipping and select someone from your group to report to the class about the article. Select another person to point to the country or region in Africa that is mentioned in your article. You may use either the map or the globe. I will give you a few minutes to do this work in your groups, and then I will call on you to make your reports. Do you have any questions?

Jimmy: Who's going to be in my group?

Mr. Carson: I'll put you into groups just as soon as I'm sure you understand what to do.

Jake: What if we can't find our country on the map?

Mr. Carson: I'll help you. You may come up ahead of time to try to find it. Any other questions? (pause) I think we're ready to start now.

1. Suppose that Mr. Carson had not thought to use the map and globe and that he had not brought the clippings. What would have happened to his lesson?
2. What are some other ways that Mr. Carson might have introduced his unit without the slides?
3. At what point was Mr. Carson about to lose control of the class? How did he manage to retain control?
4. Compare and contrast the lessons of Mr. Ray and Mr. Carson according to the following criteria: preparation, class management, effectiveness of introducing a unit, and flexibility.

COMPUTERS

Obviously, computers are the specific focus of computer literacy and computer programming classes. In addition to these classes, however, computers are now being used extensively in many schools for a variety of purposes. A school's computers may be located in individual classrooms, but sometimes they are available only in a computer laboratory that has scheduled times for different classes or specific purposes.

Some teachers use drill-and-practice programs, tutorial programs, simulations, interactive literature programs, game programs, word processing programs, desktop publishing programs, electronic databases, electronic spreadsheets, electronic reference sources, web development programs, e-mail programs, and Internet search programs as a part of their regular class instruction. They may be central to instruction or may be used for special situations, depending upon the equipment and software available.

Types of Computer Programs

Computer programs perform many functions in classrooms. Figure 8–2 shows some types with which you should be familiar. Drill-and-practice programs do not teach new material; they simply offer practice on skills that you or your cooperating teacher have previously taught. Students are often provided with drill-and-practice programs on mathematics, language, reading and other skills in order to free the teacher from the repetitive drill and allow her or him to work at *instructing* students who need extra explanation and attention.

Tutorial programs do offer skill instruction, and they also generally include a practice component. Tutorial programs may be used for students who need extra instruction in an area that has already been covered in class, for students who were absent when initial instruction occurred, or for gifted students who are ready for more advanced materials than is the class as a whole.

There is instructional software that helps students move through the writing process, from generating ideas to producing the final product. This is a specialized type of tutorial program. Some networked software allows students to comment upon each other's writing in a kind of electronic peer writing conference. Such software makes it possible for students to discuss literature online, and to discuss different aspects of each other's writing. There are also Internet sites that allow students to post their work to be critiqued by others.

Simulations replicate on the computer the important aspects of real-life situations with which the students can interact. Simulations in science, health, and social studies are available in fairly large numbers, and they can offer many experiences that students could not otherwise have. For example, simulations of chemistry experiments that use dangerous materials can provide learning experiences without danger; simulations of running businesses can help students learn economic principles without an actual outlay of money or a need for space and equipment; and simulations of ecosystems can allow students to view such phenomena as food chains without leaving the classroom.

Interactive literature programs are available on CD-ROM. Many of them allow students to have material read to them, to record and play back their own reading of the material, to click on words to get

FIGURE 8–2
Types of Computer Programs

Drill and practice programs—Offer practice on skills that have been previously taught

Tutorial programs—Offer instruction (may have a practice component)

Simulation programs—Provide situations that simulate real life

Interactive literature programs—Allow students to interact by having the material read to them, letting them record themselves reading the material, and/or letting them click on words or items to get information or see animations

Game programs—Provide recreation or skill practice in game format

Word processing programs—Allow the user to produce and easily revise text (may have desktop publishing features also)

Desktop publishing programs—Designed to allow the mixing of text and graphics in a document

Database programs—Allow creation and/or searching of organized collections of information

Spreadsheet programs—Perform calculations on organized sets of numbers, according to formulas that the user enters

Presentation software—Allows the development of multimedia presentations that can be presented on the computer

Web development software—Aids in development of web pages by converting text into HTML code

pronunciations and definitions, and to click on pictures to get animations or explanations.

Games provide recreation, but, if playing them successfully requires content knowledge, they may also reinforce classroom learning. Games are often used as a reward for successful completion of work as well as for enjoyable skill practice.

Computers with word processing software may be available for students to use in preparing class assignments in creative writing, reports in content areas, or class or school newspapers or magazines. Word processing programs allow students to make corrections in their written assignments quickly and easily, thereby making it more likely that they will attempt such corrections. These programs make inserting or deleting material and moving blocks of text easy, and many programs have spelling checkers and grammar checkers that help students find problems in their papers.

Computers with word processing programs can also be helpful to you as a teacher. You can use them to prepare study guides, review sheets, and tests and to write letters to parents. For the benefit of both you and your students, learn about the word processing software available to you, and make use of it.

Desktop publishing programs are valuable resources for developing class newspapers, class magazines, and other publications. Students can enter text, scan in pictures, incorporate clip art, and per-

form other activities that allow them to produce attractive output for creative or functional writing. Many of the current word processing programs now offer these functions, blurring the distinction that was previously made between desktop publishing programs and word processing programs.

Be careful that you are not fooled by fancy fonts, color graphics, and neat page layouts so that you fail to evaluate the information in papers that students prepare on desktop publishing or sophisticated word processing programs. Students may have beautiful papers that are empty of ideas or filled with incorrect ones (Holland, 1996).

Computer databases are also becoming an important part of instruction in many schools. A database is a "collection of related data organized to address the information needs of a variety of users" (Heide and Henderson, 1994, p. 154). The information within a database is filed under categories for easy access. A computer database can be electronically searched to locate information of interest. There are many preexisting databases that may be used in schools; as a matter of fact, classes equipped like the one in the opening vignette have numerous databases available on CD-ROM and have a program for creating databases as a part of AppleWorks or possibly some other software package on the computer's hard drive. Some school libraries are putting their card catalogs on computer, producing very useful databases. Many useful databases are available on the Internet, and they can be accessed by students in classrooms with Internet connections. Students can also create their own databases on topics of study. Doing so gives students experience in categorization of material. It is beneficial for students to know how to search existing databases and how to create their own databases for class projects. If your school has database software, learn how to use it so that you can help your students to use it effectively. You might also use database software to record information about your students or units that you plan to teach, making the effort of learning about it worthwhile for you.

In some classes, students may be learning to use spreadsheet programs. A spreadsheet program is an electronic accounting pad that can automatically perform calculations such as addition and subtraction on rows and columns of numbers. Users can enter calculation formulas to perform mathematical operations on the data. When new data are entered into the spreadsheet, the program automatically recalculates the results.

Use of Electronic References

With the advent of multimedia computers with CD-ROM drives, electronic reference materials have become much more common in schools. Electronic encyclopedias, dictionaries, thesauruses, atlases, and almanacs are among standard reference tools in many school libraries and some classrooms. There are also electronic reference materials that can be accessed on the Internet, if the classroom or library has an Internet connection. For example, the concise version (not the full version available on CD-ROM) of *Microsoft Encarta* is available free on the Internet at http://www.encarta.msn.com (Buchleitner, 1999). These reference sources are available for different grade ranges, and they need to be chosen with the potential users in mind.

Students can use Internet searches to do research for content classes. As a teacher, you can search the Internet to collect information for use in classes. For example, C-SPAN's American Presidents website (http://www.americanpresidents.org) has an in-depth look at each president. Teachers can download free guides to use with this material (Notebook, 1999). In addition, many PBS programs have teaching materials available on the PBS website (http://www.pbs.org; Sourcebook, 1999).

Students need to learn how to use a web browser, such as Internet Explorer or Netscape Navigator, to locate information on the Internet. They may locate Internet sites by entering Uniform Resource Locators

(URLs), which are the addresses of the Internet sites, in the browsers' dialogue windows, if they know the specific addresses. Once the users are at specific sites, the web browsers allow them to click on icons or words that act as links to other sites, without actually having to enter the URLs for those sites. If they do not know the URL for a needed site, are not on a site that has a link to that site, or do not know if a site with the information that they seek actually exists, they need to learn to use search engines, such as Yahooligans!®, Ask Jeeves℠, Yahoo!®, AltaVista®, and Dogpile, that "check terms that a user enters into the computer against keywords found on web pages indexed by the search service" (Roe, Stoodt, & Burns, 2001, p. 151). Different search engines use different search techniques and therefore may find different sites. Yahooligans!® is a search engine designed for use by children. It is "filtered" for their use by editors who check the sites for potentially offensive material (Buchleitner, 1999).

Online research projects make possible the collaboration of students in classrooms all over the world in common research activities. Many projects are available for classes at all levels and in a variety of subject areas. Students may collect data about water pollution in their respective areas, about temperature and weather patterns, or about some other topic of general interest to students in various courses. All students may contribute collected data to a common data bank, and the data may be analyzed in a variety of ways by the various classes. Results may be posted on a website designated for the project.

In classrooms with connections to the Internet or other wide-area networks, you can use e-mail to communicate with teachers all over the world and to consult experts in your field for advice. You can also use e-mail as a tool for students to use in lessons that you plan. Students can use e-mail to communicate with other students or resource people in remote locations. Keypal (computer pen pal) projects are frequent in the area of literature study, in which students correspond electronically with their peers or mentors in university classes about literature selections that they are reading in common (Roe & Smith, 1997). Keypal activities could be designed for any area of the curriculum.

Virtual field trips are available at a number of websites. Students can visit art museums, archeological digs, Antarctica, and countless other sites that coordinate with curricular studies. (See the discussion of field trips for more information, and for ideas about preparing students for any kind of field trip.)

Students can design and implement home pages for their classes on the Internet. These home pages can be constructed using hypertext markup language

(HTML), special software that is designed to produce HTML code for users without the users having to know the specific code (for example, FrontPage, which works well for secondary school students or Sarah's Page Web Builder, designed for ages 9 and up), or many word processing programs (such as Microsoft Word®) that can convert text files to HTML files. These home pages may be used to post creative writing, news stories, poetry, and art by class members. They may be used to present the results of class or group projects, making use of photographs taken using digital cameras, images scanned into the computer from print sources, and clip art available on the Internet or on CD-ROMs.

FOR YOUR PORTFOLIO

Design a home page for your class. Download it to disk to use in your portfolio.

For ideas about integrating the Internet into the classroom, visit *http://www.prenhall.com/methodscluster*, "Topic 15: Technology and Teaching" and look for "Uses in the Classroom" under the web links.

Expanding Computer Use

Obviously, computers can provide enrichment in school subjects for all students, offer challenges for bright students, and give special assistance for remedial and compensatory purposes. Computers that have programs in languages other than English can be helpful in enriching the learning of students for whom English is a second language and for introducing other students to the languages of various countries and cultures. Students with special needs can be helped by computer programs that offer such features as enlarged print, synthetic speech, Braille translation programs, special input devices, and even speech recognition.

Computers can be used to reinforce teaching that is not heavily dependent on textbooks and lectures. For example, computer labs can be an avenue to hands-on science and, in general, a constructivist approach to learning (Hancock & Betts, 1994).

Preparing for Computer Applications

As a student teacher, you may find that computer applications are an important component in the classes you are assigned to teach. You should have your cooperating teacher or the media specialist orient you to the particular computers and peripheral devices used in your school. You may, for example, have to know how to attach a projection device to a computer to allow you to demonstrate a program for an entire class.

You will need to know how to run commercial computer programs and what the special keys on the computer keyboard mean. You also need to know what to do if a student "crashes" a program (causes it to cease to operate).

You may also be introduced to the world of scanners, laserdiscs, digital cameras, modems, and Internet connections. If you don't already know how to do so, you will have to learn to use browsers, such as Lynx (a text-only browser) or Netscape Navigator® or Microsoft's Internet Explorer® (browsers with a graphical user interface) to locate information on the Internet. Previewing sites that you may want to use for instruction and "bookmarking" them for use during classes is a good technique. Many sites offer lesson plans for teachers of different subject areas and grade levels. These plans can give you good ideas to use in your own classes. They often provide lists of appropriate Internet sites for your students, as well.

You should know how to construct multimedia presentations for your classes and how to guide your students in constructing such presentations, if your school has appropriate hardware and software. You can learn to use programs such as HyperStudio®, mPower, or PowerPoint® to form presentations that involve text, sound, animation, and pictures to enliven your classes. Your students can learn how to construct such presentations as class projects. Today's multimedia technology—which allows, among other things, manipulation of images—can make separating reality and fiction harder for students; for example, a multimedia presentation consisting of a picture composed from parts of several other pictures may look like an authentic representation of an actual situation. Students need to realize that someone can construct such an image. They will understand this better if they are allowed to compose images themselves (Research/Center for Children and Technology, 1994).

FOR YOUR PORTFOLIO

Prepare a multimedia presentation to teach a lesson to your students. Include a copy of the presentation in your portfolio.

Judging the students' multimedia projects will also be a challenge for you. Brunner (1996) has been addressing this problem. Here are some questions you may ask about such projects, based upon her ideas:

1. Can students explain the importance of their topic?
2. Did they plan their report section by section, using a storyboard, before they started?
3. Did they use a variety of appropriate sources for the presentation?
4. Did they document their sources?
5. Is the material organized well? Is it tied together effectively, and is it easy to access?
6. Is the text easy to read?
7. Can users easily navigate the report? Are there good conceptual links?
8. Can the students explain why they chose different images, sounds, animations, videos, or text to make their points and how each one relates to the others and to the overall theme?
9. Were their choices of media appropriate, or did they waste time with "fun" animations or "interesting" videos that did not enhance the information presented?

You should also know the proper way to handle and care for the computer equipment and software. Recognize that dust, food, and drinks can be lethal to equipment. Use equipment covers when computers are not in use, and enforce regulations about not eating and drinking in the vicinity of the computer.

Be sure to read the documentation for each program your students are using. This will enable you to help students run programs, enter answers properly, and understand error messages. Some programs can be adjusted to the particular student; for example, response time or number of items can be varied. Usually, the accompanying documentation tells the teacher how to make these adjustments.

Some tutorial and drill-and-practice programs provide you with an analysis of students' performances and may move the students through new instructional sequences without your direct intervention. Obviously, such programs give you valuable aid. If the programs you are using do not provide the teacher with a performance record, you may wish to check the results on the screen before each student ends the program.

Students are unafraid of tackling computer applications. They can do some astonishing things with word processing, desktop publishing, database, and spreadsheet programs, as well as Internet publishing, if they are given the opportunity and support. Typing tutorials are available for students who lack keyboarding skills. Many programs make extensive use of a mouse, however, minimizing the need for keyboarding for some applications.

You should be ready to monitor computer use carefully when students have Internet connections available. Although some software exists to block children from viewing inappropriate sites, you cannot depend upon it completely because of the changing state of the Internet; also, many schools do not have such software installed. Have guidelines for students' use of Internet resources, and enforce them (McGillian, 1996). Circulate as the students are using the computers to be aware of the sites that are being accessed. You may want to bookmark appropriate sites for your class and restrict class use to these specified sites.

OTHER AUDIOVISUAL MEDIA

Although computers are currently high-interest delivery systems for classroom information and activities, other audiovisual media are used more frequently in the majority of classrooms.

Print Materials

Basal readers (series of graded reading instructional books) and content area textbooks can provide structure and sequence in the school curriculum. They may be the framework for learning experiences, but they should never be considered as the total instructional program. You will want to use trade books, or library books, and reference books to supplement the material in textbooks. You may want to use magazines that focus on single topics of current interest for both informational and recreational reading. You may also want to begin a collection of leaflets and pamphlets on various topics. Additionally, you can find some pictures and photographs to mount and cover with laminating film or clear contact paper to add to your collection of resource materials.

Chalkboards or Dry-Erase Boards

Chalkboards or dry-erase boards are among the most familiar visual devices in the classroom. Both students and teachers can use these boards in a number of ways. As a change of pace, students enjoy going to the board individually or in groups to do their work. For teachers, the board is readily available for recording information, writing seatwork and homework assignments, and teaching lessons.

These boards are good for listing key vocabulary that is to be used in a lesson and webbing the words when the students have read the material, heard the discussion of it, and therefore had an opportunity to grasp the connections among the terms. They are also good for recording the results of brainstorming that often takes place before reading and writing activities are begun.

Although you are accustomed to seeing the chalkboard or dry-erase board used in the classroom, you may not feel comfortable using it yourself. It is difficult to write a lot of material on the board while you are teaching, since you cannot watch the students when you are facing the board. If you have extensive material to put on the board, you may want to do it the night before or early in the morning, when you are not rushed. It is important to form your letters correctly so that your writing will be a good model for the students to follow.

Models, Globes, and Maps

Models are three-dimensional replicas of actual objects that may be smaller (an airplane) or larger (the ear) than actual size. Globes are models of the earth, and maps are two-dimensional representations of the earth's geographic and/or political features. Globes and maps can help students visualize geographic relationships and understand world affairs. Be sure that the globes and maps are current, because political boundaries change.

Math Manipulatives

Mathematics concepts are often learned most effectively when manipulative devices are used to help the students visualize the mathematical operations. Manipulatives can help students learn place value, fractions, addition, subtraction, and other basic concepts. Counters, color cubes, shape blocks, pattern blocks, linking pop cubes, sorting sets, place value charts, magnetic calendars, base-10 blocks, fraction pieces, dice, dominoes, rulers, measuring tapes, beakers, measuring cups, measuring spoons, calculator cash registers, geoboards, play money sets, learning clocks, thermometers, and playing cards can all be used as manipulatives in math lessons. As students do their own measuring, sorting, money changing, and other such activities, they see direct applications of the concepts being presented.

Audio Media

You should use audio media when sound is of primary importance for learning or appreciation. You can use recordings of folk songs, important historical speeches, or famous symphony concerts. You might want to play recordings of town meetings or forums to use as a basis for discussions of controversial issues. In many schools, students learn foreign languages in language labs that use audio media for instructional purposes. Dramatizations, documentaries, poetry readings, and great moments from history are also particularly well suited to audio presentations.

The most common type of audio media in classrooms is the audiotape recorder. Audiotape recorders have many features that make them desirable for classroom use. Students can record themselves when they read orally or make speeches, play back the tapes to listen for errors, and make efforts to improve. You can record classroom activities such as dramatizations, interviews, panel discussions, or musical programs and play them back later. You can also record some stories or lessons for students to use individually or in groups at listening stations while you are working directly with other groups of students.

You may want to have your own audiotape recorder because there are so many good opportunities for using it during the school day. An audiotape recorder is fairly inexpensive, and tapes made in class can be erased and reused. Your school may have a tape library where you can find prerecorded tapes for various purposes.

Sometimes a radio can be a useful audio medium. It can provide immediate communication on national and international affairs through newscasts, although a television is more likely to be used for this in most classrooms. Radios can also be used to listen to foreign language broadcasts.

Projected Still Pictures

Three types of projected still pictures used in classrooms are slides, filmstrips, and overhead transparencies. Slides can be selected and arranged to suit your purpose. After you assemble them, you can add a commentary tape with background sound effects; or, instead of using a prepared narrative, you may prefer to discuss the slides as you go, taking as much time with each slide as you wish. Remote-control projectors allow you to stand at the front of the class and point to details you want the students to notice.

In recent years filmstrips are being used less and less. If you have them, you can use them with synchronized tapes, or you may prefer to read from the accompanying guides. When you use filmstrips without synchronized sound, you can hold them on each frame for any length of time to allow for discussion.

The overhead projector is simple to operate, and it can be used to project images on a screen in a normally lighted classroom. You can easily create your own transparencies by writing with a grease pencil or transparency marking pen on a clear sheet of acetate, or by photocopying material that you wish to make into a transparency and using a copy machine that is designed to transfer your copy onto a transparency. You can also use commercially prepared transparencies designed for your textbook or units. If you have never used an overhead projector, become acquainted with it during your student teaching. Practice using it by yourself before using it with your class. Remember three important points: (1) check the placement and focus of the projector before the lesson starts; (2) know how to place the transparencies so that the images on the screen are readable; and (3) identify items by pointing on the transparencies, not on the screen.

Videotapes, Films, and Videodiscs

You can use videotapes, films, and videodiscs to create interest in a unit, review and reinforce a subject, provide a vicarious experience, or initiate discussion. Many useful lessons and other types of programs can be found on these media, which are often available through the school system from the central office. For example, there are video presentations of Shakespearean plays and other literature selections. Some video presentations are springboards for creative activities; others are straightforward presentations of subject matter through illustrated lectures. As processes are speeded up or slowed down on tape, film, or disc, students can watch changes occur that would otherwise be unobservable.

In recent years videotapes have almost totally supplanted films in classrooms. The videorecorders are easier to use than film projectors, and the ability to fast-forward and rewind tapes makes them more versatile. Using videotape recorders, you can record television programs and play them back later, although you must be sure to observe the copyright laws. There are also prerecorded tapes available for use in most subject areas. For example, the National Geographic Society has a series of animal videos for grades pre-K to 4, called *Tales from the Wild*.

You can also record students' performances with portable videotape recorders and play those performances back for the students to see. The students can use these videotape recordings for self-analysis. They are particularly useful in speech, drama, dance, and physical education classes. The recordings may also be used as visible evidence of improvement in these and other areas. For example, creative dramatic performances can be recorded over a period of time, and all the performances played back in a single viewing. The students can see how their actions and speech have changed over time.

Videotape recorders are easy to operate, and they can be used to provide focused instruction for the whole class or targeted groups of students. Older students can learn to use the recorders and then assist in documenting class presentations or special programs.

Videodiscs, CD-ROMs, and DVD-ROMs provide video images and high-quality sound. They also allow random access to desired frames or video segments. This gives them an advantage over videotapes for some applications. Realize that you need to analyze educational videodiscs, CD-ROMs, and DVD-ROMs to make sure that they are not all "flash," without reliable, accurate, and well-organized information. You also must be sure that they are easy to navigate (Phillips, 1996; "A DVD Primer," 1999).

FOR YOUR PORTFOLIO

Videotape or audiotape presentations that students give in a class that you teach. Include the videotape or audiotape in your portfolio with an explanation of how your lessons led to these presentations.

Television

Two types of television programming are appropriate for instructional use: educational programming, much of which is on the Public Broadcasting System or WAM! (billed as America's "kidz network"); and commercial programming that happens to cover areas of educational interest. Students may have access to either of these types of programming during the school day, depending upon scheduling considerations, or they may be assigned programs to watch at home, outside of school hours, with the understanding that these programs will be discussed in class later.

Whether or not you make use of instructional television will probably be determined by your cooperating teacher and the availability of a television set in your classroom. Unlike filmstrips, films, and videotapes, television programs cannot be previewed if they are watched live. Therefore, you must study the manual to develop your lesson. When using a television program, turn on the set at least 15 minutes before the scheduled starting time to make sure it is operating correctly. Introduce vocabulary and concepts by writing them on the chalkboard and discussing them, and thoroughly prepare your students for what they will see. When the program starts, encourage students to respond to the television teacher by participating actively in the lesson yourself. During the lesson, take notes on points that you want to discuss later. Walk around among the students to make sure that they are actively involved in the lesson. After the program is over, don't reteach the lesson, but follow through with related activities.

If you assign regular television programs (e.g., documentaries, cultural programs, or series of educational significance) for the students to watch at home during the evenings or on weekends, you should provide the students with specific objectives. Television guides are often available for teachers to use for these types of programs; sometimes they can be downloaded from the Internet. With the help of a guide, you can assign students to watch for certain points or ideas as they view the programs. The next class day, you should follow up with a discussion or other experiences related to the programs.

As mentioned before, you may videotape television programs to view later. "Cable in the Classroom is a public-service initiative of the cable television industry. It is a joint project of local cable operators and national cable programmers to provide schools with free basic cable service and more than 540 hours of commercial-free educational television programming each month" (Cable in the Classroom Fact Sheet, 1999, p. 2). These programs have liberal copyright clearance, and they may be taped and used for educational purposes. Some allow unrestricted use; some have time limits for use, but these may be as generous as use within 1 or 2 years. For example, teachers who taped C-SPAN's *American Presidents: Life Portraits* series in 1999 are unrestricted in the time that they can show it for edu-

cational purposes. Cable in the Classroom programs are available for many curricular areas.

Calculators

In mathematics classes calculators are used extensively for time-consuming or complex computations, leaving more time for the students to perform the cognitive processes necessary to solve problems. Calculators are also often useful in science classes when lab experiments require calculations.

COMMUNITY RESOURCES

The community in which your school is located offers many opportunities for purposeful learning experiences. Use of resource people and field trips provides links between the basic skills taught in the classroom and the application of these skills in the outside world. Your community involvement while you are a student teacher may be limited, but you can still utilize many resources if you begin early to explore the possibilities.

Resource People

A resource person can often attract students' attention more effectively than the classroom teacher can. Because of the resource person's direct experience

A resource person can often attract students' attention more than the classroom teacher can, and he or she is more likely to make a lasting impression.

ACTIVITY 8.2   *Survey of Resource People*

Date _____

Student's name _____   Grade _____   Phone _____

Teacher's name _____   School _____

Address of student _____

Parent's name _____

Address (if different) _____

Are you willing to volunteer your help in your son's or daughter's classroom? _____

If so, what days and hours are most convenient? _____

Do you have any special knowledge, talents, or skills that you can share with the class? _____

If so, what are they? _____

_____

Perhaps you know someone who would be able to contribute something worthwhile to the school. If so, please fill in the information below. (Use other side for additional suggestions.)

Name _____   Phone _____

Address _____

Possible contribution _____

Thank you for your cooperation!

with a topic, the presentation is usually more credible and more likely to make a lasting impression. Since you cannot be an expert in every field, other people can sometimes supplement your knowledge. A resource person can be especially effective at the beginning of a unit to create interest or near the end of a unit to reinforce and extend concepts.

The first step in using resource people is to consider who has expertise in the topics you plan to cover. Your personal friends may have hobbies or experiences that would make them valuable resource people. If you are a student teacher in your hometown, you may already know people who could contribute to your unit. School personnel may discuss their work experiences or offer special knowledge. Your university employs specialists in many fields who may be willing to work with you. People from varied cultural, ethnic, and religious backgrounds may be available to share their heritages. Businesses and industries, banks, protective service agencies, public utilities, and government agencies at all levels often have representatives who go into the schools to provide information.

Resource people can be identified through various approaches. Your school may have a volunteer services program or a file with the names of resource people and their areas of expertise. Your cooperating teacher or other school personnel may be able to recommend a suitable resource person for your subject. Senior citizens can be recruited from retirement centers and religious and community organizations. You may wish to survey your students to see if their parents or someone else they know can be helpful. A sample survey form is provided in Activity 8.2. Before you take a survey, be sure to get permission from school authorities.

After you select someone with the appropriate specialized knowledge, you will have to contact her or him concerning the proposed school visit. Tactfully discuss the type of presentation, the need to adjust to the students' level, and the amount of time available. Discuss the students' background knowledge, attention span, and probable questions. The visitor may prefer to lecture, show slides, demonstrate a process, or talk informally. Be sure she or he understands the purpose of the visit and how it relates to what you are teaching.

You must also prepare students for resource visitors. They should be involved in the planning and may want to make lists of questions prior to visits. Students can issue invitations, arrange for any special equipment, meet guests upon their arrival, introduce them, and assist them in their presentations. Students should be encouraged to show their appreciation at the time of the visit and later in the form of thank-you letters. As the teacher, you must relate the presentations of resource people to your unit by preparing the students for visits and following them up with reinforcing activities.

Some business and civic leaders may not be willing to come to the school but will grant interviews to students who come to see them. The experience of conducting an interview is worthwhile; however, careful and detailed arrangements need to be made prior to the interview. School personnel must approve the interview. Consent must also be given by the prospective interviewee and by the parents of the students participating in the interview. The students should draw up questions in advance, practice note-taking skills, and learn proper conduct in handling an interview. After the interview, students need to organize their notes and write summaries of the information to share with their classmates.

Students at the secondary level can become involved with resource people by taking surveys. The students can identify an issue in which they are interested and design a simple questionnaire to give to people they know. Topics might include whether or not to build a new gymnasium, establish a teen center, or extend the city limits. Students can get additional information about their topics by searching through records and interviewing city employees. The students can summarize their findings and draw conclusions that might have implications for community action. They can submit the results to the media for dissemination to the public.

Field Trips

A field trip is an organized class excursion for the purpose of obtaining information through direct observation. A child's experiences with field trips usually begin with visits to places like a fire station or dairy farm. Some classes take end-of-year trips to zoos or museums. Older students may "run" City Hall for one day of the year; each student is appointed to a position and assumes the responsibilities of the person who occupies the corresponding position in city government. Participation in field experiences during their school years gives students many opportunities to understand how their community operates and to broaden their knowledge of specific subjects. Acquaintance with different occupations can also give students direction in choosing careers.

Although a field trip can be a valuable learning experience, it requires a great deal of planning; otherwise, it can be a fiasco. Students may become disorderly and disruptive, get injured, destroy property, and generally damage relations between school and community. Unless you make careful preparations, students may not see the reason for the trip, and its educational value is therefore lost. Appropriate follow-up activities after the field trip can help to solidify learning. Students can have small-group and class discussions about the trip, write about it, prepare oral or multimedia presentations about it, or add information gleaned from the trip to a class web page. The checklist in Activity 8.3 can help you plan a successful field trip.

Field trips face other problems as well. With school budgets tightening, many school districts no longer provide free bus transportation for field trips. Increased concern about liability and lawsuits has made many teachers wary of the risk involved in taking students away from the school.

In self-contained classrooms, scheduling a field trip is usually fairly simple because only one teacher is involved. It is sometimes more difficult, however, to arrange trips in secondary schools, because of the short class periods in schools without block scheduling. Sometimes teachers of other subjects will cooperate to permit the absence of your students, but it may be necessary to plan trips at this level for after school or Saturdays.

Students who know what to expect are likely to learn more from a field trip than students who have no background information. The class should be involved in planning each trip. Even though you may have the idea in the back of your mind, you may want to let the students think the idea is theirs. For young children, a discussion about the subject and the proposed field trip may result in a set of questions on a language experience chart. These questions can be used as objectives for the trip. Older students can research the subject and develop individual lists of questions, which may ultimately result in written reports. Students of any age may be able to visit a related website in preparation for the trip. For example, if the students are going to visit an art museum that has a website, they may visit the website before they go to help them develop a list of the things they want to experience on the trip itself. On the other hand, students who are going to visit a water treatment plant that does not have its own website might locate a website that talks about what happens at such a plant before the trip, allowing them to make a list of questions about the specific facility they plan to visit.

Field trips are valuable only when they are an integral part of a total learning situation. You need to make adequate preparation and reinforce the educational value of the field trip with a variety of follow-up activities. These activities often spill over into many areas of the curriculum—social studies, science, reading, language arts, art, and music.

Field trips within walking distance of the school can provide students with new experiences. Businesses or recreational facilities, such as parks, near the school can be the focus of such trips. The students may want to consider why the business or recreational facility was located where it is, what the effect of this facility is on the community, and whether or not they personally see direct benefits from it. One elementary school is located near a business that makes ceramic items. The students walk to the business and receive a tour and sample items. Then they return to their classrooms to write about the tour and the business.

The field trip of the future may be the electronic field trip in which the students are prepared for the experience with hands-on activities and videotaped programs to provide background, and then have an interactive teleconference with the experts (Scherer, 1994). As mentioned earlier, students can go on virtual tours to many places by accessing their websites. For example, the Lincoln Park Zoo site is located at http://www.lpzoo.com (Buchleitner, 1999). Even without teleconferences with the experts, teachers can make use of such sites by careful preparation of the children before the visit and appropriate follow-up activities.

You may find an opportunity for taking a nearby field trip, or you may want to plan an electronic trip. Talk it over with your cooperating teacher; then make it work!

DISCUSSION QUESTIONS

1. Should you use a free, current, interesting video from a company that uses the video to advertise its product? If you decide to use the video, what are some ways to handle the advertising message?

2. How can you use the resources in your community? What people, places, or agencies are available that relate to your subjects? How can you find out?

3. What do you do if one student's parent offers to share information with your class that you feel is inappropriate? How can you avoid offending the parent and the student? Is there another way you could use the parent's services?

4. What is the policy regarding field trips in your school? Are they permitted? How is transportation arranged? What regulations are in effect? Would a field trip be a good learning experience for your students?

5. Choose one of the selected references below that is concerned with use of computers or videotechnology. Read it and answer this question: How can the ideas presented in this source help me in my teaching assignment?

ACTIVITY 8.3   *Checklist for Field Trip*

1. _____ Permission to take a field trip has been granted by the school.

2. _____ Personnel at the destination have been contacted, and a time has been set for the visit.

3. _____ Transportation has been arranged.

4. _____ If you are using private cars, insurance and liability regulations have been checked.

5. _____ An adequate number of adults have agreed to accompany the students.

6. _____ Proper arrangements have been made regarding the facilities at the destination: restrooms, cafeteria, picnic tables, parking areas, size of observation areas.

7. _____ Lunch money and other fees have been collected (if applicable).

8. _____ Parental permission notes have been sent home.

9. _____ Parental permission notes have been returned.

10. _____ Students have been told how to behave and what to wear.

11. _____ Students have been told what to expect and have adequate background knowledge to understand what they will see.

12. _____ A list of questions has been prepared to set purposes for the visit.

13. _____ Tape recorders and notepads are available for recording specific information.

14. _____ Safety hazards, if any, have been noted and appropriate precautions taken.

15. _____ A first aid kit is available for emergencies.

16. _____ A signal (such as a whistle or raised arm) has been agreed upon for getting students' attention.

17. _____ Students have been paired and assigned buddies (if appropriate).

18. _____ Policy manual regarding field trips has been read, and policies have been followed.

6. What kinds of software can be used by students for multimedia presentations? What are the pros and cons of assigning multimedia presentations to students?

7. How can you use a student-developed web page to advance your teaching objectives?

SELECTED REFERENCES

Allen, D. (1994, November/December). Teaching with technology: Literature and software. *Teaching K–8, 25,* 20–23.

Allen, D. (1995, January). Teaching with technology: Creative problem solving. *Teaching K–8, 25,* 18, 22–25.

Allen, D. (1996, February). Teaching with technology: Break the language barrier. *Teaching K–8, 26,* 16–18.

Anderson-Inman, L. (1998, February). Electronic journals in technology and literacy: Professional development online. *Journal of Adolescent and Adult Literacy, 41,* 400–405.

Betts, F. (1994, April). "On the birth of the communication age: A conversation with David Thornburg." *Educational Leadership, 51,* 20–23.

Betts, F. (1994, April). Review: Making decisions about CD-ROMs. *Educational Leadership, 51,* 42–43.

Brunner, C. (1996, May/June). Judging student multimedia. *Electronic Learning, 15,* 14–15.

Berwick, B. (1994, April). Kids behind the camera: Education for the video age. *Educational Leadership, 51,* 52–54.

Buchleitner, Warren. (1999, May/June). Teaching with technology: Exploring nature on the Web. *Early Childhood Today, 13,* 14–15.

Cable in the Classroom Fact Sheet. (1999, March). *Cable in the Classroom, 9,* 2.

A DVD primer. (1999). *T.H.E. Journal, 26* (6), 23.

Dwyer, D. (1994, April). Apple classrooms of tomorrow: What we've learned. *Educational Leadership, 51,* 4–10.

Edinger, M. (1994, April). Empowering young writers with technology. *Educational Leadership, 51,* 58–60.

El-Hindi, A. E. (1998, May). Beyond classroom boundaries: Constructivist teaching with the Internet. *The Reading Teacher, 51,* 694–699.

Focus on technology: The most bang for the buck. (1994, December 5). *Newsweek,* 88.

Grabe, M., & Grabe, C. (2000). *Integrating technology for meaningful learning.* Boston: Houghton Mifflin.

Hancock, V., & Betts, F. (1994, April). From the lagging to the leading edge. *Educational Leadership, 51,* 24–29.

Heide, A., & Henderson, D. (1994). *The technological classroom.* Toronto, Ontario, Canada: Trifolium.

Heinich, R., Molenda, M., Russell, J. D., & Smaldino, S. E. (1999). *Instructional media and technologies for learning.* Upper Saddle River, NJ: Prentice-Hall.

Holland, H. (1996, May/June). Way past word processing. *Electronic Learning, 15,* 22–26.

Holtzberg, C. S. (1994, May/June). The new multimedia. *Electronic Learning, 13,* 55–62.

The instructional power of an electronic encyclopedia. (1996, April). *Curriculum Administrator, 30,* 28–29.

Kanning, R. G. (1994, April). What multimedia can do in our classrooms. *Educational Leadership, 51,* 40–44.

Lapp, D., Flood, J., & Fisher, D. (1999, April). Intermediality: How the use of multiple media enhances learning. *The Reading Teacher, 52,* 776–780.

Leu, D. J., Jr., & Leu, D. D. (1999). *Teaching with the Internet: Lessons from the classroom.* Norwood, MA: Christopher-Gordon.

Mather, M. A. (1996). Exploring the Internet safely: What schools can do. *Technology and Learning, 17* (1), 38–40, 42.

McGillian, J. K. (1996, May/June). Cyber patrol: How can we make sure our young techies stay safe? *Creative Classroom, 10,* 69.

McGrath, B. (1998, April). Partners in learning: Twelve ways technology changes the teacher-student relationship. *T.H.E. Journal, 25,* 58–61.

Means, B., & Olson, K. (1994, April). The link between technology and authentic learning. *Educational Leadership, 51,* 15–18.

Mike, D. G. (1994, May/June). Interactive literacy. *Electronic Learning, 13,* 50–52, 54.

Muir, M. (1994, April). Putting computer projects at the heart of the curriculum. *Educational Leadership, 51,* 30–32.

Notebook. (1999, May). *Cable in the classroom, 9,* 3.

Novelli, J. (1994, January). Get animated! Multimedia communication for kids. *Instructor, 103,* 68–72.

Novelli, J. (1994, February). Putting (real) life into learning with technology. *Instructor Middle Years,* 30–36.

Novelli, J. (1996, May/June). Switched-on books. *Instructor, 105,* 55, 80.

Peck, K. L., & Dorricott, D. (1994, April). Why use technology? *Educational Leadership, 51,* 11–14.

Phillips, M. (1996, May/June). Beyond the "best CDs" list. *Electronic Learning, 15,* 16.

Rekrut, M. D. (1999, April). Using the Internet in classroom instruction: A primer for teachers. *Journal of Adolescent and Adult Literacy, 42,* 546–557.

Research/Center for children and technology: Teaching visual literacy. (1994, November/December). *Electronic Learning, 14,* 16–17.

Rock, H. M., & Cummings, A. (1994, April). Can videodiscs improve student outcomes? *Educational Leadership, 51,* 46–50.

Roe, B. D., & Smith, S. H. (1997). University/Public Schools Keypals Project: A collaborative effort for electronic literature conversations. In *Rethinking Teaching and Learning through Technology.* Murfreesboro, TN: Proceedings of the Mid-South Instructional Technology Conference.

Roe, B. D, Stoodt, B. D., & Burns, P. C. (2001). Secondary school literacy instruction: The content areas. Boston: Houghton Mifflin.

Scherer, M. (1994, April). Review: Electronic fieldtrips. *Educational Leadership, 51,* 38.

Sharp, V. (1996). *Computer education for teachers.* Madison, WI: Brown and Benchmark.

Smith, M. M. (1996, May/June). The creative edge. *Electronic Learning, 15,* 47–54, 68.

Sourcebook. (1999, May). *Cable in the classroom, 9,* 17.

Sullivan, J. (1998, September). The electronic journal: Combining literacy and technology. *The Reading Teacher, 52,* 90–92.

Taggart, L. (1994, April). Student autobiographies with a twist of technology. *Educational Leadership, 51,* 34–35.

Willis, W. (1998). Software: Focus on videotapes. *T.H.E. Journal 25* (6), 24–25.

Zorfass, J., Corley, P., & Remz, A. (1994, April). Helping students with disabilities become writers. *Educational Leadership, 51,* 62–66.

Teaching Strategies

The Challenge of Teaching Students Who Differ in Needs

Ralph is a ninth-grader reading at a fourth-grade level in Mrs. Kelsey's remedial reading class. During the year, Mrs. Kelsey and Mr. Sunas, the intern, have tried to encourage Ralph to read by finding him easy materials and offering rewards for progress. Ralph has not responded and has shown no interest in reading. Mr. Sunas is determined to find some way to reach Ralph before the end of the year. This morning Ralph had come to school unusually tired.

Mr. Sunas: What's the matter, Ralph? You seem so tired today. Did you have a rough weekend?

Ralph: We were out planting soybeans all weekend, Mr. Sunas. I'm beat.

Mr. Sunas: I don't know much about growing soybeans, Ralph. Tell me about it.

Ralph: Gosh, there's so much to tell. I don't know where to begin. My folks've been raising soybeans for as far back as I can remember.

Mr. Sunas: Is that what you plan to do, too?

Ralph: You bet! I want to grow the best soybeans around here. That's why I'm just waiting to be 16 so I can drop out of school. I want to get out and work with the soybeans and not just sit here all day doing nothing.

Mr. Sunas: Ralph, if you really want to be the best producer of soybeans in the area, how are you going to go about it?

Ralph: I guess I'll just do what my dad and his folks have always done.

Mr. Sunas: But Ralph, the Agricultural Experiment Station is developing better ways of raising soybeans all the time. There's a lot to know about disease control, fertilizers, soil conservation, and marketing. I'll bring you some information about it.

Ralph: No, don't bother. I don't want to read about it.

Mr. Sunas (a few days later): I found some pamphlets on how to raise soybeans. I thought you might want to look at them.

Ralph: Maybe later. (Ralph yawns, leans back in his chair, and stares out the window.)

Mr. Sunas (20 minutes later): Ralph, have you looked at those pamphlets yet?

Ralph: No, not yet. (He picks up his pencil and starts doodling on a scrap of paper.)

Mr. Sunas: Did you have any trouble with blister beetles last year? I hear they're supposed to be bad again this year.

Ralph: Yeah. They really gave us problems last year. (pause) Why? Does it say something about them in here?

Mr. Sunas: Yes. It tells you what to do to prevent having so many and how to control the ones you do have.

Ralph: No fooling? I bet my dad would really like to know about this.

Mr. Sunas: Why don't you read about it for the rest of the period? I'll help you with the words you don't know.

Ralph: Hey, here's a picture of one of the beetles. This is really neat. What's this say here, Mr. Sunas? I really need to know this stuff.

Florinda was a bright, eager child who came to first grade already knowing how to read. At age 3, she was reading signs on franchises along the highway, and at age 4, she was picking words out of the storybooks her father read to her. By the time she was 5, she could read simple books by herself. Mrs. Cho, Florinda's teacher, had 29 students in first grade that year and had her hands full working with a large number of immature children. Mrs. Cho realized that Florinda knew how to read, but she didn't think she could afford the time to work with Florinda on a different level. Florinda was placed in a regular reading group with the other first-graders who were not yet reading, then in a beginning readers' group.

Florinda (one morning before school starts): Look, Mrs. Cho, this is the book my daddy read me last night—*Where The Wild Things Are!* It's so exciting, and I can read it all by myself.

Mrs. Cho: That's fine, Florinda. It *is* a good book. Now put it away. It will be time for reading group soon.

Florinda: But Mrs. Cho, those stories in reading group are too easy. They're no fun to read.

Mrs. Cho: I'm sorry, Florinda, but you'll just have to read what the other boys and girls are reading. I don't have time to listen to you read your books.

Florinda: Well, okay.

Mrs. Cho (observing Florinda reading her book during class time later that morning): Florinda, I told you to put that book away. This isn't the time to read. You have four worksheets to do.

Florinda: But I don't want to do them. They're dumb.

Mrs. Cho: Give me your book, Florinda. Do your work like the other boys and girls. I don't want you causing any trouble.

1. What motivational techniques were mentioned in the vignette about Ralph? Which one seemed to be successful? Why do you think it worked?
2. Was Ralph internally motivated? If so, why didn't he respond positively to the school situation?

How are both intrinsic (internal) motivation and extrinsic (external) motivation a part of the story about Ralph?

3. Does Ralph's interest in the blister beetle mean that he is now motivated to learn? Is there a danger that his interest in learning will pass? How could his interest be extended until it becomes a part of his intrinsic motivation?

4. How could Ralph's interest in soybeans be used to increase his achievement in other areas, such as math and science?

5. What was Mrs. Cho doing to Florinda's intrinsic motivation? What might happen to Florinda as a result of her teacher's attitude? What are some choices Mrs. Cho had for keeping Florinda's interest in reading alive?

6. How did these two teachers differ in dealing with their students' needs and interests? What long-term effects do you think their different strategies might have on their students?

HELPING THEM LEARN

Now the groundwork has been laid. You know about lesson plans and discipline, as well as your resources, coworkers, and students. It's time to analyze teaching strategies. In this chapter, you'll find many different approaches to teaching and ideas for ways to motivate students and help them learn effectively. Student teaching is a good time to experiment with new ideas and find out what works for you.

Remember that you cannot teach your students all there is to know. What is important is that, through your teaching, you help students discover how to learn. Provide them with strategies for solving problems, and teach them to think for themselves. This way of teaching goes along with a constructivist theory of learning, which holds that students actively build knowledge, rather than merely receiving it passively. They use their past experiences and personal purposes to construct the meaning of their lessons. If you embrace this theory, you will try to connect the instructional material to your students' interests and prior experiences. In other words, you will try to build bridges between the new and the known. You will ask students to take part in authentic, purposeful learning experiences that connect with their own lives (Henderson, 1992).

STUDENT-CENTERED LEARNING

When students plan cooperatively and make decisions about their own learning experiences, they are assuming the kinds of responsibilities that will enable them to become productive citizens in a democratic society. Students at all levels have the capacity to make some decisions about their learning. If given such opportunities, they are likely to improve their problem-solving, critical thinking, and language skills. In addition, they will be more motivated to learn because they are actively involved. To repeat, this active involvement is congruent with a constructivist theory of learning.

Most students have a sense of wonder and are naturally curious. *Inquiry learning* allows them to identify topics that interest them and to pursue these topics in depth. Students eagerly explore self-chosen subjects by collecting information, conducting research, and presenting their findings. They might investigate such topics as why dinosaurs became extinct, how birds migrate vast distances, or how to find alternative sources of energy. Inquiry learning can occur at any grade level and across the curriculum. Listening to what children want to know and designing your lessons to enable them to find out should become part of your teaching. Although what you teach is often mandated by the curriculum or your cooperating teacher, try to give students opportunities for inquiry learning.

Student-centered learning does not mean that you should abandon all plans and preparations; after all, you have knowledge and experience that are useful for helping students learn. It does mean, however, that you should find opportunities to let students grow in their ability to direct their own learning. The term *negotiated learning* means that you, with your expertise, and the students, with their increasing ability to assume responsibility, work together to plan, direct, and assess learning experiences (see Activity 9.1).

An example of negotiated learning is the theme cycle, a way of integrating the curriculum. Together, students and teacher select a topic for study. The teacher offers choices based on the curriculum for that grade level, and the students select the topic of greatest interest to them. For example, if the curriculum mandates study of states within the United States, the students might choose Hawaii. Instead of providing the plan for the unit and related resources, the teacher asks students such questions as:

What do we already know?

What do we want to find out?

Where can we find resources?

How can we organize the class to get the information we need?

What are some ways to present the findings of individuals or groups to the rest of the class?

What time frame should we establish?

At the end, how should we evaluate what we learned?

Kerr, Makuluni, and Nieves (2000) and Hicks, Montequin, and Hicks (2000) describe a research project that involved parents, children, and teachers in investigating questions of interest. Research groups were based on the children's interests, with help from the teacher in refining the research questions. Data-collection methods included reading from traditional print materials, using computer resources, conducting direct interviews, and doing experiments. This student-centered project allowed participants to learn about research procedures, as well as their topics of interest.

As a result of these problem-solving and decision-making activities, students not only learn content, but also discover ways to work independently and cooperatively. They may complete much of the work in cooperative learning groups, in which there is positive interdependence as well as individual responsibility for learning. (See Chapter 4 for an extensive discussion of cooperative learning.)

It would be a mistake to assume that all students are ready for negotiated learning, because some may never have had opportunities to make choices and decisions at school. Cooperative teacher-student planning and decision making works best if the teacher makes careful preparations and follows guidelines such as these:

1. Create a learning environment that enables students to make reasonable choices, take risks, assume responsibilities, and use their imaginations.
2. Act as a facilitator, not a director, of learning, and be ready to serve as a resource person as needed.
3. Begin with small tasks, building gradually to larger tasks as you observe that the students are ready.
4. Involve each student as much as possible, and encourage each one to take a leadership role at some time.
5. Be sure that students perceive their activities as meaningful and important.
6. Before involving the students, be well prepared yourself: know the subject, available resources, and desirable outcomes.
7. Be accepting of students' attempts, intervening only when requested or as necessary.
8. Participate with the students in evaluating the final product.

Beginning in kindergarten, children can make choices, lead "show-and-tell" activities, work with partners, and so forth. As children mature, they are able to assume more complex roles in classroom plan-

ning and decision making. Grade level alone, however, does not indicate students' preparation for directing their own learning; their prior experiences, personalities, and social interactions, as well as the teacher's attitude toward student-centered learning, are also important considerations. In the following list, you will find some types of negotiated activities.

Student-Centered Learning Activities

1. Determine what learning strategies to use (e.g., brainstorming, demonstrating, sharing, interviewing, using reference materials, etc.).
2. Identify reasonable time frames for projects, allowing for flexibility.
3. Decide what forms final products will take.
4. Lead activities, workshops, and games.
5. Direct independent studies with input from the teacher and students.
6. Set daily schedules and rules for behavior.
7. Participate in projects, such as making videos, writing computer programs, and conducting science experiments.
8. Be responsible for establishing and managing learning centers.
9. Participate in record keeping and evaluation.
10. Provide peer assistance.
11. Create bulletin boards, displays, and visuals for the classroom.
12. Choose topics for investigation.

Remember that even when you turn a great deal of the responsibility over to the students, your guidance and support are essential components of successful student-centered learning. Bomer (1998) believes that teachers should not be afraid to teach. He says that some teachers use vague language with students when giving directions because they think they cannot have a teaching agenda in "student-centered classrooms" without the children's permission. According to Bomer, "It would be useful for teachers . . . to say what they mean when giving students directions. Even though we do want students to be active and intentional, we also want to affect what they're doing, often to turn them in completely new directions" (p. 17). He sees the teacher's place in the classroom as not authoritarian, but still authoritative.

FOR YOUR PORTFOLIO

Describe a student-centered learning activity that you have used. Write your reflections about its effectiveness with your class.

ACTIVITY 9.1   *Student-Centered Learning Activity Sheet—Plan for Negotiated Learning*

Date:

Type of activity:

Teacher's involvement:

Students' involvement:

Assessment of activity:

Recommendations for improving students' responsibilities and decision making:

MOTIVATION

One of your greatest challenges as a teacher will be to motivate your students. All learning is motivated in one way or another. Highly motivated pupils almost teach themselves, in their eagerness to learn. Poorly motivated students are unlikely to learn much of anything, no matter how well you teach.

Intrinsic versus Extrinsic Motivation

Motivation comes both from the student's inner self and from external forces. *Internal* or *intrinsic* motivation arises out of a student's needs, personality, attitudes, and values. Students who are internally motivated may be driven by the need to be popular, curiosity, the desire to excel, or the fear of failure. Intrinsic motivation is generally long-lasting; it is a part of the individual that drives that person toward her or his goals. Successful experiences tend to increase a student's internal drives, but repeated failures may eventually destroy inner motivation.

Intrinsic motivation is part of a student's basic personality and changes very slowly, if at all. This means that you will probably have little opportunity to change the underlying motivational patterns of students in the short time you will work with them. By stimulating their curiosity and building on their interests, however, you can lay the foundation for lasting internal changes.

External or *extrinsic* motivation originates in the learning environment and causes the student to want to do certain things. As the teacher, you may want to employ various types of external motivation to modify students' behavior. Be aware, however, that this type of motivation is usually short-term and may disappear when the student reaches the immediate goal.

You can use incentives as extrinsic motivators to make students want to work or behave better. Rewards are generally more effective incentives than punishments. Positive incentives that you may find useful are free time, extended recess periods, recognition on the classroom bulletin board, and prizes or awards. Students can also be motivated by earning good grades and seeing their names on the honor roll.

Keep in mind that external incentives are only artificial ways of getting students to try harder. Such incentives should never become the major reason for doing schoolwork, or students will value the reward more than the learning. Most learning tasks don't require incentives. Students should develop self-discipline to get their work done. If you decide to use incentives, learn which types work best for your students; then use them sparingly and for only short periods of time.

Be careful about giving awards or prizes as incentives for top achievers. These students are usually internally motivated anyway, and poor achievers become even more frustrated when competing against them. One way to overcome this problem is by having students compete against their own records instead of trying to be the best in the class. For instance, students can keep charts of their daily or weekly grades and try to show improvement. Another way to avoid the problem is to have one group or class compete against another group or class. Students work together to win a reward, and all students have a chance to win. Recognition can also be given for increased effort and for improvement in attitude.

Who Is Motivated?

You will be able to observe different levels of motivation among your students. Those who seem poorly motivated will need more patience and skill to get them interested. If you aren't sure which students are well motivated and which are not, use the following lists of questions as you observe students. The more "yes" answers you get on the first list, the more positively motivated the student is. On the second list, a large number of "yes" answers indicates a poorly motivated student.

Highly Motivated Students

Does the student:

1. Appear to use good study skills?
2. Read or seek information during free time?
3. Ask questions in class?
4. Listen attentively?
5. Express curiosity and interest when given new ideas?
6. Take a lively part in class discussion?
7. Do extra work beyond regular class assignments?
8. Think independently instead of following the crowd?
9. Persist in solving problems until reaching a solution?
10. Send off for information?

Poorly Motivated Students

Does the student:

1. Seem inattentive and appear to daydream a lot?
2. Give up on a test or just guess at answers?
3. Try to avoid participating in class activities?
4. Cause disruptions by distracting other students?
5. Waste time?
6. Not do homework or other assignments?
7. Jump to conclusions instead of thinking something through?
8. Seem unable to work independently?
9. Read assigned pages without understanding what has been read?

Setting Goals

All your students need approval, acceptance, and achievement. Most of them also have special interests, such as taking care of a new puppy or rebuilding a car engine. These needs and interests become the bases for setting goals. If you can develop a relationship between students' goals and your instructional program, the students will be motivated to learn. That is what Mr. Sunas tried to do with Ralph in this chapter's opening vignette.

You can set goals for your students, but if you expect them to work toward those goals, they must accept the goals as their own. The students should see that *your* instructional goals will help them achieve something *they* want; otherwise, they will not be motivated to do their best work.

One eighth-grade teacher was frustrated because, even though her students could pass tests on the correct use of English, they used poor grammar as soon as they were outside the classroom. She realized they didn't see any point in speaking Standard English. One day she asked them, "Can you think of any reasons for needing to speak correct English?" Finally, one student said, "Well, I guess so. I plan to earn money next summer by selling books. If I don't speak right, people may not buy books from me." Another student said, "When I go to church, sometimes they call on me to make a prayer. I get embarrassed in front of the preacher if I make a mistake in English."

Using their interests in establishing goals is a good way to motivate students. You can learn about students' interests by taking a simple written or oral survey. You may have a problem if the interests in your class vary widely, but students' interests usually tend to cluster around a few general topics. Once you identify these topics, you can begin to relate instructional objectives to them. If you find this procedure difficult, build on the students' interests until you make a connection with what you need to teach. For instance, if several students are interested in race cars, let them: (1) read books about race cars, (2) solve math problems that involve race cars, (3) do research reports on the history of race cars, and (4) investigate the construction of race cars. Common interests, such as holidays or community and school events, also make good focal points for setting instructional goals.

Students must also view goals as reasonable and attainable. Unreasonably long assignments will only frustrate them and discourage most of them from trying. If you want to assign work that will take a period of time to complete, break the work down into small steps. For instance, research reports can be broken down like this: (1) select a topic, (2) read about it in different sources and take notes, (3) organize the report (web or outline), (4) make a rough draft, and (5) write the final report. Goals do not seem so difficult to reach when they become a series of small, related tasks.

Motivational Strategies

You may want to use some of these specific suggestions for motivating students.

1. Keep records of progress made, books reviewed, or tasks completed, so that students can see what they have accomplished.
2. Encourage students to identify their own problems; then help them solve the problems creatively.
3. Arouse their curiosity. Vary teaching strategies so that students will be eager to see what you do next.
4. Work in some riddles and jokes. It takes intelligence to appreciate humor, and you will keep the students interested.
5. Vary the types of activities. Follow a quiet study session with a song or physical activity.
6. Be enthusiastic. Enthusiasm is contagious, and your students will catch it.
7. Create failure-proof situations for slow learners and poorly motivated students. Offer challenges to highly motivated students.
8. Use educational games, concrete objects, and audiovisual media to create interest.
9. Write brief messages to students when you return their papers, instead of assigning only a letter grade.
10. Videotape a special presentation, debate, panel discussion, or activity.
11. Set up a mailbox or communications bulletin board for each class so that you and the students can exchange messages.
12. Use a popular song (choose carefully!) as a basis for a lesson in language arts. Look for new vocabulary words, synonyms, antonyms, rhyming words, alliteration, and special meanings.
13. Instead of the textbook, teach from a newspaper. It can be used for any content area.
14. In a foreign language class, translate the school menu each day from English to the foreign language, or play "Password" in the foreign language.
15. Encourage home economics and science students to prepare projects for competitions, such as county fairs and science fairs.

16. Compute averages, figure percentages, and make graphs in math class from data the students collect. Sample topics include height of students, size of rooms, students on the honor roll, and male and female faculty members.
17. Let students set up and carry out experiments in science class. Be sure the students can explain what is happening and why.
18. In social studies class, assign different groups of students to present daily news broadcasts.

Now do Activity 9.2.

For other ideas about motivating students, visit *http://www.prenhall.com/methods-cluster,* "Topic 7: Instructional Strategies" and check out the web links under "Motivating Students."

RELATING INSTRUCTION TO STUDENTS' BACKGROUNDS

Schema theory is a term in education that may sound technical and theoretical, but actually is very simple in meaning and application. Essentially, your schema for a particular idea or thing is a combination of your knowledge, experiences, and impressions related to it. For instance, your schema for *teacher* includes memories of teachers you have had, information from your education classes about what teachers should do and be, and your own thoughts based on experiences in which you were the teacher. It may also include sensory impressions, such as the smell of chalk dust and the ache of hurting feet. Your schema for *teacher* should be rich and full, because of your association with the teaching profession, but your schema for *paleontologist* or *philatelist* may be limited or nonexistent.

A student's *schemata* (plural of *schema*), or clusters of information about various topics, are important factors in determining how well that student learns the material you are presenting. Students with many well-developed schemata bring a great deal of knowledge and understanding to the learning situation and are likely to absorb related information readily. On the other hand, students who have poorly developed schemata will generally have difficulty understanding new concepts. In other words, they cannot relate new learning to old when they have little prior knowledge or understanding of a subject.

If students lack relevant schemata for a unit you are teaching, they will be seriously limited in their ability to understand your presentations, the textbook, or other instructional materials. Therefore, it is important to assess the knowledge the students already have of the topic and then, if necessary, provide additional experiences to fill in gaps before proceeding with the lesson or unit.

You can determine your students' prior knowledge about a subject by listing key vocabulary words on the board and asking the students what they know about each term. They will reveal both their current knowledge and the gaps in it.

The K-W-L approach uses a similar technique in its initial step (Ogle, 1986; 1989). In this approach, the students chart "What I *Know*," "What I *Want* to Know," and "What I *Learned*" about the topic of the reading material. In the *K* step, the students list everything that they think they already know about the topic, activating their schemata; in the *W* step, they list the additional things they want to find out from the reading, setting authentic purposes for the reading; in the *L* step, they list the things they learned from the reading, filling in gaps in their prior knowledge and correcting misconceptions that they may have had originally. A blank K-W-L chart is shown in Figure 9–1.

Another way to determine prior knowledge is through semantic mapping. With this technique, the teacher puts the main topic in the center of the board and has students provide information that can be clustered around the main topic. In Figure 9–2, the main topic is farms, and related clusters are farm buildings, farm animals, farm work, and crops. Students who contribute answers such as these evidently have some background knowledge of farms, and you will not need to provide much additional information. However, you will need to enrich the backgrounds of students who could tell you little or nothing about farms. A semantic map such as Figure 9–2 not only checks prior knowledge, but also serves as a good introduction or overview for a unit.

If you discover that your students have very little prior knowledge of a topic, you may wish to provide vicarious or direct experiences for them. In the example of farms, you might take a class to a dairy farm, have a farmer visit the class, view a video about farms, read stories and show pictures of farms, or do some other activity that would help students understand what a farm is.

In any situation, you should try to relate new knowledge to what students already understand by making meaningful connections. For instance, you might point out how one concept is similar to or different from another by comparing a familiar concept, such as football, with another sport, such as rugby. As students build bridges of meaning between new concepts and old, they are expanding their schemata and establishing a base of knowledge for acquiring new ideas.

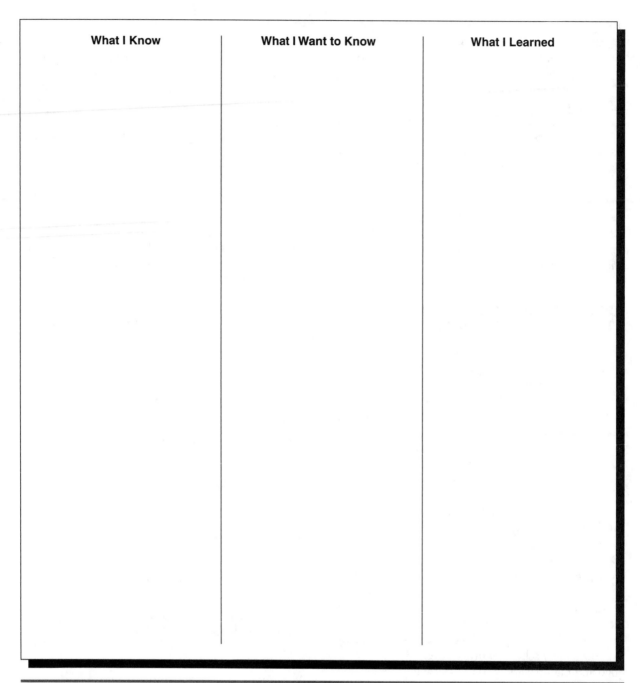

What I Know	What I Want to Know	What I Learned

FIGURE 9–1
K-W-L Chart

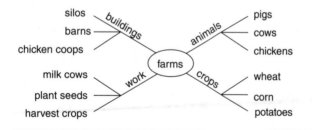

FIGURE 9–2
Semantic Map for Farms

INDIVIDUAL DIFFERENCES THAT AFFECT STUDENTS' LEARNING

Not all students learn in the same way. Just as you probably learn better in some situations than in others, all students have preferred ways of learning. Each person develops a set of strategies for acquiring information that remains fairly constant throughout life. You can improve the effectiveness of your teaching by understanding how each student learns best

ACTIVITY 9.2   **Motivational Strategies**

Read the following list of motivational strategies, taken from the list in the text, and mark those you have tried. Put a checkmark (✓) beside those that have worked well and the letter X beside those that have been ineffective.

1. _____ Keep progress records.

2. _____ Encourage students to participate in solving their problems.

3. _____ Arouse curiosity. Use variety in your lessons.

4. _____ Add humor—jokes and riddles.

5. _____ Alternate quiet and active periods.

6. _____ Let students use manipulatives and media for independent learning.

7. _____ Be enthusiastic.

8. _____ Challenge motivated students and guarantee success for slow learners.

9. _____ Write messages on papers you return to students.

10. _____ Videotape special events.

11. _____ Exchange messages with students.

12. _____ Teach with popular songs.

13. _____ Teach with a newspaper.

14. _____ Use foreign language lessons for authentic purposes.

15. _____ Let home economics students prepare special meals.

16. _____ Make math lessons meaningful by using real data.

17. _____ Let students conduct science experiments.

18. _____ Ask students to present daily newscasts.

and using that knowledge to individualize instruction whenever possible.

In terms of cognitive factors that affect learning, some students are analytical learners and learn best by examining details and studying each element of a situation; others are global or holistic learners who look at large chunks of information. Analytical students are likely to learn better with instruction in discrete basic skills, whereas global or holistic learners may learn better by first considering an entire problem or reading selection and then breaking it down into smaller elements.

Affective factors, such as a student's sociability, willingness to take risks, sense of responsibility, and motivation, may help you choose appropriate motivational strategies and provide suitable opportunities for group or individual work.

Students also vary widely in their preference for such physiological or environmental factors as level of classroom lighting, time of day when they learn best, need to snack and move about while working, classroom noise level, and classroom temperature (Dunn & Dunn, 1987). Although it is impossible to consider all these variables for each student, you can provide a variety of learning situations and sometimes give choices for working conditions.

According to Howard Gardner's theory of multiple intelligences, all of us possess at least eight distinct intelligences (Gardner, 1983; Nicholson-Nelson, 1998). We are stronger in some and weaker in others, but all intelligences can be cultivated. These intelligences are as follows:

1. *Verbal-linguistic:* Spoken or written language
2. *Logical-mathematical:* Scientific thinking, reasoning, deductive thinking, numbers, and abstract patterns
3. *Visual-spatial:* Visualizing objects and creating mental images
4. *Bodily-kinesthetic:* Physical movement, bodily motion
5. *Musical-rhythmic:* Sensitivity to rhythm, recognition of tonal patterns
6. *Interpersonal:* Person-to-person relationships and communication
7. *Intrapersonal:* Inner states of being, self-reflection, spirituality
8. *Naturalist:* Understanding the nature of living things

Because students have many different areas of strength, you should prepare lessons that incorporate a variety of intelligences so that all your students can find ways to be successful. In school, we tend to use linguistic and logical-mathematical intelligences more than the others, so students whose strengths lie in other areas may not be able to demonstrate their understanding. For an example of how you can plan a theme study that uses a variety of intelligences, see Figure 9–3. After you have examined this figure, complete Activity 9.3.

FOR YOUR PORTFOLIO

Describe a lesson that you taught in which the students used three or more intelligences. You may want to refer to Activity 9.3.

CLASSROOM TECHNIQUES

There are many techniques available for helping students learn. Some are more appropriate for slow learners than for bright students, for younger children than for older students, or for some subject areas than for others. As a student teacher, you should try a variety of techniques to find out which ones work best for you. Then complete Activity 9.4.

Lecture

"Good morning, class. Today our topic is. . . ." And so the familiar lecture technique begins. The teacher does the telling, and the students listen.

Lectures can be divided into two types: formal and informal. You can probably recall some of your college professors who delivered highly structured, carefully worded, inflexible, uninterrupted lectures. The formal lecture is generally inappropriate for public school teaching, except occasionally for classes of college-bound students who are good listeners. On the other hand, informal lectures are often effective for getting information across. An informal lecture is usually brief and often involves use of audiovisual materials along with minimal participation by the students.

You will probably want to do some lecturing because it is often the most direct and efficient way to convey a message. Lectures are particularly appropriate for history and literature classes and can also be used to explain an experiment in science. Brief, informal lectures can provide background information when you introduce a new topic or summarize what has happened during a learning experience.

When you prepare to lecture, keep certain points in mind. Remember that elementary children and slow learners have short attention spans and cannot listen very long. Even older, bright students probably

Verbal-linguistic
Examine old records (e.g., courthouse documents, newspapers).

Make a scrapbook of your community's historical events.

Read historical books written about your region.

Logical-mathematical
Compare weather charts. Is the climate changing?

Create a time line that identifies major events.

Compare life styles of people over the last century (e.g., dress, food consumption, work habits, travel).

Compare population figures. How much has the community grown in population?

Compare areas included. How much has the community expanded in area covered?

Visual-spatial
Find and display old postcards and photographs.

Locate early maps. What roads have been built, paved, widened, or extended? How have road patterns changed?

Create sketches of what you think your community looked like 100 years ago.

Bodily-kinesthetic
Re-create a corner of your classroom to resemble a classroom from a century ago. Collect artifacts from attics.

Dramatize opening exercises and lessons from early school days.

Make a model of how the downtown area looked a century ago.

Musical-rhythmic
Compare old hymnals with today's. What changes are there?

Create a musical history (may be a rap or story told in rhythm).

Learn folk songs that people sang long ago.

Interpersonal
Interview elderly people in your community. Take good notes.

Work in groups to conduct research about your community.

As a member of a team, plan ways to present information.

Intrapersonal
Reflect on whether you would prefer living in your community today or in the "good old days." Record your thoughts.

Set personal goals for how you might improve your community.

Keep a journal on what you like about your community.

Naturalist
Locate and identify trees that may be 100 years old.

Make a scrapbook of pressed leaves and flowers.

FIGURE 9–3
Theme Study Using Multiple Intelligences

ACTIVITY 9.3   *Lesson Using Multiple Intelligences*

Design a lesson that enables students to use at least three intelligences. For example, if your goal is to help students understand story sequence, you might read them "*Little Red Riding Hood*" (lesson focus). Then you might ask them to act out the story with attention to the order of events (interpersonal-social intelligence used as students meet in a group to plan their enactment and bodily-kinesthetic intelligence used as they act out the story), retell the story in sequence (verbal-linguistic intelligence used), and make a drawing of Little Red Riding Hood's route through the forest, beginning with her departure from home and ending with her arrival at Grandmother's house (visual-spatial intelligence used). You may make this lesson for any subject area.

Write each type of intelligence involved in your lesson in the spaces provided. Then describe the activity that illustrates that type of intelligence.

Subject: _____   Grade level(s): _____

Goal: _____

Lesson focus: _____

Intelligence: _____

Activity: _____

_____

_____

Intelligence: _____

Activity: _____

_____

_____

Intelligence: _____

Activity: _____

_____

_____

ACTIVITY 9.4   *Classroom Techniques*

In order to meet the diverse needs and interests of the students in your class, you should use a variety of teaching strategies. Listed below are several classroom techniques that you might try. For each technique you attempt, write a statement about its effectiveness.

Lecture:

Discussion:

Demonstration:

Guided study activities—supervised study:

Guided study activities—drill:

Guided study activities—review:

Guided study activities—project:

Homework:

Questioning:

Programmed instruction:

Case method:

Can you think of other teaching strategies to use? If so, what are they?

Reflect on the methods that you have used and identify the most effective ones. Why do you think these methods work best? What methods will you want to learn to use better? Which ones might you want to discard?

won't want to listen for more than about 20 minutes without a change of pace. Get to know your students well enough so that you can adapt your lectures to their interests and needs and relate the lectures to their background experiences. Then prepare and organize your material carefully so you can make a concise, easy-to-understand presentation.

Delivery makes the difference between a boring and a stimulating lecture. Keep your voice pitched low, use expression, and make sure every student can hear you. Maintain eye contact, and occasionally interject a student's name to recapture the attention of a student who appears to be drifting away from you. Speak in Standard English, and use vocabulary the students understand.

You can use several techniques to hold students' interest as you lecture. Begin by making sure that students remove all unnecessary items from their desktops so that they will not be distracted. Introduce your topic in such a way that you arouse curiosity and activate the students' prior knowledge, making it possible for the students to construct knowledge by joining the new information with previously known material. Use audiovisual materials or demonstrations to supplement the lecture. Emphasize major points by writing them on the board, and encourage secondary students to take notes. Occasionally ask a question to get students involved and to check on how well they are listening to your presentation.

Although a lecture is often a quick way to transmit information, it has many dangers. It does not encourage much student creativity or problem solving, nor does it enable students to practice applying the knowledge that is being passed along to them. During this one-way communication process, many teachers get carried away with their own speech making while students sit passively and daydream.

Discussion

Guided discussion is also a teacher-centered technique, but it affords greater opportunities than a lecture for students to participate. Students can exchange ideas and consider the pros and cons of issues. Guided discussion is a natural and informal way for students to communicate their thoughts.

By engaging students in guided discussions, you can help them achieve many worthwhile goals. They learn to see different points of view and to keep their minds open. They begin to think critically about important issues and question whatever they are told or see in print. They develop speaking and listening skills by reacting to what their classmates say. They also develop tolerance for other people's ideas when they hear different opinions expressed.

If you want to conduct a guided discussion in your class, first decide whether you want a whole-class discussion or several small-group discussions. In the latter case, you will need to divide your class into three or four groups and appoint a leader for each group. You should move from one group to the next, checking to see that students are making relevant comments. After small-group discussion, each leader can summarize the group's ideas for the rest of the class. Students who are afraid to speak out in front of the entire class are usually willing to participate in small-group discussions.

In a discussion with the whole class, you have several responsibilities as the discussion leader. Choose a topic familiar to your students so they can discuss it intelligently. Create a supportive atmosphere where students are not afraid to say what is on their minds, but control the discussion so that it doesn't deteriorate into pointless conversation. Encourage widespread participation by asking questions directed toward students of different ability levels. Conclude the discussion by summarizing the points that were made and suggesting a solution that seems acceptable to most of the class.

A good topic for discussion by secondary science students might be "What sources of energy should we pursue for future development?" Possible answers include solar, nuclear, geothermal, synthetic fuel, wind, and biological sources. You could consider these sources in terms of their cost to develop, the length of time before they would be available for independent use, their impact on the environment, and their safety. The whole class could consider these issues, or you could divide the class into groups, with each group discussing one source and making recommendations as to its feasibility.

During a guided discussion or another type of lesson, students may raise questions you cannot answer. Rather than take a chance and give a wrong answer, admit that you don't know the answer. Then, depending on the situation, you can look the point up in a reference source immediately, tell the students you will try to find the answer, or suggest that they find the answer and discuss it in class the next day. Of course you should know your lesson, but no one knows all of the answers all of the time.

Panel discussions and debates are variations of the discussion approach. In panel discussions, students prepare in advance to discuss issues related to a specific topic in front of the class. One student usually serves as chairperson and directs the discussion. Debates call for two teams of students to present opposing sides of a topic. There are rules for presenting arguments and rebuttals. With both procedures, make sure the participants understand the ground rules and are well prepared. At the conclusion of the activity, ask the rest of the class to respond to the presentation.

Demonstration

Another teacher-centered instructional activity is the demonstration. With this technique, students learn by watching as well as by listening. You can use demonstrations in every part of the curriculum and at any age level. In the elementary grades, you might need to show some children how to form cursive letters or how to dribble a basketball. At the secondary level, you can demonstrate how to mix oil paints in art class. If you teach science classes, you will have many opportunities to demonstrate scientific processes by performing experiments yourself or helping students set them up.

Demonstrations have a special attraction for students. They create a feeling of anticipation. Students welcome the change from routine lessons and give their full attention to what you are doing.

To demonstrate a process that involves decision-making and risk-taking, such as are involved in writing a poem or critiquing a piece of writing, you may well want to perform the process in front of the students *without prior preparation,* so that they can view your mental struggles and decisions as you "think aloud" about it. This type of demonstration can be threatening for you, but very effective for the students.

In preparing for a demonstration, make sure it relates clearly to your objectives. Try to keep it simple and to the point—it's a mistake to try to teach too many concepts in a single demonstration. If your demonstration could cause injury, be sure to take safety precautions; then practice it several times until you are confident that nothing will go wrong.

Now you are ready to present the demonstration to your class. Collect all the materials you need, and provide a good viewing area for the students. Prepare them for what you will be doing so that they will know what to expect. During the demonstration, you can ask questions or point out what is taking place. Afterward, review what happened and why it occurred as it did. If something went wrong, ask the students if they can tell you why.

Guided Study Activities

By offering opportunities for students to study material to be learned in class, with you available to guide and monitor their efforts, you can help students overcome some of the hurdles to learning that they may face if left to their own devices.

Supervised Study. As the teacher, you may want to supervise occasional study sessions in which students are responsible for mastering content you have assigned. Be sure to make reasonable assignments

A demonstration creates interest in learning new concepts.

that all students can complete successfully if they apply themselves to the task. You may have to individualize some assignments according to students' different ability levels. You should walk around among the students while they study, stopping occasionally to answer questions, offer suggestions, and head them in the right direction. Your guidance during a supervised study session can help students learn to use study time efficiently when they are on their own.

Supervised study during class time is a useful teaching technique if you are introducing a new subject or type of assignment. You are there to offer encouragement and make sure students are getting off to a good start. It is also valuable if an assignment requires the use of resources in the classroom or the school library.

Because of its limitations, however, you should use this approach infrequently. It can easily become boring and routine and may seem unrelated to real-life situations.

Drill.   Nine times 2 is 18, 9 times 3 is 27, 9 times 4 is 36. On and on, over and over. This is known as drill, or organized practice. Is it really necessary? Why do we do it?

Drill can be a valuable instructional technique when it is based on solid understanding of a concept. It provides practice through repetition to the point of overlearning. In such areas as math, spelling, grammar, and motor development, repeated practice is helpful for mastering skills.

Although drill is often boring, it doesn't have to be. Here are some ways to keep drill from becoming tedious. Think up games for practicing skills. Keep a drill period short—don't go beyond the time when it ceases to hold the students' attention. Vary the amount and kind of drill according to students' needs. Give slow learners more repetition than fast learners—because they generally need it. Make sure students see the reason for complete mastery of the concept. Let students keep individual charts to record their progress. Intersperse drill with other types of instruction to avoid monotony.

Review.   Review is similar to drill. It is based on previously learned concepts and makes use of recall. While drill simply provides practice in skills, however, review explores students' attitudes, understandings, and appreciations. Review is essentially a group process that extends initial learning by bringing out relationships and applications of the topic. Use review before tests and whenever you want to pull together the major concepts you have been teaching.

Projects.   Another type of guided study activity is use of projects. In this approach, students have more freedom to direct their own work and can become more actively involved in the learning process. Usually several groups work simultaneously on different but related projects. Groups may conduct research, construct models, or solve problems, and then prepare a report to present to the class. Your role as the teacher is to provide focus and to support, encourage, and assist the groups as they work toward completing their projects. Quite often, course content is not covered as thoroughly in this approach, so you will need to fill in the gaps with other techniques.

Computer technology is often involved in project-based learning. CD-ROMs or DVD-ROMs are available with information for the different subject areas. The Internet has many sites that contain much pertinent information, and there are even coordinated global Internet projects in some areas of interest. See Chapter 8 for more on this topic.

Homework

"Can't tonight. I've got tons of homework to do." Sound familiar? Educators disagree about whether or not homework is of any value. Research reports indicate, however, that achievement increases when students conscientiously do regularly assigned homework (Bennett, 1986). To be most effective, homework should relate to and go beyond what students are learning in the classroom. Also, teachers should carefully prepare the assignments, thoroughly explain them, give reasons for doing them in terms of enhanced learning, and promptly return them with comments.

To keep your assignments from becoming boring and meaningless, vary the type of homework that you give. There are two major types of homework: (1) practice and preparation and (2) extension activities. Practice and preparation homework includes most independent activities. It can allow you to provide extra practice for students who need it and to give assignments that are compatible with the needs of different students. However, it is often difficult to manage such individualized assignments. Extension activities often involve group work such as mapmaking, conducting surveys, doing long-term science experiments, and working on community projects. Use a combination of these types of homework so that students don't always have to work math problems or answer questions from the text. Instead, sometimes allow the students to investigate, discover, interview, work on projects, work with computer programs, and solve problems dealing with real-life situations.

Remember that some students have little time or opportunity to do homework. They may have jobs or chores to do after school. The home may be so crowded and have such poor study facilities that doing homework is impossible. There may be no one at home for some students to turn to for assistance or clarification. If you are uncertain about the homework you assign, ask some of the dependable students how much time they are spending on homework and if the assignments seem beneficial. Their answers may guide you in making realistic assignments.

Questioning

You can use questioning with almost any type of lesson, including an informal lecture, a discussion, a demonstration, a recitation, discovery, and inquiry. Questioning sessions should generally offer students time for thoughtful, reflective responses. Students benefit more from recitations which allow time to consider the implications of higher-order questions.

Suppose you want to try your skill at leading a questioning session. How would you start? First, choose an appropriate topic. It should be one that your students already know something about, that is important and interesting to them, and that is within their level of understanding. Get their attention before you begin, and then ask your questions clearly. Ask each question only once, so that they will know they must listen carefully. Once the session begins, keep to the subject. Try to include all the students in the questioning, even those who don't volunteer.

One way of ensuring participation by all students is to use the every-pupil-response technique. In this approach, you ask questions that all pupils can answer at the same time by indicating one of two or more choices. You may read a list of statements and ask students to put their thumbs up if they agree, down if they disagree, and to the side if they aren't sure. Or you may make cardboard strips with "yes" or "true" on one end and "no" or "false" on the other end for each student to hold up in response to questions or statements. Other applications for cardboard strips include the following:

1. "Long" and "short" to indicate the vowel sound
2. Two strips with "add," "subtract," "multiply," or "divide" to show the appropriate mathematical process
3. "Fact" or "opinion" to indicate the dependability of a statement
4. "Vertebrate" or "invertebrate" to indicate the type of animal
5. "Acid" or "base" for the appropriate chemical property
6. "Deciduous" or "evergreen" to indicate the type of tree
7. "Before" or "after" to show the place of an event in history

Although this technique affords full participation by students and can offer a fast-paced review, it does not allow for creative responses. You may want to follow up the initial question with "why" questions for students who disagree with each other, encouraging analytical thinking.

It is not easy to ask good questions. Write down in advance some questions designed to achieve certain purposes. Phrase them simply and clearly so students will know exactly what you want. Don't be afraid to include a question for which you don't know the answer—you and the students can seek it together. As the session progresses, you may find yourself discarding your prepared list and asking spontaneous questions that arise from students' responses. Be sure that, if you do so, you do not ask only literal-level, detail questions.

The types of questions you ask determine the kind of thinking your students will learn to do. You need to include diverse types of questions, stressing higher-level thinking and in most cases avoiding questions with only "yes" or "no" answers. Table 9–1 lists purposes for various types of questions and words or phrases to use to begin appropriate questions that meet these purposes. Activity 9.5 helps you become aware of the kinds of questions you ask.

Asking questions is only half of the process; the other half is obtaining responses. Give your students plenty of time to answer—at least 3 seconds. "Wait time" encourages more students to think through the question and consider the answer. Don't rush on after an answer has been given; leave the door open for other students to express their views. Extend a thought by asking "Are you sure?" and "How do you know?" Be willing to accept reasonable answers even if they don't agree with your preconceptions.

One aim of a good questioning session is to let students ask questions of you and each other. Foster this purpose by setting an accepting, noncritical classroom atmosphere in which honest questions, no matter how silly they seem, are welcome. If students ask you something you don't know, encourage them to join you in finding the answer. A really productive questioning session involves a lively exchange of ideas in an effort to reach a logical and satisfying conclusion.

You can use questions to promote convergent or divergent thinking. When things converge, they come to a point. When they diverge, they go off in many directions. A convergent question is narrowly focused and usually has a single correct answer. An example of a convergent question is "Who was the first president of the United States?" If you use many convergent questions, you will be checking knowledge of facts, but you will not be helping your students think creatively or critically.

TABLE 9–1
Questions and How to Begin Them

Purpose	Questions
If you want to:	Ask questions that begin with:
Assess knowledge	Define, Describe, Tell, List, Who, When, Where, Identify
Check understanding	Compare, Contrast, Explain the relationships, How do you know
Help analyze problems	How, Why, What procedures, What causes, What steps in the process
Lead students to explore values	Why do you feel, What is important, Why do you prefer
Promote creative thinking	How else, What if, Just suppose, Create a new, Design an original
Help evaluate situations	Judge the following, Select, Evaluate the result, Rate as to good or bad
Show how to apply knowledge	Demonstrate, Show how to solve, Construct, Use the information to

Divergent questions, on the other hand, challenge students to think of many possible solutions. These questions are the type used in reflective thinking or discovery inquiry. A good divergent question is "How many ways can we think of to help make our community more attractive?" You may want to begin a questioning session with divergent questions, then move toward more convergent questions as students approach a decision or reach a conclusion.

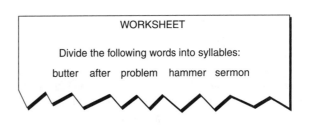

FIGURE 9–4
Sample Syllabication Worksheet

Deductive and Inductive Teaching

You should also be familiar with deductive and inductive teaching. Both types are useful, but many teachers depend heavily on deductive teaching. You can probably remember that many of your teachers told you rules and even made you memorize them; then you applied them. Here is an example of a deductive lesson on syllabication.

Deductive Lesson: Syllabication

Say: "Today we are going to learn a new rule for dividing words into syllables. The rule states that whenever a word has two consonants with a vowel on either side, you divide the word between the two consonants. Here is an example.

In the word *comfort*, we divide the word between the *m* and the *f*. Now I want you to divide the words on this worksheet into syllables." (See Figure 9–4 for a sample worksheet.)

Say: "When you finish your worksheet, be sure you can say the rule that tells you how to divide these words into syllables."

Inductive teaching calls for an inquiring mind and leads students to make their own discoveries. It is based on the use of examples. By asking students questions about the examples or helping students form their own questions, you can guide them toward a solution. The discovery inquiry approach challenges students to think for themselves and pull together clues for discovering the answers. Students internalize what they discover for themselves; it becomes a part of them, and they aren't likely to forget it. An example of an inductive lesson follows. By using your ingenuity, you will be able to come up with other examples of inductive lessons that are pertinent for your class.

Inductive Lesson: Syllabication

Say: "Sometimes we need to divide words into syllables. How do we know where to divide them? Look at these examples on the board."

but/ter   af/ter   prob/lem   ham/mer   ser/mon

"How many syllables are in each word?"

"What do you think the slash mark means?"

"What do you notice about the position of the slash mark in each word in relation to consonants and vowels?"

"Does it make any difference whether the two consonants in the middle of the word are alike or different?"

"State a rule that tells where to divide words into syllables. Using this rule, where would you divide these words into syllables?"

suppose   sister   content   channel   blunder

Programmed Instruction

Programmed instruction is implemented through many types and combinations of media. It is most commonly administered through workbooks or computers. (See Chapter 8 for information on using computers for instruction.) Programs are either *linear* or *branching*. Linear programs consist of a series of small steps in the development of a skill or concept, with frequent provisions for the student's responses. These programs are easy to use and provide good practice in areas such as spelling and word recognition, math problems, and literal translations of foreign words.

Branching programs are much more complex. Students answer multiple-choice questions, and each answer determines what question they see next. If the student answers incorrectly, he or she leaves the main line of the program and is branched to a track where the concept is retaught. When the student is able to answer the questions on the branched track correctly, he or she returns to the main line to continue the work. With branching programs, a student selects answers and moves to the next steps on the basis of his or her answers.

If you plan to use computer programs for practicing skills, you will need to evaluate the software carefully in order to choose programs that give clear directions and are user-friendly. The software you select should offer practice on skills related to classwork at levels of difficulty appropriate for your students. Programs should be interesting enough to sustain attention, and they should provide immediate feedback.

The effectiveness of programmed instruction depends on how you use it. Don't expect programmed instruction to be the total instructional program; it should be used along with other learning activities. While students are engaged in programmed learning, you need to check their progress and help them with any difficulties they may be having.

The Case Method

The case method is suitable for teaching students to analyze real-life situations. Case studies allow students to extend and apply information from their textbooks. To discuss the issues in each case, the students also must pull together knowledge from different subject areas. The case method encourages them to think critically and acquaints them with problem-solving techniques.

Cases are built around problem situations. They describe actual problems and supply facts related to the situations. Some cases may be open-ended, with no solution given; others may be closed, with one solution or several alternative solutions. The incident case, a short, three- to five-paragraph description of a situation, is more appropriate for young students than the more complex case studies used at the college level. Some of the vignettes and case studies in this book could be used as incident cases in your college class or seminar. The case method is appropriate for almost any subject area, but is particularly effective in history, economics, sociology, psychology, and business courses.

If you want to try the case method with your students, first select a fairly simple situation that will interest them, such as the development of a well-known fast-food franchise or the promotion of a famous rock star. Then learn all you can about the subject. Draw up a set of questions that will lead students to define the problem, analyze different aspects of it, reach one or more possible solutions, and evaluate the possible consequences of their conclusions. You can start with a simple case that can be completed in one class period, then work up to a more complicated case that could last for several days.

As the teacher, you must play an active role in presenting and developing a case. Lively discussion is the key to learning through this method. You must be knowledgeable about all aspects of the subject so that you can supply additional information as the students begin asking questions about the case. After students have arrived at a tentative solution, you may need to offer alternative proposals to stimulate further critical analysis of the problem. You should guide the class in making a decision based on facts rather than personal prejudices or hunches. Finally, you will need to help the students evaluate their decision and look at its long-range implications.

ACTIVITY 9.5   *Types of Questions*

Tape-record one of your discussion or question-answer lessons. Play back the tape and write down the questions you asked. Listen for the opening words of each question, and identify the purpose for the type of question you asked (see Table 9–1). Count the number of questions for each category and fill in the second column for each of the purposes listed below.

PURPOSE	NUMBER OF QUESTIONS
1. Assess knowledge	
2. Check understanding	
3. Help analyze problems	
4. Lead students to explore values	
5. Promote creative thinking	
6. Help evaluate situations	
7. Show how to apply knowledge	

Look at the number of questions for each purpose and find out what purposes you are meeting with the questions you ask. Consider whether you are selecting your questions to meet just one or two purposes or covering a wide variety of purposes. Are there any types of questions you should add? Do your types of questions relate to your instructional goals? Write a statement about your use of questions and any changes you might make.

DISCUSSION QUESTIONS

1. How can you involve your students more in your lessons? What kinds of responsibilities can they assume?

2. Are you motivated to be a good teacher? What motivates you to do your best? Is your motivation primarily intrinsic or extrinsic? Explain your answer.

3. Select a student in your class who appears to be unmotivated. What are some ways you might try to motivate her or him? Looking back through this chapter, can you find some strategies that might work with this student?

4. How would you assign homework so that it relates to what you are studying but doesn't involve the use of textbooks? Can you design it so that it requires problem solving or creative thinking?

5. Select a goal that you and your students would like to achieve. From Table 9–1, find the purpose that most closely relates to that goal. Can you compose a set of questions appropriate for reaching your goal?

6. Why are schemata important for understanding topics presented in school? What schemata are directly related to the next unit you plan to teach? How will you enrich the experiences of students who may be deficient in their knowledge of essential concepts?

7. What are some ways that you might accommodate students' individual differences?

8. What are some lessons in which you could use the every-pupil-response technique for answering questions? How would you implement this technique?

9. What kinds of homework could you assign that would extend learning through group work on long-term projects? How would such assignments benefit the students?

10. What is your response to the article by Schifter, "A Constructivist Perspective on Teaching and Learning Mathematics," cited in the Selected References? Would this approach to teaching mathematics be a good one for you to try? Why or why not?

SELECTED REFERENCES

Bennett, W. J. (1986). *What works.* Washington, DC: United States Department of Education.

Bomer, R. (1998, September). Transactional heat and light: More explicit literacy learning. *Language Arts, 76,* 11–18.

Dunn, K., & Dunn, R. (1987, March). Dispelling outmoded beliefs about student learning. *Educational Leadership, 44,* 55–62.

Emig, V. B. (1997, September). A multiple intelligences inventory. *Educational Leadership, 55,* 47–50.

England, D. A., & Flatley, J. K. (1985). *Homework—And why.* Bloomington, IN: Phi Delta Kappa Educational Foundation.

Gall, M. (1984, November). Synthesis of research on teachers' questioning. *Educational Leadership, 42,* 40–47.

Gardner, H. (1983). *Frames of mind: The theory of multiple intelligences.* New York: Basic Books.

Granston, R., & Wellman, B. (1994, April). Insights from constructivist learning theory. *Educational Leadership, 51,* 84–85.

Henderson, J. G. (1992). *Reflective teaching.* New York: Macmillan.

Hicks, B., Montequin, L., & Hicks, J. (2000, January). Learning about our community: From the underground railroad to school lunch. *Primary Voices K–6, 8,* 26–33.

Kerr, A., Makuluni, A., & Nieves, M. (2000, January). The research process: Parents, kids, and teachers as ethnographers. *Primary Voices K–6, 8,* 14–23.

Melton, L., & Pickett, W. (1997). *Using multiple intelligences in middle school reading.* Bloomington, IN: Phi Delta Kappa.

Melton, L., Pickett, W. & Sherer, G. (1999). *Improving K–8 reading using multiple intelligences.* Bloomington, IN: Phi Delta Kappa.

Nicholson-Nelson, K. (1998). *Developing students' multiple intelligences.* New York: Scholastic.

Ogle, D. M. (1986, February). K-W-L: A teaching model that develops active reading of expository text. *The Reading Teacher, 39,* 564–570.

Ogle, D. M. (1989). The know, want to know, learn strategy. In D. Muth (Ed.), *Children's comprehension of text: Research into practice.* Newark, DE: International Reading Association.

Ross, E. P. (1998). *Pathways to thinking.* Norwood, MA: Christopher-Gordon.

Schifter, D. (1996, March). A constructivist perspective on teaching and learning mathematics. *Phi Delta Kappan, 77,* 492–499.

Sweet, S. (1998, November). A lesson learned about multiple intelligences. *Educational Leadership, 56,* 50–51.

Moving On

Continued Professional Growth

Carmen and Mike, both student teachers at Jefferson School, walk together to the parking lot after school.

Mike: Have you observed in any other classrooms yet?

Carmen: Yes, I have. I observed Miss Page and Mrs. Lansing. I guess I chose them because they were both my teachers when I went to school here.

Mike: I've observed both of them, too—what a contrast! Mrs. Lansing seemed to be using all the latest ideas we learned about, but Miss Page's class seemed to be strictly traditional. When I was in Mrs. Lansing's room, her students were playing a simulation game on appreciating cultural diversity, but when I observed Miss Page, her students were simply looking up the definitions of 10 vocabulary words and copying them directly from the dictionary.

Carmen: I noticed the same thing. Miss Page taught her class exactly the way she did when she was my teacher years ago, but I hardly recognized Mrs. Lansing's class. Students were working in groups, with some using computers to find information for research papers. I mentioned to her something about how things had changed, and she said, "You never stop learning how to be a better teacher." She has gone back to the university and gotten a master's degree since I was her student, and she still takes occasional classes. She also showed me several professional journals she subscribes to. She said they have wonderful teaching ideas in them.

Mike: Miss Page made a disparaging comment about college courses when I had my conference with her. I don't think she's done any advanced work at the university.

Carmen: I don't either. I also doubt that she gets many journals, and I heard her mention to another teacher that she wasn't going to waste her money on useless professional organizations.

Mike: My university supervisor said it's possible to get 20 years of experience in 20 years or to get 1 year of experience 20 times. It looks as if he was right.

Carmen: It really does. I want to make sure I get a new year's experience for every year I teach. I guess that means taking more college courses and getting involved in professional organizations.

1. Did Mike and Carmen learn something from their observations besides teaching techniques? If so, what was it?
2. Do you agree with Carmen's analysis of the situation? Why or why not?

EMPLOYMENT

After you complete your student teaching, you need to search for employment and consider your continued professional growth. In this section, we will talk about searching for employment—finding a potential position, developing résumés and letters, getting letters of reference, and handling interviews.

How to Find a Position

One of the best sources for locating a position is the college or university career services office; it should have a complete and current placement file. This office probably offers services such as providing placement files to employers who request credentials, arranging on-campus interviews with school systems, providing current listings of job opportunities, and making job-search resources available.

You will also find a career library in the career services or placement office, with such materials as brochures and applications, directories of community service organizations, encyclopedias of associations, audiovisual tapes on interviewing, information on writing résumés, overseas teaching literature, and the *AAEE Job Search Handbook,* available through the American Association for Employment in Education, P.O. Box 1265, Columbus, OH 43216-1265. This handbook provides a wealth of information, including articles on such topics as interviewing and writing résumés, a list of U.S. State Teacher Certification Offices, and advertisements of openings.

Some private employment agencies specialize in placing teachers, and job vacancies are often advertised at professional meetings. If you have contacts among teachers or school administrators, they may be able to help you locate vacancies or suggest locations where teachers are needed. At employment fairs you can have interviews with a number of prospective employers who represent schools in various geographic areas. If you are unsuccessful in obtaining a regular teaching position, apply for a substitute teaching position. An effective substitute often gets a full-time position when an opening occurs.

Developing Letters and Résumés

When you apply for a teaching position, you need a résumé and a cover letter. You should also send a thank-you letter to each interviewer and to anyone else who helps you obtain a job.

Letter of Inquiry. Send a letter of inquiry in response to a known vacancy to show that you possess the qualifications for the position. This letter is generally accompanied by a résumé and a list of references.

Here is a general outline for a letter of inquiry or an application for an existing position.

- *Paragraph 1*—Give your reasons for writing, indicating the position for which you are applying.
- *Paragraph 2*—State concrete reasons for wanting to work for this employer. Give evidence that you understand the requirements of the position and that you possess the qualifications necessary for success.
- *Paragraph 3*—Refer the reader to your enclosed résumé and emphasize relevant personal qualities not cited elsewhere.
- *Paragraph 4*—Refer to an attached list of at least three references with complete names, job titles, addresses, and telephone and fax numbers so that the interviewer can contact them easily.
- *Paragraph 5*—Request a response and ask for an interview. Figure 10–1 provides a sample letter of inquiry.

If you don't know if a vacancy exists but wish to teach in a particular school system, you might begin the letter of inquiry with an opening similar to this:

I would like to inquire about employment opportunities in your school system because I plan to relocate in your area. Please notify me if a vacancy exists. I am sending you my résumé to keep on file in case a vacancy occurs.

Résumé. A résumé is a brief statement about your abilities and experiences to help a prospective employer assess your potential for success in a school system. The résumé can serve as a general introduction to accompany your letter of inquiry or application. The résumé should be confined to one page, if at all possible, and it should tell at a glance what a prospective employer needs to know. Many employers prefer concise, bulleted information instead of paragraph-style descriptions. You may want to use a word processing program that has a résumé format. Here are some general tips for writing a résumé.

- Keep computer graphics simple. Use nondecorative typefaces and a font size of 10 to 14 points.
- Use standard-sized white paper, printed on one side only. Make sure it is immaculately clean (no smudges or fingerprints).
- Be consistent in the format and style you use.
- Organize the information logically.
- Place your name, address, and phone number at the top of the page.
- State your objective.
- Give information about your education.
- List experience in reverse chronological order.
- Check carefully for correct grammar and spelling.

FIGURE 10–1
Sample Letter of Inquiry

Box 145
University of Parkersburg
Parkersburg, Tennessee 55519
May 2, 2001

Dr. John Doe
Superintendent of Schools
Cumberland County Schools
Hillside, Delaware 24970

Dear Dr. Doe:

It has come to my attention that a teaching position in mathematics will be open next year at the Parkview School. I plan to graduate in June from the University of Parkersburg with an M.S. Degree in Mathematics Education and would like to apply for this position.

Your school system is often cited as outstanding because of its strong instructional program. The extensive use of electronic media in your school system and the availability of high-quality facilities and equipment are impressive. My program of study included media courses that provided practical information for using audiovisual aids and computers in the classroom. I am eager to put my educational experiences into practice in a full-time teaching position.

Enclosed is a copy of my résumé, which will give you some insight into my background, education, and experience. A videotape of my teaching performance is also available upon request, and a copy of my placement file can be obtained from our Office of Career Services.

Attached is a list of three references whom you may contact about my qualifications for the position. I have received permission from all three to use them as references.

I will be available at your convenience for an interview and will look forward to hearing from you. Thank you for your consideration.

Sincerely,

Robert J. Alfred

Robert J. Alfred

Activity 10.1 will help you see what should be included in your résumé. Figure 10–2 is a sample résumé showing an acceptable format and what data to provide; you can modify it according to your specific experiences and qualifications.

Thank-You Letter.   Show appreciation for your interview by sending a thank-you letter to your prospective employer shortly after the interview. This letter establishes goodwill, reminds the interviewer of your visit, and strengthens your candidacy. It should be warm and personal. It can be brief, but it should make the following points:

- Express your appreciation for the interview.
- Reemphasize your qualifications, pointing out how they meet the requirements of the position.
- Provide supplemental information not given before.
- Restate your appreciation.

FIGURE 10–2
Sample Résumé

Robert J. Alfred
Johnson Avenue
Corbin, ME 44407
(207) 123-4567

Professional Objective:

To secure a mathematics teaching position in a secondary school that encourages innovation and creativity.

Education:

2000–2001   Course work toward M.S., Mathematics Education, University of Parkersburg, Parkersburg, Tennessee—anticipated completion date June 10, 2001

1999   B.S., Mathematics Education—University of Highpoint, Greenville, North Dakota
Certification: Grades 8–12
Major: Mathematics Education
Minor: Physical Science
GPA: 3.8

Honors and Awards:

Received Maxwell Student Teacher of the Year Award (1999)
Was in top 10 percent of secondary education graduating seniors (1999)

Experience:

Teaching assistant (for tenth-grade class), Parkersburg Secondary School, Parkersburg, Tennessee, 2000
Student teacher, Marks Secondary School, Greenville, North Dakota, 1999
Math tutor for gifted children during the summer, Greenville, North Dakota, (1999)

Activities:

Debate captain
Active member in Student Teacher Association
Volunteer worker for Special Olympics

Interests:

Sports
Computers

Placement File:

Available upon request from:
Office of Career Services, University of Parkersburg, Parkersburg, TN 55519

You may also want to follow up your interview with a phone call to make sure that all necessary materials have been received and to inquire if further information is needed. A follow-up phone call may also help you land the job!

Getting Letters of Reference

Letters of reference increase an employer's confidence in an applicant's ability. Avoid including references who might be considered biased, such as relatives. Letters from appropriate persons (your adviser, student teaching supervisor, or cooperating teacher; professors of courses you have taken; and the like) should reflect the writers' knowledge of your academic preparation and career objectives and should be positive statements of support for the position you seek. Be sure you ask permission of each individual you list as a reference. If you want the career services

ACTIVITY 10.1   **Writing a Résumé**

Study the sample résumé in Figure 10–2. Then note, for each heading below, the information that you would be able to include on a résumé if you had to write one now.

Professional objective:

Education:

Honors and awards:

Experience:

Activities:

Interests:

Placement file:

office to keep letters of reference in your file, provide the person writing the reference with any required checklist of pertinent personal characteristics and a stamped envelope preaddressed to the placement office. With an "open file" (nonconfidential), you can read the letters; with a "closed file" (confidential), you are unable to read your letters of reference.

Interviewing Skills

CASE STUDY 10.1

A Fruitless Interview

John had just graduated from college with a bachelor's degree in elementary education. He wanted to teach at Sanford, an elementary school close to home, and work with fifth-grade students.

John was busy during his last semester, so he didn't investigate ways to apply for a teaching position. He decided to telephone Mr. Jenkins, a teacher at Sanford, to ask if he knew of any openings for the coming year. Mr. Jenkins thought there might be an opening in first grade, but he wasn't sure.

One day at a party, John overheard someone discussing the possibility of a job opening in the fourth grade at Brookside, another school in the same system. John wasn't really interested in teaching at Brookside, but he decided to see the superintendent anyway.

Before going for the interview, John decided he would compile some kind of résumé. He took a few minutes to write it, and this was the result:

Name: John MacKay
Age: 24
Sex: Male
College: City University
Degree: B.S. in Education
Experience: I student-taught in the third grade at Cordell Elementary School. They were nice kids, but I like the higher grades, like fifth, better.

On his way to the superintendent's office, John thought, "I've heard that they need men teachers in the elementary school. There weren't many guys in elementary education in my graduating class, so they should be glad to get me. Maybe they will give me a fifth-grade job at Sanford and move somebody else."

John walked into the Board of Education building and asked to see the superintendent. The secretary told John he would need to make an appointment because the superintendent would be busy with meetings all day. John argued with the secretary, but finally agreed to set an appointment for the next day.

Traffic delays caused John to be late for his appointment, but he saw no need to apologize. Shaking hands with the superintendent, John took a seat and answered questions about his school experience and his interest in the job. John admitted that he was not really very interested in the open position, but would rather teach fifth grade at Sanford. The superintendent said that he could not offer John a job teaching fifth grade at Sanford, but a first-grade position might be available there. John said he didn't think he wanted to teach first graders, and he wasn't really interested in teaching at Brookside. The superintendent said that he would do his best and would let John know if any openings became available.

Before John left, the superintendent asked him for references. John said he did not have a reference list, but would give the superintendent the names of teachers he had worked with who might give him a good recommendation.

As John left the office, he had the feeling that the superintendent did not intend to call him. He shrugged and thought, "I don't need either of those jobs. I can find a better one if I get in touch with the right people."

What suggestions would you make to John about the following?

1. How to go about finding a job
2. Developing a letter of inquiry and résumé
3. Procedures for applying to a school system
4. Getting letters of reference
5. Interviewing skills.

This part of the chapter suggests ways to improve on John's interviewing skills.

Before going to an interview, check with the career services office for videotapes and books on interviewing. Use a mirror, or ask a friend to look for characteristics that could detract from an interview session. Here are some tips for successful interviews:

- Dress conservatively. Be neat and well groomed.
- Arrive promptly for your appointment.
- Know the name and position of the interviewer.
- Make a good first impression. Look the interviewer in the eye as you give a firm handshake.
- Look alert and interested.
- Use correct grammar and diction.
- Listen carefully to the interviewer's questions and answer thoughtfully and directly.
- Avoid saying "um" or "uh" to fill gaps in conversation, and try not to end sentences with "okay?" or "you know." Sound sure of yourself and confident of your abilities.

The best advice for interviewing successfully is to *be prepared.* One way to prepare is to find out about the school's reputation, organizational structure, teacher-pupil ratio, benefits and services, and other considerations, such as relationships between school and community. Another way is to think through answers to questions you can anticipate, such as those in Activity 10.2. You will have a chance to ask questions also, so think of some you may wish to ask, such as these:

What are your discipline policies?

What kinds of in-service programs will be offered to help me during my first year?

How are teachers evaluated?

What types of schools and situations are new teachers placed in?

What is the beginning salary, and what are some benefits?

Completing Activity 10.2 will help you prepare for an interview.

Portfolios

Take a professional portfolio to the interview. It should be a collection of your very best work that is relevant to the job you are seeking. It might also include your résumé, transcript, statement of your teaching philosophy, sample lesson and unit plans, overview of a special project you developed, and student evaluations. Throughout this book there are additional suggestions for items to include in your portfolio. Be selective, so that you don't overwhelm your interviewer with too much material, and organize your portfolio carefully, perhaps providing a Table of Contents. Some topics you may want to include are "Teamwork," "Interpersonal and Personal Qualities," "Management Abilities," "Technical Skills," "Community Involvement," and "Lifelong Learning" (Sherbet, 2000). A three-ring binder lets you tailor the contents to each job description by adding or removing items. Many prospective teachers now include videotapes of themselves teaching lessons so that potential employers can evaluate their classroom performance.

An electronic, or digital, portfolio provides another option. It includes essentially the same content, but it offers additional ways for you to display your abilities. Wiedmer (1998, p. 586) defines this type of portfolio as "a purposeful collection of work, captured by electronic means, that serves as an exhibit of individual efforts, progress, and achievements in one or more areas." It has the potential for using animation, scanned images that show selected projects, and voice-over explanations of your performance. Web editors, designed to create multimedia material, and web browsers are practical programs that you can use to create and display electronic portfolios. You can store and display information on CD-ROM, which makes distribution, copying, and storage easy—a clear advantage over bulky paper portfolios. Another advantage of the electronic portfolio is that you have an opportunity to demonstrate your technological skills for your prospective employer.

CONTINUED PROFESSIONAL GROWTH

After you actually have a job as a teacher, you may be tempted to settle into a routine, much like Miss Page at the beginning of this chapter. It is, after all, easier to use the same lesson plans year after year without bothering to revise and update them. If a plan worked the first time, it ought to be good enough now, right?

Wrong! Every year, you will have students with different abilities and needs, and you must adjust instruction if the students are to benefit fully. Educational research is continually revealing more effective strategies, organizational plans, evaluation techniques, and teaching procedures. There will always be changes going on within your discipline that could enhance the effectiveness of your teaching. A teacher like Miss Page will never know.

Professional Organizations and Publications

Professional organizations for teachers abound today—general organizations, encompassing all grade levels and disciplines; and specific organizations, focusing on particular grades or subject areas. These organizations frequently have local, state, regional, and national activities, and your involvement can vary. Activities usually include regular meetings (discussions, speakers, panels), conferences and conventions, and service projects. Members often receive benefits such as reduced rates for conferences and conventions, journals and/or newsletters, and group study opportunities.

Two large general professional organizations are the National Education Association (NEA) and the American Federation of Teachers (AFT). The NEA promotes professional development of educators and improvement of educational practices. The AFT is an affiliate of the American Federation of Labor, and it functions primarily as a teachers' union by promoting better working conditions and higher salaries. Analyze

ACTIVITY 10.2   **Preparing for an Interview**

Think about the following questions that you may be asked during an interview, and write some possible responses. You may want to rehearse your responses with an experienced teacher or supervisor who could help you polish them.

1. Why did you select teaching as a career?

2. How do you believe discipline should be maintained in a classroom?

3. What class organizational pattern do you prefer, and why?

4. How will you take individual differences into account in your classroom?

5. What are some instructional materials that you would like to use in your classroom? Why?

6. What types of student evaluation will you use? Why?

7. How do you plan to remain up-to-date in your field?

8. What is your philosophy of education?

9. Where do you see yourself 10 years from now?

the goals and functions of these organizations to decide which, if either, is more oriented toward your personal philosophy.

A list of some professional organizations available to educators follows. This list is far from comprehensive, but it gives you an idea of the diverse organizations available to you.

American Association of Physics Teachers, 1 Physics Ellipse, College Park, MD 20740-3842

Association for Childhood Education International, 17904 Georgia Ave., Suite 215, Olney, MD 20832

Association for Educational Communications and Technology, 1025 Vermont Avenue NW, Suite 820, Washington, DC 20005

Council for Exceptional Children, 1920 Association Drive, Reston, VA 20191-1589

International Reading Association, 800 Barksdale Road, PO Box 8139, Newark, DE 19714-8139

Modern Language Association of America, 10 Astor Place, 5th Floor, New York, NY 10003

National Association of Agricultural Educators, 1410 King Street, No. 400, Alexandria, VA 22314

National Association for the Education of Young Children, 1509 16th Street NW, Washington, DC 20036

National Association of Geoscience Teachers, c/o Dr. Robert Christman, Dept. of Geology-9080, Western Washington University, PO Box 5543, Bellingham, WA 98227-5443

National Communication Association, 5105 Blacklick Road, Building E, Annandale, VA 22003

National Council for the Social Studies, 3501 Newark Street NW, Washington, DC 20016

National Council of Teachers of English, 1111 West Kenyon Road, Urbana, IL 61801-1096

National Council of Teachers of Mathematics, 1906 Association Drive, Reston, VA 20191-1593

National Education Association, 1201 16th Street NW, Washington, DC 20036

National Science Teachers Association, 1840 Wilson Boulevard, Arlington, VA 22201-3000

Teachers of English to Speakers of Other Languages, 1600 Cameron Street, Suite 300, Alexandria, VA 22314-2751

Many professional publications can benefit the individual teacher, and quite a few of them are connected with professional organizations. Articles in journals cover a wide range of topics, including classroom management, methods, materials, teachers' liability, accountability, curriculum revision, new developments in different disciplines, and many others. Search out articles related to your situations and needs, read them, and grow professionally. Completing Activity 10.3 will help you to identify some organizations that would be most beneficial to you.

In-Service Opportunities and Graduate Work

To keep their teachers up-to-date, school systems budget a certain amount of money each year for in-service education. Some systems ask teachers to attend a variety of professional functions to earn a certain number of in-service "points" each school year. You may be able to earn points by attending the meetings and conferences of the professional organizations of your choice, participating in specially planned activities at your school, or working on curriculum development or textbook review committees.

Graduate courses can also help you improve your teaching; in fact, many states require a certain amount of graduate work for renewing teaching certificates or licenses. Certification or licensure in additional areas expands your knowledge and increases your employment opportunities. If you actually enroll in a degree program and steadily take relevant courses, your advanced degree may also lead to a salary increase. The *Graduate School Guide* (available at 210 North Avenue, New Rochelle, NY 10801) is a directory of advanced professional degree programs offered by more than 1,000 colleges and universities.

FOR YOUR PORTFOLIO

Identify some specific ways you plan to continue your professional growth after you graduate.

PROFESSIONAL ETHICS AND LEGAL STATUS

During your student teaching and practicum experiences, your cooperating teacher and university supervisor guided you in ethical and legal matters. As you become a full-fledged teacher, however, you need to rely on your own knowledge of ethics and school law. You may wonder: Am I allowed to express my own political opinions when I teach? Can I do anything I want to do in my free time? Should I talk about my students with other teachers? What should I do if I suspect that a student in my class is using drugs or being abused?

CASE STUDY 10.2

Suspected Child Abuse

Miss Cooper notices that Debbie is dull and listless in class and sometimes is bruised. She is concerned about Debbie and wants to help.

Miss Cooper (trying to gain Debbie's confidence): Debbie, tell me what you like to do when school is out.

Debbie: Nothing.

Miss Cooper: Where do you live?

Debbie: Over by the cannery.

Miss Cooper: You must do some things for fun.

Debbie: Nope.

Miss Cooper (2 weeks later, still patiently trying to bring Debbie out of her shell): Debbie, you really look nice today.

Debbie: Yeah. My cousin gave me this new shirt.

Miss Cooper: I think you could be a really good student in class, but sometimes you look so sleepy. What time do you go to bed?

Debbie: About midnight, sometimes later.

Miss Cooper: Couldn't you try to get to bed earlier than that? I'll bet you could really do well if you got enough sleep.

Debbie: I can't ever get to sleep before then.

Miss Cooper: Why? Surely you can go to bed earlier than that?

Debbie: I don't want to talk about it.

Miss Cooper (after another 2 weeks): Debbie, have you tried to get to bed any earlier? You know, it would really help you. You fell asleep during English today.

Debbie: I know. I really want to, but I just can't.

Miss Cooper: Why don't you tell me about it?

Debbie (sighing and looking doubtful): Would you promise you wouldn't tell anybody? Anybody at all?

Miss Cooper: I promise. I won't ever tell anybody.

Debbie: Well, see, it's like this. My dad comes home; then he starts drinking. He's okay at first, but then he starts getting real loud and mean. Then he starts beating on me and my mom. We try to get away from him, but he's too strong. There ain't nothing we can do about it. Now don't tell anybody, because that'll only make it worse.

Miss Cooper, very concerned after this disclosure, decides to tell Debbie's story to the principal. He shares her concern and realizes that this is probably a case of wife and child abuse. The principal notifies people at the Department of Human Services at once, and they agree to investigate the matter. Miss Cooper is now worried that Debbie will think she told them and asks them to be discreet.

Debbie (1 week later, with dark bruises on her arms and a bruise under her left eye): I thought I could trust you not to tell. I should've known better. All you teachers are just alike. You sent the welfare person out, and she asked my dad a bunch of questions. He figured I'd been blabbing, so he really laid into me and my mom last night. Now it's worse than ever. I wish I'd never told you!

1. Do you think Miss Cooper did the right thing? Are there laws about reporting suspected child abuse? Check with your local agency, and find out how this situation should be handled.
2. Should Miss Cooper have consulted the principal before she promised not to tell Debbie's story?
3. Is there anything Miss Cooper can do now to restore Debbie's trust? How might she try to do this?
4. Do you believe it is ever right to share a student's confidences with someone else after you promise not to tell? If so, under what circumstances?
5. What would you have done in a similar situation?

Ethical Responsibilities to Students

Each student is entitled to your courtesy and consideration, regardless of her or his physical appearance, socioeconomic status, or ethnic origin. Because it is easier to get along with some students than with others, you will be tempted to have "teacher's pets." Students may compete for your attention with notes and little gifts, but you should be impartial in the way you treat your students. Never embarrass or humiliate students who do not measure up to your expectations.

Your classroom should have a democratic atmosphere. Students should be allowed to express their opinions and different points of view. Don't impose your own religious or political views on your students, and be careful to present both sides of controversial issues.

Students who confide in you expect you to keep their secrets. It would be unethical to take advantage of the information they share with you, or to embarrass them by revealing their information to other people. There may be times, however, when you feel the information they confide in you may bring harm to them or to others. They may be concealing information sought by the police, or they may need psychological help you cannot provide. In these cases, as in the case of Debbie and Miss Cooper, it is usually a good idea to discuss the information with someone in

ACTIVITY 10.3 *Professional Organizations and Publications*

Research the professional organizations cited earlier in the chapter and others that you have heard about in class or from your cooperating teacher. For a more comprehensive list of professional organizations, you can go to *http://www.prenhall.com/methods-cluster* on the Internet and select "Topic 11: Professional Development." Look for the link "Professional Organizations" under "Education Resources." List up to four organizations that you believe might be good for you to join. Indicate for each one the focus of the organization and its publication or publications.

1. Name:

   Focus:

   Publication(s):

2. Name:

   Focus:

   Publication(s):

3. Name:

   Focus:

   Publication(s):

4. Name:

   Focus:

   Publication(s):

authority who will respect the student's confidence and know what to do.

You may overhear teachers talking, particularly in the faculty lounge, about some of the students. It is unethical for you to openly and informally discuss a student's character, personality, appearance, or behavior in a disparaging way. Such conversations violate students' rights to privacy, and you should avoid them.

Students also have the right to confidentiality in the grades they receive. You shouldn't post grades or read them aloud unless you use some identification other than the students' names. When you return papers, make sure that only the student receiving the paper can see the grade.

Ethical Responsibilities to the Profession

You should be proud to be entering the teaching profession, and you will want to act appropriately. Dress and behave in such a way that your students and colleagues will respect you. Try to get along with your coworkers, and show respect for people in authority, even if you don't always agree with them.

Observe ethical standards regarding tutoring. Don't tutor students assigned to your classes for pay unless no other qualified person is available.

As you look for a teaching job, be completely honest with school district personnel about your qualifications and professional preparation. Don't apply for any position already held by a qualified teacher.

FOR YOUR PORTFOLIO

Write your own Code of Ethics, based on the ideas given in this section and on your personal experiences and values.

The Law and Student Teaching

You need to know your legal rights, responsibilities, and liabilities as a teacher. Since local and state laws differ and change frequently, be sure to find out what your legal status is in the school system where you will be teaching. (See Activity 10.4.)

If a serious problem arises, document the evidence as soon as possible. Record the time, date, and place; the names of those involved; and a brief account of the event. Be objective and accurate in your report, and avoid personal opinions and judgments. Such evidence is useful for later reference and in some cases may be used as court evidence.

Child Abuse.   Laws in most states specifically direct school personnel to report suspected child abuse. Since many cases of abuse involve school-aged children, educators can play a key role in identifying and reporting students who have been abused. Learn to recognize these signs of possible child abuse:

1. *Physical abuse*—Lacerations, missing teeth, fractures, rope burns, cigarette burns, bruises
2. *Neglect*—Constant fatigue, excessive hunger, uncleanliness, body odor
3. *Sexual abuse*—Difficulty in walking or sitting, torn or stained underclothes
4. *Emotional maltreatment*—Low self-concept, behavioral extremes, frequent temper tantrums, demands for affection

Not every child who exhibits one of these characteristics has been abused, but a combination of these factors, frequent recurrence of injuries, or serious behavioral maladjustment may justify your suspicion. If you suspect that a student is being abused, contact a school authority—perhaps the guidance counselor, school nurse, or principal—who may interview the student in a relaxed, nonthreatening manner. The interview should be conducted privately, and the school authority should assure the child that the conversation will be confidential unless it becomes necessary to contact an agency for help. If further action is necessary, school authorities will then follow appropriate procedures for reporting the situation.

If there are abused children in your classroom, you can offer support in a number of ways. Be understanding and patient with them. Be a model of behavior for them to follow so that they realize there are better ways to deal with frustrations and disappointments than physical violence. Focus on their strengths, and find ways for them to experience success. Praise them whenever there is cause. Be sensitive to their problems and willing to listen if they need to talk about their feelings.

Negligence.   School personnel are responsible for the protection of students while they are in school. When an accident or injury occurs to a student, you may be held liable if you are in charge and negligence, or extreme carelessness, can be proved. To protect yourself, report any accident and notify parents as soon as possible. In determining negligence, a court of law considers whether or not the person in charge exercised reasonable care and acted sensibly. If, for example, on a day when you are responsible for the class, an accident occurs while you are out of the classroom, you could be found negligent if your presence most likely would have prevented the accident.

Accidents are likely to occur when unusual events are taking place. When animals are brought to school, you are responsible for seeing that they are kept under control so that no students are injured. Physical education teachers must take special care to establish a safe environment, warn students of known hazards, and provide adequate supervision. When the class goes on a field trip, each student should return a signed parental permission form that shows the date, destination, and type of transportation. The note should include a statement that frees the teacher and school from liability in case of an accident, but, even so, you could be held liable if you were negligent. If the permission form is not returned, make arrangements for the student to stay at school during the event. Do not accept a phone call instead of a signed note, because you will not have a written record of permission.

Discipline. Decisions of the U.S. Supreme Court have held that corporal punishment does not violate the Eighth Amendment, which bars cruel and unusual punishment. The Court supported the teacher's right to use corporal punishment even over parental objections. Although corporal punishment has been banned in nearly half of the states and in some local districts, other school systems permit it. As a regular teacher, use it only as a last resort, however, after other disciplinary measures have failed. As a student teacher, you shouldn't use it at all.

The Supreme Court has established certain due process procedures for administering corporal punishment.

1. Corporal punishment should rarely be used for a first offense.
2. Students should know what types of misconduct could lead to corporal punishment.
3. A school official should be present as a witness when someone administers corporal punishment.
4. The student should be informed in front of the witness of the reasons for the punishment.
5. The disciplinarian should inform the student's parents of the reason for administering corporal punishment, if requested to do so (Connors, 1979).

Corporal punishment may take forms other than spanking or striking a student. It is sometimes interpreted as any action that could cause physical or emotional damage to a student, such as having a student stand with arms outstretched while holding a book in either hand.

Other forms of discipline can also result in legal action. For example, courts generally oppose a decision to punish all the students for the misbehavior of one when the culprit cannot be identified. Such mass discipline punishes the innocent as well as the guilty.

In addition, results of court cases indicate that teachers cannot lower grades as a penalty for misconduct. Grades should reflect academic performance, not behavior. Recent court cases also found that school districts could not reduce grades for absences due to suspension, or deny students the opportunity to make up final examinations because they were suspended (Hobbs, 1992).

Individuals with Disabilities Education Act (IDEA). The Individuals with Disabilities Education Act (IDEA) has significantly affected services to all students with disabilities in public schools. The section "Mainstreaming and Inclusion" in Chapter 3 explains the provisions and implications of this law. If misbehavior relates to a student's disability, you can't punish the student for the misbehavior.

Search and Seizure. Courts have generally ruled in favor of allowing school officials to conduct searches and seizures. Searches consist of looking for illegal goods; seizures involve confiscating illegal goods. Some of the items usually prohibited in schools are drugs and drug paraphernalia, weapons such as knives and guns, and obscene materials.

The Fourth Amendment to the Constitution gives individuals freedom from unreasonable searches and seizures. Weighing this freedom against a safe and drug-free school environment, however, the courts usually rule in favor of the schools. Searches and seizures are increasing as drug use and violence in schools become greater problems.

If you suspect that a student possesses something illegal and the evidence warrants an investigation, you can ask a school official to search the student's locker. Do not conduct the search yourself, and do not search a student's body or clothing for suspected harmful items.

You may find that your students are bringing things to school that distract their attention and interfere with their schoolwork, such as comic books or toys. You have a right to remove these things from them, but you must return them to the students at the end of a period of time or to parents whom you ask to come to school for them.

Liability Insurance. You need professional liability insurance to protect yourself from lawsuits. Liability insurance is available through many of the professional societies listed earlier in this chapter.

Before you drive students anywhere in your own vehicle, make sure that you have adequate insurance

ACTIVITY 10.4 **Legal Status of Teachers**

Because states differ in their laws, and because new legal decisions are made from time to time, it is important for you to know your legal rights and responsibilities. Check the law on the following issues and write a brief statement about each.

Child abuse (responsibility for reporting and to whom to report):

Negligence (use of permission notes, extent of responsibility):

Discipline (status on corporal punishment):

Individuals with Disabilities Education Act (IDEA) (involvement in preparing an IEP):

Liability insurance (availability, coverage, cost):

Self-defense (reporting procedures, what is considered "excessive force"):

First aid and medication (when to act, administering medication):

Copyright laws (photocopying rights, "fair use"):

Private lives of teachers (rights and responsibilities):

Academic freedom (censorship; prayer and other religious issues):

coverage. If there is an accident and you are found negligent, you could be sued. Your school may provide coverage for you, but if you are not covered, you should not transport students in your personal vehicle.

You should check the school's insurance policies regarding coverage of personal losses or damages. You may want to bring your own tape player or Uncle Jack's priceless African mask to enrich your lessons, but if these items are stolen or damaged, you may have no recourse. Never bring anything potentially dangerous to school.

Physical Intervention.   Physical intervention generally takes one of three forms: protecting yourself against a student who threatens bodily harm (self-defense), preventing one student from physically injuring another, and stopping a student from destroying school property. If a student is injured as a result of any of these actions, the courts will generally support you if you used "reasonable force." However, if you act out of anger and lose your temper, you may apply unreasonable force and eventually lose a court case. Whenever possible, avoid a physical confrontation, but if you must intervene, avoid excessive force when dealing with a physically aggressive student.

Consider any threats made against you for their potential danger. For example, a student to whom you have given a bad grade may say, "I'm going to kill you!" Although this is likely to have been said in a moment of anger or frustration, you need to consider threats to you or your personal property seriously and report them to the proper authorities.

First Aid and Medication.   The best guideline for a student teacher to follow in administering first aid is to act only in case of emergency, such as choking or bleeding. Whenever there is an injury, notify someone in the school, such as the school nurse (if there is one), another teacher, or the principal. Try to make the student as comfortable as possible, but avoid treating an injury unless absolutely necessary, since you could be sued for improper treatment.

Some students must take prescription medication under certain conditions, but you should not administer the medication. Don't give students aspirin or cough drops either, because they could be harmful for some students. If a student needs an insulin shot during the school day, the school nurse or the child's parent should give the injection.

Copyright Laws.   The U.S. Copyright Act contains certain provisions for photocopying material. You need to know what you can copy and how many copies you can make without violating the copyright law. Some magazines and journals state their photocopying policies on the title page of each issue. When reproduction of certain material is clearly prohibited, you may still write to the publisher for permission to use the material.

There are several guidelines for determining if material can be photocopied under the "fair use" policy. Generally, "fair use" is observed when photocopying material has no effect on its demand. For instance, you can make a copy of an article or selection, but you can make multiple copies of only a very small portion of a work. You are not permitted to copy consumable materials, such as workbook pages and standardized tests, unless permission is granted by the publishers. You cannot reproduce substantial parts of materials for public performances, including sheet music and plays. If a work is out of print or unavailable, however, the policy of "fair use" generally allows you to photocopy it.

Cautions about videotaping copyrighted television programs have been mentioned in Chapter 8.

Private Lives of Teachers.   Concern about teachers' private lives has changed considerably since the days when teachers were forbidden to drink or smoke, and married women were not permitted to teach. Today, teachers are granted much more privacy, but their behavior is still sometimes challenged and brought before the courts.

Some general guidelines for behavior have been established as a result of case law. Out-of-school dress, grooming, and private sexual behavior usually come under the teacher's right to privacy, unless it can be proved that the teacher's appearance or lifestyle affects her or his teaching. Teachers, as well as students, have the right to refuse to participate in patriotic ceremonies. They are also free to oppose school policies by speaking out against them or writing letters that appear in local newspapers. As a new teacher, however, you would be wise to act with discretion and avoid antagonizing people.

Freedom of Expression.   "Congress shall make no law respecting an establishment of religion, or prohibiting the free exercise thereof; or abridging the freedom of speech, or of the press; or the right of the people peaceably to assemble, and to petition the government for a redress of grievances" (First Amendment, United States Constitution).

A great deal of controversy has arisen over recent interpretations of the First Amendment. Many court cases have dealt with censorship of materials and subjects for instruction, as well as with school prayer and

Bible reading. The issues of morality, politics, racism, and religion form the basis of most attacks by censors. Find out about your school's policy on controversial materials and if there are procedures to follow when a book is contested.

Teachers sometimes face the dilemma of either using uncontroversial and generally acceptable materials, or using materials relevant to living in contemporary society that may offend some citizens of the community. When you deal with controversial issues, you risk confrontations with parents and public criticism. Teachers who use books or teach subjects that have been specifically forbidden by the board of education may be dismissed. These are some questions to consider in determining whether or not to use controversial materials in your classroom:

1. Is the material you plan to use appropriate for the maturity and age of the students?
2. Is there a valid educational reason for using the material?
3. Is there any policy established by the board of education to prohibit use of the material?

In *Abington Township School District* v. *Schempp*, 1963, the U.S. Supreme Court ruled that some school prayer and Bible reading violated the constitutional provision for separation of church and state. Because of different interpretations of the law, some schools ban all school prayer, whereas other schools permit silent periods of meditation or voluntary school prayer.

Students are also entitled to certain freedoms, as long as they don't disrupt class activities, infringe on the rights of others, or endanger others. Speech outside the classroom is generally protected, but students may be punished for offensive or lewd speech. If you are an advisor to a student publication, you may restrain the publication of some materials if you believe the materials may seriously disrupt classwork or violate the rights of others. Recent court cases have dealt with students' appearance, including restrictions on hair length and clothing associated with gang membership.

FOR YOUR PORTFOLIO

Drawing on your own educational experiences, describe an incident related to a legal issue. Critique how the incident was handled and perhaps suggest alternatives for dealing with it.

LOOKING AHEAD

Consider not only your first teaching position, but also your long-range goals. How do you view yourself as an educator in the years ahead, what contributions would you like to make to the field of education, and how can you achieve your long-term goals?

You can grow while helping others. Speaking at professional meetings or writing for professional journals will help you clarify your thinking, and working as part of a team to develop themes and locate related resource materials will benefit both you and your students. Serving on committees at the local, county, or state levels gives insights into teaching and enables you to share your ideas. You may want to become a classroom researcher by experimenting with new teaching methods, carefully observing and recording the results, and then sharing them with others.

After a few years of teaching experience, you might want to apply for a position in a related field. You might add certification or get an advanced degree in order to become a school librarian, a guidance counselor, a speech therapist, or an administrator. You could teach in a state correctional institution, work for a state Department of Education, join the Peace Corps, or work for the Bureau of Indian Affairs (teaching on a reservation). You might want to teach overseas through the U.S. Department of Defense or the Teacher Exchange Program (under the Fulbright-Hays Act), or work in a school operated by an American firm conducting business overseas. Textbook publishers employ teachers in several capacities, including as sales representatives, demonstrators of materials, leaders of in-service sessions, and writers for manuals and workbooks. Many challenging opportunities exist for educators, which may either improve their effectiveness as classroom teachers or help them move into other educational endeavors.

DISCUSSION QUESTIONS

1. What options and resources should you consider when looking for a position?
2. What factors should you consider in developing a résumé and a letter of inquiry? How can you present yourself effectively during an interview?
3. How can you keep up-to-date in your field after you leave the college classroom?
4. What contributions can professional organizations make to your growth as a teacher?
5. Find a current directory of job opportunities, or check with your placement office about the availability of positions. What good prospects are available?

6. Role-play an interview with a peer. How could you improve your performance?

7. Role-play what you should do if you join the teachers in the faculty lounge and hear them discussing one of your students in a way you feel is unfair to him or her. Should you get up quietly and leave, sit there quietly and not enter into the discussion, speak out and defend the student, or mention that you think it is wrong to talk about students that way?

8. Do you believe the school is responsible for providing education in values, sex, systems of government (including communism), morality, and religion? If so, how should these matters be handled? What would your approach be? Discuss this issue in small groups.

SELECTED REFERENCES

AAEE 2000 job search handbook for educators. (2000). Columbus, OH: American Association for Employment in Education.

Banis, W. (1996). The art of writing job-search letters. *Planning job choices: 1996, 39,* 46–53.

Bolles, R. N. (1997). *The 1997 what color is your parachute? A practical manual for job-hunters and career changers* (Rev. ed.) New York: Ten Speed.

Connors, E. T. (1979). *Student discipline and the law.* Bloomington, IN: Phi Delta Kappa.

Cramer, G., & Hurst, B. (2000). *How to find a teaching job.* Upper Saddle River, NJ: Merrill.

Goethals, M. S., & Howard, R. A. (2000). *Student teaching: A process approach to reflective practice.* Upper Saddle River, NJ: Merrill.

Head, S. (2000). Portfolios go electronic. In *2000 job search handbook for educators.* Columbus, OH: American Association for Employment in Education.

Hobbs, G. J. (1992, March/April). The legality of reducing student grades as a disciplinary measure. *The Clearing House, 65,* 204–205.

Hurst, B., Wilson, C., & Cramer, G. (1998, April). Professional teaching portfolios. *Phi Delta Kappan, 79,* 578–582.

Interview to win (1996). *Planning job choices: 1996,* 54–60.

Levy, J. (1996). Graduate school in your plans? *Planning Job Choices: 1996, 39,* 85–88.

Lyons, N. (1999, May). How portfolios can shape emerging practice. *Educational Leadership, 56,* 63–65.

May, A. (1996). The professional performance portfolio. In *The job search handbook for teachers* (30th ed.). Evanston, IL: ASCUS.

Medley, A. (1991). *Sweaty palms: The neglected art of being interviewed* (Rev. ed.). New York: Ten Speed.

1995 deskbook encyclopedia of American school law. (1995). Rosemount, MN: Data Research.

Rosenberg, M. S., O'Shea, L., & O'Shea, D. J. (1998). *Student teacher to master teacher* (2nd ed.). Upper Saddle River, NJ: Merrill.

Rossow, L., & Hininger, J. (1991). *Students and the law.* Bloomington, IN: Phi Delta Kappa.

Schaerer, J. (1996). Wave of the future: Televideo interviewing. In *The job search handbook for educators* (30th ed.). Evanston, IL: ASCUS.

Schmidt, P. J. (1991). *Making it on your first job: When you're young, ambitious, and inexperienced* (Rev. ed.). Princeton, NJ: Peterson's Guides.

Sherbet, S. (2000). Portfolios for the educator's job search. In *2000 job search handbook for educators.* (pp. 22–23). Columbus, OH: American Association for Employment in Education.

Thomas, S. B. (Ed.). (1994). *The yearbook of educational law.* Topeka, KS: National Organization on Legal Problems of Education.

Wiedmer, T. L. (1998, April). Digital portfolios. *Phi Delta Kappan, 79,* 586–589.

Write the résumé employers want to see. (1996). *Planning job choices: 1996, 39,* 33–38.

APPENDIX A

Assessment Instruments

This appendix contains instruments for the cooperating teacher in the school and the university supervisor to use to aid in assessing the student teacher's or practicum student's performance.

Overall Assessment

Student _____

Cooperating Teacher _____

College Supervisor _____

Grade Level and/or Subject Area _____

Date _____

KEY TO ABBREVIATIONS:

EE = Exceeds expectations
ME = Meets expectations
NI = Needs improvement
BE = Below expectations

	EE	ME	NI	BE
1. Conducts self in an ethical manner				
2. Handles the stress of teaching appropriately				
3. Has positive relationships with:				
a. Students				
b. Supervisors				
c. Peers				
d. Other school personnel				
e. Parents				
4. Learns from classroom observations				
5. Plans effectively for instruction				
6. Uses a wide range of instructional resources well				
7. Is effective in teaching content				
8. Handles discipline well				
9. Understands how to use various organizational plans				
10. Supervises study effectively				
11. Maintains a positive classroom environment				
12. Motivates students to learn				
13. Adjusts instruction to meet students' needs				
14. Evaluates students' progress well				
15. Assists with extracurricular activities as appropriate				
16. Has a good knowledge base				
17. Has good communication skills				
18. Maintains a professional appearance (appropriate dress, neatness, and cleanliness)				
19. Has a positive attitude toward teaching				
20. Seeks continued professional growth through professional reading, attendance at meetings, and/or conferences with professionals				

Early Progress Check

Student _____

Cooperating Teacher _____

College Supervisor _____

Grade Level and/or Subject Area _____

Date _____

KEY TO ABBREVIATIONS:

EE = Exceeds expectations
ME = Meets expectations
NI = Needs improvement
BE = Below expectations

	EE	ME	NI	BE
1. Shows enthusiasm for student teaching				
2. Is punctual in arriving at school and for each class				
3. Is becoming familiar with the faculty of the school				
4. Has learned students' names				
5. Shows readiness to help in classroom in a variety of ways				
6. Asks questions designed to prepare him or her for teaching				
7. Investigates the instructional resources of the school				
8. Interacts positively with other student teachers				
9. Knows school rules, routines, and disciplinary procedures				
10. Is planning for future participation				

Periodic Progress Check

(File Sequentially for Comparison Purposes)

Student _____

Cooperating Teacher _____

College Supervisor _____

Grade Level and/or Subject Area _____

Date _____

KEY TO ABBREVIATIONS:

EE = Exceeds expectations
ME = Meets expectations
NI = Needs improvement
BE = Below expectations

	EE	ME	NI	BE
1. Plans lessons thoroughly				
2. Has clear objectives for lessons				
3. Ties new material to previous learning				
4. Motivates students to study material				
5. Chooses content wisely				
6. Has good grasp of content				
7. Uses a variety of materials and resources				
8. Uses appropriate materials and resources				
9. Budgets time well				
10. Evaluates students' learning appropriately and accurately				
11. Has enthusiasm for teaching				
12. Relates well to other school personnel				
13. Handles noninstructional activities willingly and effectively				
14. Accepts constructive criticism and learns from it				
15. Shows signs of effective self-evaluation				

Discussion Topics for Conferences between Student Teacher and Cooperating Teacher or Student Teacher and College Supervisor*

Questions for Cooperating Teachers or College Supervisors to Ask

EARLY IN THE EXPERIENCE

1. Have you become familiar with the physical layout of the school? If not, how do you plan to accomplish this goal soon?

2. Have you met the other school personnel with whom you will be working? Do you have any questions or concerns about these working relationships?

3. Have you gotten to know the students whom you will be teaching? If not, how can you get to know them better in a short time? Do you have any concerns about dealing with any of the students to whom you have been assigned? If so, what are they?

4. Are you networking with the other student teachers or practicum students in your group to share concerns, problems, and solutions? If not, how could you begin to do this? Do you see the benefits of such networking?

5. Do you understand what is expected of you during your student teaching or practicum experience? If not, what things need to be clarified?

LATER IN THE EXPERIENCE

1. What have you learned from observing your cooperating teacher or other school personnel?

2. Have you been devoting enough time and effort to planning your lessons? What makes you think so?

3. Have problems surfaced during your teaching that you did not know how to handle? What were they? Where did you turn for help? What else might you have done?

4. Have you had any problems with class control? What kinds of problems? How might these problems be handled, considering both the structure of the class to which you have been assigned and your status as a student teacher or practicum student (rather than a regular classroom teacher)?

5. Have you been using a variety of instructional resources and teaching approaches in your lessons? What have you used? How could you make use of other strategies and resources to facilitate the learning of your content?

6. What have you learned about teachers' responsibilities that go beyond teaching?

7. Do your students have special needs that must be considered? What kinds? How have you tried to accommodate them?

8. Have you promoted a positive classroom atmosphere? How have you attempted to do this? How have the students responded?

9. Have you been able to evaluate your students' learning effectively? What problems have you had with evaluation? Are there appropriate forms of evaluation that you have not tried? What might you try next?

NEAR THE END OF THE EXPERIENCE

1. Do you feel comfortable performing the duties of a teacher? If not, with which ones are you uncomfortable? What can you do in the time remaining to correct this problem?

2. Have your students been learning from your lessons? If not, have you analyzed your lessons for possible flaws? Have you retaught lessons that were not effective?

---

* Note: These are just some suggestions that can help to keep a conference focused on important concerns. No conference would be likely to use all of the questions in a category, but all of them might be addressed over time.

3. Have you helped your students to enjoy learning? What are some ways in which you have accomplished this?

4. How have your career goals been affected by your experiences? Are you comfortable with the students and subject matter with which you have been working, or will you seek employment at another level or in another teaching area?

5. Has your philosophy of education been changed by this experience? If so, how? If not, how did the experience reinforce your original position?

Questions for Student Teachers or Practicum Students to Ask

EARLY IN THE EXPERIENCE

1. Am I doing the types of things that will best prepare me for the responsibilities I will have?

2. Are there people who are using different strategies and materials in the school that I could observe?

3. Am I assuming the correct amount of responsibility for this point in the term? If not, what should I be doing?

4. How can I interact with students more effectively?

LATER IN THE EXPERIENCE

1. Do my plans look complete, coherent, and effective? If not, how do they need to be changed?

2. Am I overlooking resources that would enrich my lessons? If so, what are they?

3. Am I being responsive enough to my students? If not, what more should I be doing, or what should I be doing differently?

4. Do my evaluation procedures appear to be appropriate? If not, what should I try?

5. Is my classroom management plan appropriate and effective? If not, what do you suggest?

6. Am I carrying my share of the noninstructional responsibilities? If not, what should I be doing?

NEAR THE END OF THE EXPERIENCE

1. Have I met your expectations in my noninstructional activities? Please explain why or why not.

2. Have my lessons been well planned and delivered, so that you have felt that the students were learning? Please explain why or why not.

3. Have my evaluation procedures been good enough to provide you with the information about the students that you need for reporting purposes? Please explain why or why not.

4. Has my attitude promoted a positive feeling in the classroom? Please explain why you feel that way.

5. Do you believe that I have the qualities to be a successful teacher? Please explain why or why not.

Discussion Topics for Seminars*

1. What different types of students does this school serve? What types of adjustments need to be made for this student body?

2. What things have happened in your classes that have caused stress? How have you handled them? In what other ways might they have been handled?

3. Should teachers be involved with extracurricular activities? Why or why not? What have you learned while working with extracurricular activities in your situation?

4. How have you seen teachers work together for common goals? Can you think of other ways that you could work with peers for common goals?

5. Why is it valuable to observe in the classrooms of a variety of teachers and at different grade levels? What have you learned from such observations?

6. What instructional resources have you used in your lessons besides textbooks? How effective were they? What other resources do you plan to use? Where will you obtain them?

7. What problems have you encountered with time management? How might you avoid these problems in the future?

8. What discipline problems have you encountered? How have you handled them? How effective were your techniques? What else could you have done?

9. In what ways have you organized your classes for instruction? Have you tried whole-class, small-group, and individual organizations? Have you tried cooperative learning? Were some patterns more effective for certain types of lessons than others?

10. What assessment procedures have you used? Did you encounter any problems in using any of them? Which ones were most effective?

11. What motivational techniques have you used in your classes? Which ones have been most effective? What else do you intend to try?

12. What teaching strategies have you used? Have you tried both teacher-centered and student-centered strategies? Do you see a difference in students' involvement when different strategies are used? How will this affect your teaching?

13. What part does homework play in your teaching situation? What kinds of homework are most effective? Why?

14. How does your use of questions affect what students learn? Are you including enough higher-order questions in your lessons?

15. Do some of your students have trouble reading their textbooks with understanding? What can you do to improve their chances of learning the material?

16. Where can you obtain ideas for teaching strategies that will enhance your teaching skills?

* Note: One form of assessment is observation of the responses that student teachers make during discussion of important topics. Here are some discussion topics that may be used in seminars, from which much assessment information can be gleaned. The discussion questions at the end of each of the chapters in the book are also good for this purpose.

Sample Unit and Lesson Plans

In this appendix we have examples of a unit overview and a sample lesson plan in math, a unit introduction and a sample lesson plan in health, a lesson plan in social studies, and a lesson plan in science. They can be used as models to stimulate the development of other plans.

Math Unit Overview

Janet Wheeler

I. Unit topic: Graphs and ordered pairs—4th grade

II. Instructional Objectives:

    A. Given a bar graph, the learners will answer questions about the graph with few errors.

    B. Given a pictograph, the learners will answer questions about the graph with few errors.

    C. Given a line graph, the learners will answer questions about the graph with few errors.

    D. Given a grid, the learners will locate points and ordered pairs with few errors.

    E. Given a card with information, the learners will construct the correct graph or grid with few errors.

III. Required Prior Knowledge and Skills:

    A. Prior skills: The student should be able to add, subtract, and compare two like groups of numbers.

    B. Teaching strategies: I will use the inductive method of teaching. I will give examples, then let the students draw their own conclusions. I also will use the guided discovery approach if I think the students need more structured help.

    C. Materials and media:

        Monday: unifix blocks, paper, and chalkboard

        Tuesday: bar graph quiz, poster board, squirt guns, pins, and paper

        Wednesday: pictograph quiz, poster board, and paper

        Thursday: line graph quiz, poster board, and paper

        Friday: ordered pairs quiz, graph paper, note cards with information, paper, and rulers

THURSDAY'S LESSON PLAN
(Excerpted from the entire unit plan as a sample)

IV. Instructional Procedures:

    A. Set:

        1. Have students think of an object in the classroom.

        2. Ask students to describe the location of the object using two clues. (Let several students do this orally and let a student guess what the object is.)

        3. Say: "Over the last few class meetings we have been studying graphs. Today we will be discussing grids, which are drawn on graph paper, and how to plot points on them. Grids are often used with maps."

    B. Instruction:

        1. Say: "I want you to look around the room and see if you find something that looks similar to a grid. A grid is one large rectangle or square shape with smaller square shapes inside it. I will draw one on the board for you. Point to something in the room that looks like a grid." Ask several people what they are pointing at.

        2. Say: "I have made a grid on this poster board. As you notice, the grid is numbered on the left side and across the bottom. I have three letters on the grid with dots beside them."

        3. Say: "Look at the letter J. Who can tell me how we would locate this letter?" (Wait for responses.)

        4. Say: "The dots on the grid are called points. Notice how the zero is in the corner of the grid, then the next number on each side is 1."

5. Ask: "Who can tell me how to find the B? The W?" (Wait for responses.)

6. Ask: "If I had the numbers (6, 4), where would the point go? (9, 6)? (1, 3)?" (Wait for responses.)

7. Say: "The two numbers I have just put on the board are called an ordered pair. Thinking about the examples that we have just done, in what direction do we go for the first number in the ordered pair?" (to the right) "The second number?" (up)

8. Let several students come to the board and plot points. Then have them tell the ordered pairs for those points.

C. Closure:

Ask the following questions:

1. "What is the name of the graph we are working with today?" (grid)

2. "What are the dots called on the grid?" (points)

3. "What are the two numbers called?" (ordered pair)

4. "In what directions do we move on the grid?" (right, then up)

    Then tell the students:

5. "In our next class meeting, we will be constructing graphs and grids."

V. Evaluation:

Monday: Assign pages 138–139 of text. (Pages cover bar graphs.)

Tuesday: Give quiz over bar graphs; assign pages 140–141 on pictographs.

Wednesday: Give pictograph quiz; assign pages 144–145 on line graphs.

Thursday: Give line graph quiz; assign pages 146–147 on ordered pairs.

Friday: Give ordered pairs quiz; review for test; quiz will be a grid with points on poster board. Ask class 10 questions about grid. (Example: "What letter is located at (6, 8)? What is the ordered pair for point J?")

Evaluate the students throughout the unit by checking homework and giving daily quizzes. In some of the daily lessons require them to make graphs or answer questions about a graph done in class. Collect this work with the homework.

Final evaluation (test):

Questions 1-32 count 3 points each. Question 33 (constructing a bar graph) counts 4 points: 1 point for the title, 1 point for correct form, 1 point for correct numbers, and 1 point for correct labeling. There is a 5-point bonus—if the student writes 4 questions about the graph, then he/she receives all points. Each counts 1 point. Students receive 1 point for trying.

Stress and Exercise Unit Introduction
LEVEL: Seventh and Eighth Grade

Cindy McCloud

GOAL: The learners will become familiar with stress and how exercise can minimize neurological and biological stress.

OBJECTIVES:

1. Given a diagram of the circulatory system, the learners will label the appropriate parts with 100% accuracy.

2. Given an essay test, the learners will explain how exercise can relieve stress from the heart with 100% accuracy.

3. Given a multiple choice test, the learners will identify appropriate symptoms of stress with 100% accuracy.

REQUIRED PRIOR KNOWLEDGE: Basic health awareness

SET:

Say: "When I say the word stress, you may think about weight stress on a house's foundation, stress on a heart due to excess fat, or excess mental stress due to the test you will be taking tomorrow."

Demonstrate stress by popping a balloon. Explain that this puts a small amount of stress on your nerves and might even have made your heart jump.

Say: "Today we are going to discuss the inner workings of your heart and how aerobic activity helps reduce mental and physical stress."

INSTRUCTION:

Ask students to define stress.

Briefly discuss how the circulatory system works.

Ask: "What type of exercise is best for the heart?" (Answer: aerobic exercise such as dancing, biking, walking, or running.)

Ask: "Why is this the most effective type of exercise in strengthening the heart? What does psychological stress mean? How can exercise help reduce depression?"

Be ready to explain that anxiety before a test or depression can be a form of stress and that exercise can help reduce depression by enhancing self-esteem, increasing wellness and vigor, promoting clear thinking, enhancing quality of life, causing a person to have more energy and vitality, taking care of extra energy that could be applied to worry. In other words, you sleep better and feel better!

Say: "Stress, like fat, is a necessity in our lives. Too much or too little can be detrimental. This is why exercise plays an important role in managing stress. Exercise helps keep stress manageable."

Have students name situations involving stress and write these on the board. Ask students how each situation can benefit from exercise.

Say: "Exercise can also be harmful, if overexertion occurs. What do I mean by this? How often is it reasonable to exercise? What are some ways to avoid overexertion?"

Be ready to explain that 30 minutes a day is a reasonable amount of exercise and that warming up, stretching, and cooling down can help to avoid overexertion.

Perform a classroom experiment: Hand out a chart that shows a set number of days students should keep track of their exercise schedule. Have them fill it out for these days. They can personally see if they sleep better, feel better, and handle levels of stress better after exercising. This applied activity gives them the chance to see exercise benefits for themselves.

CLOSURE:

For review, provide the class with a trivia game, asking them questions reviewing the heart, stress, and management of stress through exercise.

Say: "In the next lesson, we will discuss your charts and certain warm-up techniques for exercise."

MATERIALS AND MEDIA:

Exercise schedule

Four articles from the journal *Quest*

One article from the magazine *The Physician and Sports Medicine*

Lesson Plan on Stress

GOAL: The learners will gain knowledge concerning the different aspects of stress.

OBJECTIVES:

1. The learners will recognize different life causes of stress and categorize them under physical and mental stress.
2. The learners will work in pairs to formulate different areas of stress in their life and work with partners in deciding the best methods to deal with their stress.
3. The learners will participate in a relaxation technique.

INSTRUCTION:

1. Pop balloon. Collect reactions from class and write them down on the board.
2. Pop second balloon. Ask: "Was your body more prepared for the second pop? Why or why not?"
3. Say: "Sometimes stress can be predicted, and other times we have absolutely no idea what's about to take place. Today we will decide together some ways you can reduce stress, and by the end of the lesson, you should have enough information to help you deal with expected and unexpected stress." Pop third balloon.
4. Write the words *physical* and *mental* on the board. Ask, "What do these two words have to do with stress? Are the two categories related? Can some of these reactions go under both *mental* and *physical*? Why?"
5. Have students form pairs. Tell the students: "Come up with a list of things that are causing stress in your own life. Exchange papers. On your partner's paper and/or orally, state some ways that would help reduce stress."
6. Say: "Pages 210–211 in the Gardner text discuss some mental, physical, and spiritual ways that you can deal with stress. For this week's journal entry, choose one of your greatest causes of stress and tell how you will deal with it in a positive way."
7. Demonstrate the "guided imagery" technique for relaxation.

Lesson 1—American History
Chapter 12—"The Civil War 1861–1865"
The Battles of Chattanooga and Chickamauga

Tezra Volkmar

GOAL: The learners will understand the important themes, aspects, trends, and conflicts related to the battles of Chattanooga and Chickamauga during the Civil War.

OBJECTIVES:

1. Given a list of vocabulary words, the learners will define major aspects of this lesson and will be able to analyze meanings of and relationships among words. For example, they will identify the regional and geographic relationships and proximity of Chattanooga and Chickamauga. They will also clarify relationships among words by use of semantic mapping (such as *missing in action* and *casualties*).

2. Given a blank United States map, the learners will identify (in the following order) Tennessee, by outlining the state with a pen; Chattanooga, Tennessee, by placing a *C* on it; Georgia, by outlining the state with a pen; and the battle site of Chickamauga, by marking it with an *X*.

3. After watching a videotape of the Civil War monuments of Chattanooga and of Chickamauga battlefields while listening to Johnny Horton's "Johnny Reb," Dwight Yoakam's "I Sang Dixie," and Vince Gill's "Go Rest High on the Mountain," the learners will analyze their opinions on these two battles and their opinions on the Confederacy by completing a semantic differential data sheet.

4. After completing the semantic differential, the learners will analyze and be ready to participate in a class discussion on the topic.

5. After completing the reading on the "Cost of Chickamauga," the learners will answer a series of questions which will prepare them for a class discussion on the topic.

PREREQUISITE KNOWLEDGE:

The students must have prior knowledge of European colonization of America and American history (including the Civil War) up to the fall of 1863. In addition, students should have a general concept of the social, economic, and cultural differences and conflicts existing between the United States' northern and southern regions prior to the war.

MATERIALS:

Vocabulary list, blank United States map, a reading on "The Cost of Chickamauga," questions to coincide with the reading on "The Cost of Chickamauga," videotape of the battlefields of Chattanooga and Chickamauga with Johnny Horton's "Johnny Reb," Dwight Yoakam's "I Sang Dixie," and Vince Gill's "Go Rest High on the Mountain," and the semantic differential data sheet

PROCEDURES:

1. I will begin the lesson by asking the students a variety of questions which will lead into the discussion about the Civil War, especially the battles of Chattanooga and Chickamauga.

2. I will then inform the students that they are going to learn about the battles of Chattanooga and Chickamauga and how these battles affected the outcome of the Civil War by helping to seal the fate of the South.

3. First, I will hand out the vocabulary list and discuss the words and definitions with the students by asking a different student each time to define the term in his/her own words. I will also put the terms on the overhead projector. When needed for clarity, I will add important points to each term.

    Then, I will ask the students to circle two words they feel are related (for example, *casualties* and *missing in action* or *mass graves* and *national cemeteries*). I will then ask a student to come to the overhead to show the class what he/she did and why.

I will then ask each student to draw a line on the left side of the paper to a word which is similar to the two he/she just circled. Then, I will call on someone to come to the overhead to demonstrate to the class what he/she just did on his/her paper and to explain to the class why. (For example, a student may draw a line between *tragedy* and *mass graves*.)

I will continue this process of connection, drawing lines to words, circling words, etc., until all the relationships among the words have been indicated.

4. Next, I will hand out a blank United States map. I will then ask the students to outline the state of Tennessee with their pens. Then I will ask for a volunteer or call on someone to come up to the overhead and demonstrate for the class what he/she did on his/her paper. I will then ask the class members to raise their hands if they had the same answer.

   I will then ask the students to place a *C* on where they think Chattanooga, Tennessee, is. Then I will ask for a volunteer or call on someone to come to the overhead to demonstrate for the class what he/she did on his/her paper. I will then ask the class members to raise their hands if they had the same answer.

   I will then ask the students to outline the state of Georgia with their pens. Then I will ask for a volunteer or call on someone to come up to the overhead to demonstrate for the class what he/she did on his/her paper. I will then ask the class members to raise their hands if they had the same answer.

   At this point, I will hand out a modern-day map of the National Military Park at Chickamauga in Georgia; however, I will not tell the students the battlefield is in Georgia. The map is a limited one and only shows Chickamauga battlefield and the immediate surrounding area (not including Chattanooga). From the information that they have, I will ask the students to draw a square and put an *X* in the center of the square in the location where they think Chickamauga battlefield is. I will then ask for a volunteer or call on someone to come up to the overhead and demonstrate for the class what he/she did on his/her paper. I will then ask the class members to raise their hands if they had the same answer.

5. At this point, I will ask the students to put down their pens and watch, without taking any notes, the video of the battlefields of Chattanooga and Chickamauga while listening to Johnny Horton's "Johnny Reb," Dwight Yoakam's "I Sang Dixie," and Vince Gill's "Go Rest High on the Mountain."

   After the video presentation is over, I will then instruct the students to respond to their semantic differentials. I will tell the students to consider their responses carefully and to support their answers with proof from the video and their previous knowledge of the topic. I will then instruct the students to put their pens down and look up when they are finished.

   I will then call on eight people or ask for volunteers and have each one come to the overhead individually and demonstrate his/her answers for the class. I will then ask the students to explain their responses to the class. The class will discuss these answers and the support for the answers from the video and music.

6. Next, I will hand out the reading and questions on "The Cost of Chickamauga" which the students had previously seen on the videotape. I will instruct them to read silently and to complete the questions at the end of the reading. I will tell them they need to read the material carefully for detail because there will be a class discussion on the subject.

   After the reading, I will return to the videotape of Pvt. Ingraham's grave. I will turn the volume down. I will then ask the students if it is possible to determine his age. (No, there is not enough information.) I will then ask the students to write down his death date. I will then instruct the students to turn to the map on page 323 in their book *The United States and Its People*. This is a map of the battles of Chattanooga and Chickamauga. I will call on a student to tell me the date on the map. The date on the map is September 19, 1863, which signifies the first day of battle. I will then return to the videotape and have one of the students state that Pvt. John Ingraham was killed on September 19, 1863, the first day of battle. I will then return the videotape to the memorial plaque where this is stated. The class will also discuss the importance of the fact that on the tombstone it says Ingraham was a volunteer.

I will then call on students to answer each of the questions separately. I will then write the students' responses on the overhead projector. The class will discuss in detail each question and supporting details from the reading and other sources.

7. Before concluding the lesson, I will ask, "Why was a little Tennessee railroad town, like Chattanooga, an important target for the North?" (It opened up the South, especially Georgia, to the North, and the following spring Sherman burned a path through Georgia.)

8. I will ask a series of review questions about the information that the class just covered in the lesson. I will also inform the class that the next lesson will continue to cover the battles of Chattanooga and Chickamauga.

Science Lesson Plan

Elementary Science,* Energy in a Nutshell— Using a Peanut to Illustrate Forms of Energy

Catherine Massengill

Scientific processes: Observing, describing, measuring (mass and temperature), questioning, collecting, recording and analyzing data, drawing conclusions, labeling diagrams

Rural issues and technology: Farm products are renewable resources that we are looking to now and in the future as fuel sources. Using a peanut as fuel demonstrates the science processes that can be used to discover new technologies.

Elementary science: Grades 4–6, Physical Science. Related Tennessee Science Curriculum Guide Objectives: 454N1, 551D4, 554N2, 651D1, 651C4, 654N3

Materials: Balance or scale for weighing equal amounts of peanut and peanut shell, empty soup can, metal coat hanger, paper clip, matches, thermometer, styrofoam cup, raw peanuts in the shell (roasted and salted in shell will work also)

Vocabulary: Temperature, thermometer, heat energy, light energy, potential energy

Instructional Procedures (Directions for Teachers)

SET:

Show students a peanut in its shell, and ask them if it has energy stored in it. Tell students that today we will experiment to see if we can prove that a peanut has stored (potential) energy.

LESSON:

If all students agree that the peanut has energy (they will usually say that it does because you can eat it and get energy), discuss the following questions before the experiment. If some questions cannot be answered by students, write the questions on the board, and say they will be answered by our experiment.

How could we measure the potential energy in a peanut? (Hint: How do we measure the potential energy in a stick of wood?)

When we burn a peanut, the potential energy is changed to what form(s) of energy? (heat energy and light energy)

When we eat a peanut, the potential energy is changed to what form of energy? (chemical energy)

Which do you think has more potential energy, a peanut or peanut shells? (Some students will say a peanut because it weighs more; some will say the shells because they burn faster.)

How can we make sure we are burning the same amount of peanut and peanut shells? (We can weigh them.)

What instrument do we use to measure heat energy?

How are we going to contain the heat energy given off by the burning peanut in order to measure it? (Listen to students' suggestions; then explain that we can use the burning peanut and shells to heat water and then measure the rise in temperature of the water.)

---

* "Energy in a Nutshell: Using a Peanut to Illustrate Forms of Energy," from *SPRITES*. Sponsored by TTU/TVA Environmental/ Energy/Science Education Center, and TTU Rural Education Research and Service Consortium. Developed by Catherine Massengill, 1987.

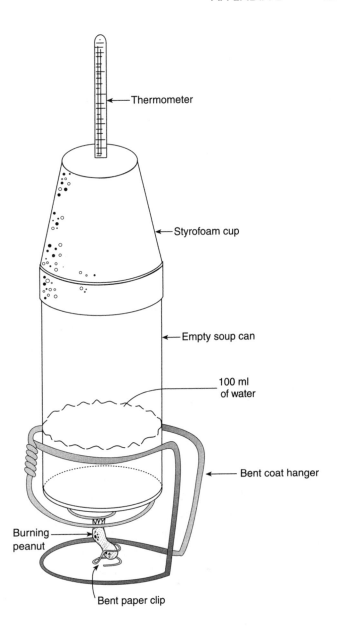

Thermometer

Styrofoam cup

Empty soup can

100 ml of water

Bent coat hanger

Burning peanut

Bent paper clip

THE EXPERIMENT: Show students the homemade apparatus that will be used, and have them draw and label it in their science notebooks.

Have students make a chart like the following to record the data.

Fuel	Temperature of Cold Water	Temperature After Burning	Difference in Temperature
Peanut			
Peanut shells			

PERFORM EXPERIMENT:

1. Weigh equal amounts of peanut and peanut shells, and attach paper clip stands to each.
2. Put 100 ml of cold water in can; record temperature in chart.
3. Burn peanut underneath. (You may also want to record time it takes to burn peanut.)
4. Take temperature of water, and record it.
5. Repeat with fresh water and peanut *shells*.

CLOSURE:

Which had more potential energy, the peanut or the peanut shell?

Why?

Which burned faster?

What if we compared peanut oil and fuel oil? Could you design an experiment to do this?

Are peanuts a renewable or non-renewable resource?

Where did the peanut get its stored energy in the first place, and why is it there? (from the sun; stored for the young plant to get started)

What is gasohol? What agricultural products is this fuel made from?

RELATED ACTIVITIES:

Language arts: Who was George Washington Carver? Did he make a fuel from peanuts?

Math: Weigh your peanuts on a gram scale. Can you figure out how many peanuts are in a pound of peanut butter? (one pound = 454 grams)

Social studies/geography: Which state produces the most gasohol?

PLAN BOOK ENTRY FOR ENERGY LESSON:

Objective: To demonstrate forms of energy.

Materials: Balance scale, empty soup can, metal coat hanger, paper clip, matches, thermometer, styrofoam cup, peanuts

Procedures: Do experiment on energy with peanut. (See Science Curriculum Guide, p. 97)

Assignment: Learn about George Washington Carver.

Sample Learning Center:
Fabulous Fables

Sample Learning Center:
Fabulous Fables*

Noralyn Parsons

OBJECTIVES:

1. To acquaint students with fables.
2. To encourage students to analyze and explore fables.
3. To enable students to have fun with fables.
4. To offer some creative challenges through fables.
5. To relate fables to students' personal lives.

MATERIALS AND RESOURCES:

1. An area (counter or table) with activities and resources attractively displayed
2. Collections of fables
3. Tape recorder
4. Paper, pencil, scissors, glue
5. Activity packets, task cards, and/or assignment sheets
6. Resources for art project (such as cardboard cartons, old magazines, scraps of fabric and colored paper, and miniature animals)

DIRECTIONS:

Work independently or with a partner on the activities that you find displayed here. Complete five of the seven activities. If an activity has * beside it, it is required. Take a file folder, write your name on it, and put your completed work in it (except for the art project, which you can leave on the table in the back of the room). You should finish your activities by _____ .

ACTIVITIES:

*1. *Introduction*—Read "The Hare and the Tortoise," "The Town Mouse and the Country Mouse," and any other two fables. Then complete these statements about fables.

   a. A fable is usually a _____ (long, short) story.

   b. The main characters are usually _____ (people, animals, witches).

   c. A fable usually ends with a _____ (moral, joke, question).

2. *Character traits*—Read "The Ant and the Grasshopper" and "The Fox and the Crow." Think about the main characters. When you finish reading these two fables, cut out the words at the bottom of the page. Then look at four of the characters from "The Ant and the Grasshopper," "The Fox and the Crow," and "The Hare and the Tortoise." Glue the words that you might use to describe each character in the appropriate column. (Some words might be used to describe more than one character.)

* Adapted from "Fabulous Fables," a Learning Center by Noralyn Parsons, 1987. Tennessee Technological University, Cookeville, Tennessee.

Ant	Grasshopper		Fox	Tortoise
Industrious	Slow	Lazy	Crafty	Frivolous
Hardworking	Sly	Steady	Foolish	Persistent

3. *Find the moral*—Read "The Lion and the Mouse" and "The Fox and the Grapes." Consider the morals in the fables you have read. (A moral is a statement dealing with right and wrong behavior.) Then match the story to the appropriate moral.

_____ The Hare and the Tortoise

_____ The Ant and the Grasshopper

_____ The Town Mouse and the Country Mouse

_____ The Fox and the Crow

_____ The Fox and the Grapes

_____ The Lion and the Mouse

a. Better to eat plain food in safety than rich food in danger.

b. Slow and steady wins the race.

c. It is best to prepare for times of need.

d. Little friends may be great friends.

e. Do not trust flatterers.

f. It is easy not to want what you cannot get.

Read another fable, and write your own moral for it.

Name of fable: _____

_____

Moral: _____

_____

4. *Art project*—Make a collage or diorama illustrating one of the fables. You may work with a partner. Use the materials at the center, or find other materials.

*5. *Think of it!*—Choose one of the following ideas, and write a story.

a. *Invent-a-fable.* Write an original fable to fit one of these morals:

(1) It pays to be kind.

(2) There is always a way.

(3) Don't be greedy.

b. *Add-a-character.* Pretend you are another hare in "The Hare and the Tortoise." What might you do or say? Would the race have a different winner? Rewrite the story with this character.

c. *Change-an-ending.* Choose one of your favorite fables. Change the story so that it has a different ending.

6. *Characterize and vocalize*—Find a partner, and rehearse a scene from a fable. Say the parts the way you think the animals would speak them. When you think you know what to say and how to say it, tell your story into the tape recorder. Some sample scenes might be those that follow.

    a. The fox flattering the crow

    b. The hare challenging the tortoise

    c. The grasshopper persuading the ant to stop working so hard

    d. The town mouse persuading the country mouse to dine on fine food

*7. *It's a lesson for you*—Fables have been used for a long time to teach lessons to people. The morals from fables can help you make smarter decisions, be a better citizen, or be a better friend.

Choose a moral from one of the fables you have read. Write the moral and the name of the fable it came from on your paper. How might you use this moral to help you make a decision in your life or solve a problem? Describe a situation (pretend or real) in which you might use this moral.

Moral: _____

_____

Fable:_____

Situation:_____

EVALUATION

The student should have completed five activities, and the activities should show the student's familiarity with several fables, knowledge of the characteristics of fables, appreciation of the worth of fables as a guide for living, and ability to relate morals to stories.

Subject Index

Name Index

Ban, J., 103
Bennett, W. J., 217
Betts, F., 184
Bodine, R., 74
Bomer, R., 200
Brown, Marcia, 162
Browning, Robert, 162
Brunner, C., 184–185
Buchleitner, Warren, 183, 192
Burns, P. C., 183

Canning, C., 14
Canter, L., 113, 123
Canter, M., 113, 123
Carlsson-Paige, N., 74
Charles, C. M., 103
Clark, R. W., 126
Coelho, E., 62, 65
Coffey, J., 162
Connors, E. T., 240
Crawford, D., 74

Dewey, John, 14
Dover, 153
Dreikurs, 102–103
Dunn, K., 209
Dunn, R., 209

Fogarty, R., 74
Frank, Anne, 162

Gardner, Howard, 209
Glasser, W., 107
Goodlad, J., 23
Guild, P., 62

Hancock, V., 184
Heide, A., 182
Henderson, D., 182
Henderson, J. G., 199
Hicks, B., 200
Hicks, J., 200
Hobbs, G. J., 240
Hodne, P., 74
Holland, H., 182

Johnson, D., 74
Johnson, R., 74

Kerr, A., 200
Kohn, A., 115
Kounin, J. S., 108

Lee, Harper, 162
Levin, D., 74

Makuluni, A., 200
Marshall, M., 115
Massengill, Catherine, 262–264
McCloud, Cindy, 256–258
McGillian, J. K., 185
Montequin, L., 200

Nicholson-Nelson, K., 209
Nieves, M., 200

Ogle, D. M., 205

Parsons, Noralyn, 266–268
Phillips, M., 187

Roe, B. D., 183

Scherer, M., 192
Shakespeare, William, 162
Sherbet, S., 232
Skinner, B. F., 114
Slavin, R. E., 79
Slobodkina, Esphyr, 162
Smith, M. M., 166
Smith, S. H., 183
Steinbeck, John, 162
Stevahn, L., 74
Stoodt, B. D., 183

Thompson, D. C., 33
Thompson, G., 102

Volkmar, Tezra, 259–261

Wasley, P., 126
Wheeler, Janet, 254–255
Wiedmer, T. L., 232
Williams, Tennessee, 162
Willis, S., 65

Zahorik, J. A., 153